WHY WE WAR

The Human Investment in Slaughter, and the Possibilities of Peace

by Al Smith

1

Acknowledgements: I would like to formally acknowledge Dr. Robert Elam, who first urged me to lecture on war. I would also like to acknowledge Professor Holly Piscopo for the invaluable input on tenor, content and style of this book. And I owe much gratitude to Dr. Kenneth White, and to Dr. Stan Spector, for encouraging the project throughout the course of all stages of completion. Thanks as well to Professor Sandra Woodside and Professor John Ulloa for emotional and spiritual support.

Printed in the United States of America

Library of Congress Cataloging in Publication Data
Paperback – ISBN: 978-1-84728-520-1
Smith, Albert 1957 –
Why We War: The Human Investment in Slaughter, and the
Possibilities of Peace

This book is dedicated to my sons;
morgan and eliot…
And to those unwitting victims of war we call
"collateral damage"

CONTENTS

4

LIST OF ILLUSTRATIONS

Cover illustration: WWII poster of the world united in war. Materials published by the U.S. Government Printing Office are in the public domain and, as such, not subject to copyright restriction. Source: Northwestern University Library http://www.library.northwestern.edu/govinfo/collections/wwii-posters/

The Great Wall of China, Wikipedia.

Nakhal Fort, one of the best-preserved forts in Oman Photographed by Andy Carvin, October 2003.

Bourtange (http://www.bourtange.nl) fortification, restored to

1750 situation, Groningen, Netherlands

American Civil War surgeons using a casualty to train other surgeons in amputation. Civil War photographs, 1861-1865 / compiled by Hirst D. Milhollen and Donald H. Mugridge, Washington, D.C. : Library of Congress, 1977. No. 0866
Title from Milhollen and Mugridge.
Forms part of Selected Civil War photographs, 1861-1865 (Library of Congress).

Princess Diana was one of many activists calling for an end to mass production and indiscriminate use of land mines, Wikipedia.

Surgery, http://www.pdimages.com/

Firearm inventor Samuel Colt was one of hundreds of weapons innovators who applied technology to efficient killing with the support of the business and governmental sectors.

The 1911 Colt .45 automatic pistol

Gatling gun illustrated in an 1885 encyclopedia in Swedish http://www.lysator.liu.se/runeberg/nfai/0122

The modern incarnation of the Gatling gun the GAU-8 Gatling gun of an A-10 Thunderbolt II at Osan Air Base, Korea, USAFNS.

Nuclear weapons test, Wikipedia.

Frederick Winslow Taylor, Wikipedia.

We Can Do it. Color poster by J. Howard Miller, World War II. National Archives and Records Administration.

Riveter at Lockheed Aircraft Corp., Burbank, CA. World War II. National Archives and Records Administration.

Alfred Palmer, October 1942. 208-AA-352QQ-5. National Archives and Records Administration.

Nuclear Reactor, Wikipedia.

United States nuclear weapons test. USAFNS.
B 52 nuclear Bomber. USAFNS.

"Tactical" nuclear weapons. USAFNS.

The "Peacekeeper" MIRV, Wikipedia.

Archery, Wikipedia.

Boxing, Wikipedia.

Doom, Wikipedia.

Full Spectrum Warrior, Wikipedia.

War poster, from RCA. NARA (NWDNS-44-PA-1795).

War poster, f rom General Motors. NARA (NWDNS-44-PA-2314).

War poster, NARA.

War poster, NARA.

pp. 238 THE FACE OF WAR GALLERY

Rameses the Great at Kadesh in 3 images, Artist(s) unknown.

Japanese woodblock print by Chikanobu Toyohara, signed Yoshu Chikanobu, published by Fukuda Kumajiro, dated Meiji year 31 (1898 in the Christian calendar).

Japanese woodblock print by Chikanobu Toyohara, signed Yoshu Chikanobu in Meiji year 31 (1898 in the Christian calendar).

Japanese woodblock print by Chikanobu Toyohara, signed Yoshu Chikanobu in Meiji year 32 (1899 in the Christian calendar).

Civil War battle victims. Photographer unknown. Photographs in the public domain from the Library of Congress.

George Bellows, *The Cigarette* (from the *War* series), 1918. Lithograph. Edition unknown.

George Bellows, *Massacre at Dinant* (from the *War* series), 1918. Lithograph. Edition of possibly 80.

George Bellows, *The Return of the Useless* (from the *War* series), 1918. Lithograph, Edition of at least 72.

George Bellows, *The Bacchanale*, 1918, lithograph

George Bellows, *The Barricade*, 1918. Lithograph

George Bellows, "Gott Strafh England"

"Starving inmate of Camp Gusen, Austria." T4c. Sam Gilbert, May 12, 1945. 111-SC-264918. NARA

"This victim of Nazi inhumanity still rests in the position in which he died, attempting to rise and escape his horrible death. He was one of 150 prisoners savagely burned to death by Nazi SS troops." Sgt. E. R. Allen, Gardelegen, Germany, April 16, 1945. 111-SC-203572. NARA

"These are slave laborers in the Buchenwald concentration camp near Jena; many had died from malnutrition when U.S. troops of the 80th Division entered the camp." Pvt. H. Miller, Germany, April 16, 1945. 208-AA-206K-31. NARA

"Some of the bodies being removed by German civilians for decent burial at Gusen Concentration Camp, Muhlhausen, near Linz, Austria. Men were worked in nearby stone quarries until too weak for more, then killed." T4c. Sam Gilbert, May 12, 1945. 111-SC- 204811. NARA

"Bones of anti-Nazi German women still are in the crematoriums in the German concentration camp at Weimar, Germany, taken by the 3rd U.S. Army. Prisoners of all nationalities were tortured

and killed." Pfc. W. Chichersky, April 14, 1945. 111-SC- 203461.
NARA

"A German girl is overcome as she walks past the exhumed
bodies of some of the 800 slave workers murdered by SS guards
near Namering, Germany, and laid here so that townspeople
may view the work of their Nazi leaders." Cpl. Edward Belfer.
May 17, 1945. 111-SC-264895.
NARA

Bombing run over Cambodia.
Photographer unknown.
NARA

The massacre of South Vietnamese civilians at
My Lai – source unknown

South Vietnamese police Chief General Nguyen Ngoc Loan
executes Viet Cong Captain
Nguyen Van Lem
Source unknown

PREFACE – After 9/11/01

War is a crime. Make no mistake; war and terrorism differ in the degree of "official" sanction by politically recognized government, but killing is killing – and the dead don't come back. They all had baby pictures. All had families that loved them. All the dead loved. Some may have patriotically volunteered to die, or were otherwise coerced by their nation, while far too many were "collateral damage" – innocent dead. All are alike in death. None care whether they were victims of committed terrorists motivated to make political statement through murder. Neither do the dead care whether or not they were made dead as a result of "official policy." This book is not about "a war," or "the war," it is about all war. I take the position that war and the forces which perpetuate war are the central crime against humanity.

War has been said to be the "extension of diplomacy by other means'" and the "health of the state." Personally, I like the Ernest Hemingway observation: "Never think that war, no matter how necessary, nor how justified, is not a crime." War simply legitimizes crime.

Crime, we are told, is a matter of a combination of means, motive, and opportunity. Civilization as we practice it has given humanity the means, and the opportunities. This book is mostly about motive. Historically, this book was written as the result of a lecture series I presented as part of California Community College Interdisciplinary Studies program in the 1990s. As such, what former Assistant Secretary of Defense Frank Gaffney calls the Fourth

World War on terrorism had not yet begun. Even before the attacks on the World Trade Towers, the Pentagon, and Washington I, like many social scientists, had been intensely concerned about the increasing frequency of war. And, perhaps more importantly, I was concerned about why humanity continues to resort to warfare at all. What is it that keeps us at it? Why and how is humanity continually motivated not to peace, but to war? What's the excuse? Where are the excuses? They got us, so we get them. "We" are preserving the peace. "They" are the evil foes of freedom. You are either with us, or against us. All of these and more are excuses we use. Finally, what does war do to us? We treat war as a necessity, as an inevitability of human nature. Because of this, the sheer social investment in conflict appears to out weigh any investment in peace and human rights. War is more "true" to the human experience since the middle of the Nineteenth Century than ever. As if in graphic correction to the myth of human progress, we have become more warlike as we have become more complex and civilized.

And now we war. Since the end of the Cold War the United States has been the sole global superpower. Yet with the threat of Soviet domination abated, the U.S. government has continued to pursue provocative unilateral foreign policies that have produced not peace, but a series of asymmetrical conflicts that we call a War on Terrorism. It is (as always) "us" against "them." The "us" – the U.S. – has the power to annihilate life on a scale unheard of in human history. Or, the power to actually begin to change to what could also be unheard of in human history (certainly in U.S. history) – a global power whose government is committed to a policy of genuine peace. Being the sole superpower, and the self-styled global police should make peace obtainable. Yet peace has continued to elude "us."

Imagine a superpower committed to making peace an institution, instead of continuing to institutionalize war. Being a "superpower" means having incredible influence, and resources. And, it means being able to project those resources anywhere in the world. How has the U.S. used this "superpower?" The Presidents of the United States had declared war on Iraq because of the ongoing Saddam Hussein regime. Because I am a citizen of the United States, I was able to record the declarations on videotape, and was able to watch the war on television in the comfort of my office. I mention this because of the unnatural realities of life in the United States. Do not overlook the irony of your relatively protected position. There was war – despite massive lack of support from the governments of the world. There was war – despite the huge popular outcry against war from citizens of the world – citizens of the U.S included. There was war because just as many governments wanted war, and because just as many citizens of the world are convinced that war is the only way. There will be more war. There will be more terrorist attacks on the U.S. – despite the fact that any conventional war will most likely be quickly won (as it was in Iraq) by the United States and its dwindling list of often anemic allies. There will be innocent people killed. And, as I write, the television commercials continue. This is because war has become a product that has been packaged for your consumption.

We are at war right now, and – if history shows anything – we will be at war again, soon. When speaking out against war at the Community College where I teach history, I once had someone yell: "support our troops!" My retort was "who said anything about the troops? I am against war! The troops didn't start it," I continued, "The troops on *both* sides and the Iraqi citizens die in it." We have to get over *this war* or *that war* if we intend to end all war. Of necessity we have to deal with the current situation and the current players. But that must not mean that we lose sight of the big picture – that humanity needs reasonable strategies for sustained peace.

This is the nature of the beast. And there is a lot to it. At the time of this writing, George Bush, Karl Rove, Richard Cheney, Donald Rumsfeld, and others of that ilk were at the head of a vast and powerfully structured apparatus. Saddam Hussein was, likewise, in control of a huge and deadly mass weapon organized to create death and destruction. These and other power brokers throughout history used their authority – spent human lives – for their continuing profit, power, and social control. Other than power, influence, and wealth, Bush, Cheney, and Rumsfeld risked little personal safety. And if the U.S. would have lost, they would still be safe and in control. Saddam Hussein would have risked little, if he had not challenged the power of the Bush clique. Either way, both used countless lives to shield their positions of power and wealth. I particularly like Michael Moore's critique (received in March, 2003). "How many pro-war congressional members risked lives intimate to them? One, that's right, one."

"Saddam could have become another Hitler," you nervously and passionately chide. "Perhaps," begins my retort. Saddam Hussein, like Adolph Hitler, was a product of history. Each had a background that gave them reality. Those backgrounds certainly included organized violence and more. Their stories and ours contain the cultural and social organization that makes these men the inevitable products of history. I am not so worried about Saddam Hussein, or Pol Pot, or Adolph Hitler. The stories of individual wars, or aggressors are mostly important for what they tell about the next war. It is this history of organized murder that this book addresses.

Without the social organization of violence, without the cultural evolution of conflict, Adolph Hitler would have just been an incompetent artist, and would have remained a minor player on the political fringe in post-World War One Germany. But, Hitler had the example of WWI to help propel him to the forefront of pre-existing institutions of organized violence. He had the perception of the denial of human rights, and the reality of the lack of economic justice as a result of the Treaty of Versailles to motivate followers in Germany. Hitler also had a global backdrop of colonial imperialism that would cause his war to be our war. And, he had a vast human history of conflict to use as a basis for constructing new and more efficient institutions of destruction. Without these, Hitler may have become a petty local gangster – as Saddam would have remained – had it not been for a human history of acquiring and maintaining both wealth and power through the social organization of violence. I believe in evil. I have seen it in many forms. Hitler and Saddam Hussein were evil. They may have become grand thugs regardless, but the pre-existing institution of war made them mass murderers. Which, then, is the greater evil?

Bush, Cheney, Rumsfeld, and the others had no genuine anointed moral status. War is war. And it is the killing of other human beings on a massive scale. Both of the major political parties share in this indictment. Democrats like Joseph Biden were just as much to blame – and were just as immune to personal threat of war – as any of the Republicans. What they all had to gain at the expense of so many lives was continued power, wealth, and influence. It is leadership that starts wars. Leadership benefits...people die. That is the nature of civilized warfare. We have become socially organized as human beings to make many things possible. War does not have to be so regular a result of social organization. "We have a responsibility," one of my students said, "to prevent another holocaust." I agree. We do have a responsibility. Our leaders have a responsibility to us to promote institutions of lasting peace. They have failed due to the very nature of their power. We have a responsibility not to let them continue.

This war is history. And, like all war, this war is the result of history. The book below presents a viewpoint on the history that has led to war. Our task is to understand how this has all come about. This is not armchair history. History has come home. It is time to increase organized activism for peace. Not for a second do I mean to dismiss or to discount vital organized peace efforts like those of Ramsey Clark and the International Action Center/A.N.S.W.E.R., and other NGO's. But, if anti-war activists are seen as "leftists" outside of the political mainstream, then it tells us some things about peace activism and the war system. One obvious conclusion is that war is more central to the system than peace. It also means that the values supporting war are still the core values of most people in society. And, finally, what it all means is that more peace activism is better. This brief history is meant as a brick in the foundation for supporting more antiwar activism and a change in the core cultural values that support war. The understandings of the history that has led to this war – and to war in general – are crucial to your future, and to the future of the people of the world. My motivations are sincere and utterly selfish. I have two children. Two sons. Men fight war. I worry that as I have been steeped in conflict, so will they be. I don't want my sons to be caught up in war – any war. And so, I advocate peace. But, it is not as simple as that, is it?

I am the center of a paradox that my life companion called hypocrisy. I own guns – not unlike many Americans.   Not an arsenal, like some Americans, but still, more than one. I have computer games that involve significant amounts of violent mayhem. I like "action" movies. I was a kick-boxer. I have three black belts. I still go to a boxing gym to work out. I was also a Sixties California Bay area kid. Raised on civil rights, peace and freedom – anti-Vietnam all the way. I have remained anti-war.   I advocate and organize against violence in the streets and against war in the world. Yet, part of my identity – a key part – is that of the warrior. My companion and I once argued over this book. She saw this book as doomed to hypocrisy. The power of patriarchy is too strong. To her, I am a victim of my own male dominant arrogance and thus cannot possibly be aware of genuine potentials for peace. After all, it is fairly indisputable that (mostly) men make war. And it may be that masculinity (the social construction of maleness) is violent. It is certain that to "be a man" in most societies means to be involved with assertion, aggression, power, and dominance. Why don't I give up my guns? My companion said that it is impossible to be a pacifist, as she is, if I come from such maleness, and that peace advocacy is for me at best uncommitted, and at worst hypocritical. For my part (short of giving up the argument entirely), I understand her position, and I feel the paradox. She suggested that the most important potential contribution of this book may be to look at myself. Not a biography, but maybe a pathology. I'm not sure I'll see what she wants me to see, but I'm committed to looking at what I can. This is why it is especially important for me to continue my hypocrisy. I loved her. I love her still. And, women along with children are among the most regular victims of war.

I am a flower child become martial artist – a warrior advocating peace. I am the same age as Osama bin Laden. I am just common enough a sort to be arrogant, and just arrogant enough to think that how I got to be this way may be important to understanding war and how to stop it. What motivated me? How did I go from peace to war, and how can I be who I have become – a gun owner advocating peace? I think that if peace ever becomes a reality, it will be because warriors truly learn to make genuine peace. Peace that is not a noun, but a verb.   -Al Smith, 2004

INTRODUCTION

WHY WE WAR

War makes no sense. There may be just causes rationalized. Heroes and villains may be identified. There may be winners and losers who are often distinguishable only by the differing levels of pain, anguish and death. There is evil in the world - to be sure - however, as former United States Secretary of Defense Robert McNamara said in *The Fog of War*: "How much evil do you have to do in the name of good?" War blurs the distinctions of good and evil into a gray continuum of carnage. Strip war of its pathos and politics. What you get are human beings organized around the purpose of the efficient systematic slaughter of other humans. Ask combat veterans. They may have reasoned that war was necessary, but no one liked being there. War makes no sense. Yet, humankind invests more energy and time on war than on peace. At the individual subjective level, peace is infinitely more desirable. War is not normal, yet seems to have become normalized as the regular state of collected human affairs. Maybe it's the way we look at it. Maybe it's the questions we ask ourselves. Aggression may be normal biological human behavior (especially among men), but war is different from aggression. Violence, especially war, is both socially structured and culturally conditioned. There is a kind of script. It is politics and pathos. War is an institution.

In spite of the social construction of masculinity

that already favors aggression and violence, war is still not an individual's first choice. An expert at killing and training others to kill, Lt. Colonel Dave Grossman, notes (132) that men have an "…instinctive resistance to killing…" and that "…killing the foe…is not a natural act; it is a repellent one." It is only through intensive training that most men become efficient and reliable killers of other men.

War is the product of social organization, and culture, not biology. Apart from aggression, humans are also empathetic. Biologically, people are quite empathetic. We would all rather just get along. It suits the human ability to organize socially and develop culturally. However, it is through social organization that individual aggression is heightened and channeled into group behavior. I question authority and I question social organization. Through them, empathy is dismissed - inherent human empathy that struggles with social mandates and cultural conditioning. More than fear, or its political cognate cowardice, people realize themselves in their (potential) victims. But, social and cultural conditioning can and does override empathy. And, still we make war. We have not yet decided to un-make war. By the clear proportion of sheer physical investment and political priority, we seem to be unwilling to make peace.

This book is not an exhaustive recollection of humanity and war. It is a reorganization of thought on the issues that surround why we war. The central purpose is to challenge the way we think of war and social organization. The unfortunate idea is that war is still conceived of by many (if not most) of humanity to be a regrettable necessity. If we accept that lasting peace is too impossibly complex a task, then this is one root of the cause of war. There are many complex problems that humanity has solved cooperatively. Warfare is as important a problem as humankind will ever face, so the complexity of war is an unacceptable excuse for not ending it. But, more than that, there is in complexity a thread of truth to why we war. There is an ever-present connection between wealth, power, and organized violence.

There is a consistent denial of human rights and social justice that enshrouds war. These connections between concentrated wealth, power, and the systematic denial of human rights are not just part of Western society and culture, but (like war) are part of all human civilization. War is a corruption of human social organization – an organization that is otherwise aimed at guaranteeing survival of the species through cooperative behavior. War serves only to concentrate wealth and power and deny human rights that social organization was meant to provide. If civilization has led the human race to thrive on this planet, then war has also made us our own worst enemy. Civilization and war must become disentangled. The social organization of peace must eclipse that for war. To do this, the social and cultural evolution for war must be reexamined, and new questions asked about why we war.

Social organization has produced many things for humanity. Agriculture may be first and foremost of the positive products of social organization. And a philharmonic symphony is a crowning achievement in social organization. And, just the other day while walking with my boys, I was marveling at how well crosswalks and crossing lights work. Many other positive advantages have developed out of the human ability to organize into groups and to divide necessary jobs. We have a collective sense of human rights that addresses satisfying human needs through collective social organization. So why war? Why the recurring destructive phenomenon that seems so contradictory to human need and human rights? Of all the products of civilization, war seems to be one of the most consistent. Ehrlich, in <u>Human Natures</u> (210) observes that:

> "The fact that such violence is virtually
> universal within human societies has
> given rise to a school of thought in which
> human beings are seen as having an
> innate drive or "military instinct" that
> leads to aggression and is the root
> cause of warfare."

While aggression may well be human, the product of war is "virtually universal within human societies" *because of human society*, not human biology. War fits social organizations that are structured around hierarchies of wealth, and power. War occurs because it is productive, perhaps second only to agriculture. But where agriculture makes prosperity and plenty possible, war makes the concentration of wealth and the consolidation of social power possible. War is productive and profitable because it has been made to be so. The point of this book is to understand how war – and not human rights – is reinforced. It is not always just the money. There is always the power. But, war can be disentangled from social organization. Understanding why we war will help to generate activism against war – a movement toward cultural evolution. We can build a different type of social organization - one that need not rely on war to reinforce it. The late Issac Asimov once wrote:

"...violence is the last refuge of the incompetent..."

So far, war is the ultimate in violence. Humanity makes war. Is humanity ultimately incompetent? Let's get a bit more personal. Let's own our actions. We pride ourselves as a species that is social. We – all of us – view ourselves as organized, progressive, and peace loving at heart. Life is sacred. And then, *we* make war. Are we a species of hypocrites? Are we a race of incompetents? Will we be a species whose absurd challenge to itself will be our final undoing? We *make* war. It does not seem to appear on its own – it's a human thing. We create it out of what was once peace. In peacetime, governments invest in warfare. We convince ourselves of the prudence of defense. *We* must be right, after all, because *they* are armed. Regardless of the often relatively peaceful tensions that precede a war, at one point we regularly decide on a course of combat.

Then, we glory in war. Our calculated capacity for the organized and systematic destruction of human life is evident at even the most basic social level. Of all creatures, only we humans have crafted special tools, to be used in ritual ways, simply for the purpose of fighting. And make no mistake – the purpose is killing. For (mostly) male humanity, aggressive and combative activity is a rule. And we have specially organized labor unions of death. The military in all its historic branches and forms is civilization's social institution of murder. Called "soldier" or "warrior," the social specialization is killing.

Individuals as well as economic, political, cultural, and social institutions organize around the principles of war. Modern businessmen read <u>Go Rin No Sho</u> (<u>A Book of Five Rings</u>) – applying the ancient samurai combat strategy to commerce. Corporate "officers" engage in hostile takeovers as part of "trade wars." Political parties use "war chests" of money to "wage campaigns" against each other. The United States government has a "war on drugs," or a "war on crime" (often a war on the poor in reality), and of course, a "war on terrorism." We speak of "strategic initiatives," our national budgets dominated by "defense" spending. War – as a word and concept – represents the ultimate to which social energy can be put.

But, even that is not quite enough. We make war gods. Examine the earliest semi-mythic legends. Then, review the modern spiritual and philosophic religions of humankind. All are concerned with war. Some religions are completely obsessed with war. Judeo-Christian-Islamic texts depict not only human conflict, but a cosmic struggle between bellicose evil and equally belligerent good. The Old Testament god is a "God of Hosts" bent on retribution, who exhorts his followers to raze cities, putting whole populations to the sword. Siddartha Gautama (Buddha) was a warrior prince, and the Rig Vedas chronicle war. Holy war. Not that there is no good or evil. When any people use any god as an excuse for murder or genocide, then there is real, genuine evil. This book is concerned with the evil that men do in any god's name.

We make war stories. The most ancient recorded traditions of humanity embrace war as either the central theme of history or as the essential punctuation. The ancient Greek Thucydides is often considered a patriarch of history in western (European) civilization. His initial contribution to human thought is a chronicle of war between his people and their Spartan neighbors. His, his, his – you will read a lot of male pronouns in this work. Gender is significant. Since early times, war and history have both been largely male pursuits. The history of Western Civilization has often been military history ever since Thucydides. Written in our own blood -- seemingly chaotic -- the record of the race is war.

We make war machines. Many of the earliest tools recovered by archaeologists are evidence of technologies that allowed humans to dominate aspects of their environments. Hunting and gathering activities permitted, if not promoted, early human proliferation. As numbers of people grew or resources became otherwise scarce, competition set in. Tools and technology could insure survival. Even more that survival, technology could produce surplus, prosperity, and wealth. Larger groups of people could get together. Choices were made. Soon these tools were used not solely on other animals, but on the human animal. Wealth needed protecting, and tools could be of use here too. Spears overcame clubs. Bows and arrows outdistanced spears. Weapons became specialized for the killing of people. Weapons were decorated and glorified as social status symbols. Eventually, a science or "art" of war developed. Guns allowed anyone lethal power. War became more political. Death became democratic. Eventually, the power of the atom became part of the machinery of war. Finally, chemistry and our own biology became weapons of mass human destruction. Technology never advances so fast as when the object is the more efficient murder of our own kind.

In the ancient or modern record, one is hard put to find a generation without skirmish, battle, or war. Somewhere a war just ended. Elsewhere a war is about to begin. North Korea and the U.S. rattle nuclear sabers. There is a war going on now. No, there are many wars going on now. Israeli fights Palestinian, Irish Catholic fights Irish Protestant, America fights a "war on drugs," and most recently George W. Bush declared a World War on terrorism, then on Iraq. Many are unclear how we all got to this point, but revenge is always a motivator. Our revenge, their revenge in return - then our revenge again. Forget that Osama Bin Ladin was a religious fundamentalist and that Saddam Hussein was a secular fascist. And, that they would normally oppose one another were it not for the unifying influence of U.S. intervention.

But, where has war taken us? Where will war lead? Certainly not to peace, if history serves. Death and destruction – and, of course, more war – appear to be the real results of war. There must be an alternative - one that realizes who we all are, what we all are, how we got here, and where we can go from here. It is not a nation that is at stake. Nor is it a people, or even a civilization at stake – as George W. Bush puts it. It is humanity. In this era of sudden mass death – of indiscriminate nuclear and biological war – humanity itself is at stake. And we may be doomed. For all that we pat ourselves on the back for – all of our cultures, and social institutions – we may be a killer species. Many still think that the human race is genetically predisposed to mayhem and murder. More likely it is culture and social organization. It could be that the main tool of humanity, namely culture, may only be a useful adaptation to mitigate our homicidal tendencies. We might be the "Killer Ape" after all. But it may only be so because we conceive of it as so. Like has been said of god, if war did not exist, we would create it.

We could cooperate with each other and the environment. However, the objective view of the world humanity assumed long ago brings with it a paradigm of struggle. Seeing the world and others in it as full of things – objects to be manipulated – has meant that human culture(s) manipulate the environment. People become objects or less than that. Private property takes on a social value. Property can be transferred, bought, sold, or destroyed. People as objects – as numbers – can and are disposed of as property. The enemy becomes a thing. Soldiers are "spent" like currency. Culture and reason has also meant conflict and strife. If our belief systems endorse war, we rationalize that people are less valuable than property.

Historically, when humanity is at peace with the environment, we war with one another. In times of plenty, "we" must defend ourselves from "them." If times are hard, and resources are few, "we" must take what "they" have. If honor or security is in question, then every patriotic militancy is in order. If there is no perceived "them," we will create one. All things being equal, "we" will fight among ourselves. Racist, sexist, and class-ist struggles erupt within a society. Even in recreation, conflict and entertainment go hand in hand. Our games are rough and violent even when we are at play. "No pain, no gain." "He who dies with the most toys, wins." Did you really think he "made a killing in the stock market?" How is it that humankind espouses peace, yet makes unceasing war? How do we talk to ourselves? There are many lies, and a few truths about war.

What, first, are the eternal truths to the absurd cycle of war? Take gender, for instance. Patriarchy – male dominance in a society – does appear from all accounts to promote war and violence as a solution to social problems. War may be a male thing. If it is a "mans world," is war his fault? Is war part of the unequal power of men in society? What about her? Are women uninvolved by nature? Or is this, too, social conditioning? Are women only victims? If hers is the hand that rocks the cradle, then why does her son grow up to be a potential killer? Blame genes or society? Who is it that supports a war effort when the men are away at the killing? It was not necessary to wait until "Rosie the Riveter." Society has been molding (all) gender in support of war for quite some time. It was a Spartan woman – a mother – who told her son to come home "bearing your shield or on it." And women are also victims of the social organization of war. In a pretentiously peaceful society like the United States, women are currently more than half of the population. Women are more than half of the votes in any election. And there is always the undervalued and under-recorded labor factor. Of what value to the war system is the un-waged labor of women? By keeping "the home fires burning," women's acceptance of patriarchy allows the economic benefits of "women's work" to support the war system. Remember *Lysistrata*? If women united in political strikes against war, would it end? If women wanted to end war, could they? In American societies, women hold less wealth and power than men. This is not a biological disparity, but a socially contrived phenomenon. Women were not "asking for it." In war, men rape. There is a tangible relationship between war, rape, and male dominance in societies that feature war as policy. Race, gender, class, and religion are all components in the human tragedy of war. Do we really want peace? It may well be that peace is the anomaly, and warfare the norm. Have we turned blind eyes to these and other truths?

Speaking of money, war always seems to generate wealth – at least for the powerful political and corporate figures that create wars, but don't fight in them. I have never known a rich soldier. On the other hand, officers often go into military service rich, and then capitalize (literally) on the military experience with political power afterwards. Political economy is an analysis of the relationships between power and wealth that has some value in understanding the unnatural frequency of organized human conflict. It has been an axiom that "war is the health of the state." Follow where authority and money intersect in a society, and things clarify. The consistent development in industrial and post-industrial societies of a military-industrial complex points to a fairly inescapable conclusion. Those with political and/or economic power work in social systems to maintain and expand their power. In this scenario, anything is rationalized. Add the intoxication of nationalism to the economic imperatives in a capitalist society. War becomes the "extension of politics, by other means" that Clauswitz spoke of. Preparation for war or engaging in war adds new vigor to industrial and post-industrial economies. Corporations can push for the highest levels of production, patriotically demanding supreme efforts from workers. Propaganda drenched labor "forces" are swept up in an undertow of nationalistic fervor often overcoming union tendencies to preserve hard-won class achievements. Many workers set aside rights just as governments relax or remove protective labor regulations. Strikes become a matter of national security. Unions are curbed, and dissidents are prosecuted. Congress (and other corporate-lobbied legislative bodies) increases "defense," military and police budgets even as they grant corporations liberal freedoms – economic freedoms that are suspended for workers. The ultimate result is corporate profits, a vigorous economy, and a body count. All too typically, it is the bodies of poor, working class poor, and middle classes that fill the graves.

The history of every generation is one of lethal and potentially lethal group-to-group confrontation. Even the great pacifist movements and religions are documents to the tenacity of institutionalized warfare. Why is this so? Why the persistent impression that war is built into the human genome? It may be that the *ability* to wage war is an inevitability of cultural evolution and diversity. Such an important question - why we war - demands that all investigative avenues be examined. A central truth to the human experience seems to be that we are ever at war. No matter the religion, governmental system, or philosophic movement humankind has either perpetuated or felt compelled to unavoidably respond to the reality of all-pervasive organized human-to-human aggression. In other words ...We War. Why we war is as ancient a riddle as we humans know. Thus far, our search for solutions to this most lethal conundrum has faltered. Our search for answers has been in vain because it rested on fallacies. But really, fallacy is a word for improper logic, when what we have actually done is lied to ourselves about war.

Lie #1; we really want peace. Ah, now – there you may have had a gut response - a kind of Frankenstein-ian "war BAD, peace GOOD!" visceral response. "Of course we want peace," you say. Or do we? Humankind's collective research into war has been overloaded with such emotion. But, is the emotion sincere? It is not nearly enough to assume that pacifism has lost to aggression because of the relative natures of the positions. It does not absolve us of responsibility because aggressive warlike types simply tend to dominate over passive ones. If people and their governments truly demanded peace, then all they must do is quit the killing. If enough people really became pacifists, the killing would stop. It has not stopped. We lie. We want peace unless it hurts. We want peace – unless we are pissed-off. Lie #2; war is dysfunctional. Either from having witnessed the horrific realities of war or from dramatic fantasies of glory, our assumption has been that war is futile. We cling to the notion that base animal instincts toward violence can be overcome through learning. Civilization is the savior of humanity. Unfortunately, it is the truly "civilized" cultures that seem to have institutionalized war. We have been smug to think peace the sole functional expression of human culture. War and peace both exist for reasons -- scientific reasons beyond viscera. Certainly, for war to have its near-organic vitality and frequency, it must have willing participants. Thus, war has some social value and cultural basis. War must also have physical consequence. Sooner or later, social and cultural behaviors acted out over thousands of years must somehow impact biology. If war has absolutely no value in a biological sense, then it would be

31

vestigial, not vital – atrophied, not active.

Civilization - first occurring in what has been called the Neolithic Age as a result of advances in plant and animal domestication. Civilization is defined as complex social organization with divisions and specialization of labor. Social institutions and cultural practices developed to stabilize the most ideal conditions for human beings to thrive in a capricious natural environment. As a species, we have not biologically changed much since the Neolithic period. Why? Organized warfare and the Neolithic agricultural revolution – same time – a coincidence? Not very likely. Social organization has affected our biology. And, one of the most regularly recurring features of social organization – of civilization – is war. If war was not originally part of the biology of humankind, it has become so through repetition. We make war, but war made us.

We are products of evolution. We have evolved as a species. War has evolved. We evolved a social and cultural strategy for dealing with the environment. Soon it was not just the natural environment that we could collectively effect, but we had created social environments to deal with – new landscapes. We had cultural complexes that dynamically influenced human beings to the degree that together; culture and society have challenged natural biologic evolution (and the environment). Social scientists have made this popular as the "nature versus nurture" problem. Are humans and their behavior products of biologically determined "hard wiring," or are they the products of social and cultural conditioning? In reality, there is no controversy – we are both. Nature and nurture operate together to produce what and who we are.

The scientific controversy is to what degree nature versus to what percentage nurture. Who and what we are and why we war is to be found in the balance, not in an either-or approach. So to figure out why we make war and what can be done about it, we need to look at society, and cultural evolution.

Men make war so violence is male, so men make war, etc., etc. - chicken and egg, again and again. War is a masculine expression, true. But, it is a human expression – also true. Human social organization makes war possible, and apparently often desirable. We cannot end it by simply dismissing war as a gender expression, or as male conditioning. The social construction of the role of the male is one thing, but institutionalized male power is another thing entirely. Masculinity and patriarchy differ in that masculinity is a role individuals play out in society, while patriarchy is the system that confers power and privilege on the male playing the proper role. Patriarchy is also a system that punishes those who do not play the proper role. They are linked, of course. One is a social behavior of dominance, the other is a social system of dominance. War happens because of male dominance, but male dominance happens because of war. Just as all civilization is not due to men, so too war is not solely due to men. Yet, patriarchy is different. It moves beyond the social construction of male-ness, into the control of society by men. When our social systems are structured around a type of male leadership and masculinity that is constructed as aggressive and violent, then civilization follows a violent lead. Patriarchy is at the center of human civilization, and cannot be discounted as a source of war. Patriarchy may lay the foundations of conflict, however a whole society supports a war. Civilization is war. But, it is because it is the way that civilization is constructed. It takes the truly civilized – groups of people organized and specialized – to make war. Indeed, currently civilization demands war, promotes conflict, intensifies violence.

We are at war – again. We are a cult of war and warriors. How do you join? How did I? Is war, with its warriors and soldiers all part of manliness and masculinity? Is it part of humanity, biology, psychology, philosophy, history? Choices...do you choose? Do you actually choose war or peace? Did I? Is there "free-choice?" Some social scientists (Martin Heidigger and others) have said no. What we call "free choice" is really selecting from a limited set of circumstances. These circumstances are limited in part by our awareness. How can one choose from what one knows nothing about? Choice is further limited in part by what those who came before us leave us, and partly by what is in our immediate environment. If human history is punctuated by power struggles and war, and all around us are indications that violence is acceptable – even rewarded under the right circumstances – then what will become of choice? No, our biological and cultural background, as well as our current environment made us. Nature and nurture, so to speak, is why we are what we are – and choice is an illusion. The principles of cultural evolution suggest that each generation modifies the (genotype and phenotype) last generation's behavior. We say we want peace, even though the leadership of this United States demands war. What have we done to make peace? Most people given the "choice" choose

34

peace. Why, then, does war persist? Not just this war, or that war, or a war, but _all_ of them.

If the cultural evolutionary approach to history is acceptable as a theory explaining humanity, then biology responds to culture and cultural practice. Humanity evolves culturally, as well as socially. The genes for aggression and war are advanced each generation by each aspect of culture and society that supports war. But war also advances when we do nothing to actively oppose it. Our social institutions are organized around war, not peace. War will perpetuate itself. It is a system. The identity of warrior or soldier is a social construct that is networked into advantages and penalties. The social advantages and penalties are conferred or levied on the soldier by those who profit from leading us into war. This means we war because we mean to war. Or, at least, that we do not really mean to make peace. To make peace, and to fashion peace as a craft of human organization seems somehow beyond us. There is so much war in history, and so much at stake because of it, that the evolution of war and the cult of conflict seem a central feature of humanity. I argue that war is so intimate a part of human civilization as be more influential than money. And, that the organization of conflict that we call war is the central disease of society.

Authors such as Barbara Ehrenreich (in <u>Blood Rites)</u> have written that the nature of the construction of masculinity in a social system may be the deciding factor promoting the frequency of warfare. Spurred and lashed continuously by private property and its merciless offspring capitalism and materialism, patriarchy (male dominance) has a history of destructive acquisitiveness. Add the rest of the features of social organization and the resulting power and status of male dominance create the conditions fostering more organized violence. These conditions are aggression, organization, and concentrations of wealth. But male dominance exists within a social system, not independent of it. The system of human social organization is superior to its parts.

The case is also made by Dr. Paul R. Ehrlich and others that the system of social organization (we call civilization) has an evolutionary history. If so, it has been a cultural evolution that centers on war, the threat of war, and the "preservation" of peace. Both war and social organization are intimately bound in co-evolution. But, this does not have to continue. War is dependent on social organization – and more importantly – on the *nature* of social organization. But social organization is not dependent on war. Society can function without patriarchy. Male dominance is an afterthought by cultural evolutionary standards. Maleness and the social construction of masculinity are prime-time tickets into the cult of the warrior, but not the exclusive tickets. And, maleness need not mean violence. All males are not warriors, just potential warriors. Without this patriarchic social organization, dominance has no meaning – no structure of distinctions, no gender based divisions of labor, wealth and status – no dominance. Patriarchy would be a meaningless term. Some think that, likewise, without masculinity war could not occur. While I am convinced by the data that a change in the social meaning of masculinity is essential to reducing war, I am not ready to go that far. War does not exist simply because of masculinity, but because of male dominance and the social nature of patriarchy. Men may often be brutish, short-sighted, and aggressive, but war only occurs if you get a group of us together under a leader who can rally the rest of society to support conflict. No matter who is dominant – a society based on dominance, private ownership, and concentrated wealth will generate the organized violence of war.

How has the rest of human society come to be organized around war? A book of particular interest that will be discussed at length later, is the fictional Report From Iron Mountain on the Possibility and Desirability of Peace. Regardless of being at root a political satire, this book revealed how tightly integrated war has become with the rest of society. If we (as some still do) are to accept this once nearly anonymous yet wholly believable 1967 publication, then war is the aim of the state. The state supports war because war supports the status quo of the state. Allegedly the result of a secret U.S. government "special study group" think tank, the Report clearly outlines a viewpoint on the functional necessity of war. That this was a work of fiction and that it was (is) widely accepted as fact reveals how deeply seated our acceptance of war is. In the account given, war is essential to civilization as we know it, and peace is the "de-stabilizing" element. It is interesting and more than a little frightening, how the specific strategies outlined in this Vietnam era Report reflect the types of government and institutional policies enacted since that time. George W. Bush, and Karl Rove – for example – could be using the Report as a manual. Extremists on the Right and the Left have supported the Report since the 1960's. The conclusion of the Report is that American Institutions will fail without regular war (Lewin/Navasky).

37

But this is not about the U.S. Humanity has institutionalized war. War is a uniquely human institution that has no cultural boundary, and no social one. All recorded histories expose the sutures binding social organization to war. Each social system confers privileges, rights, and (evolutionary) advantages on the warrior and his support network. It is the support network (from families, to farmers, to workers, to corporations, and yes the media) that makes the specialization of soldier possible. It is social organization that makes war possible. Biology may give us the ability to have aggression, culture may have given us the tools, but society has evolved war into an institution.

How then to solve the riddle of why we war? Pose new questions based on the fundamental assumption that to be so widespread and deep a part of the human experience, war must be a culturally adaptive strategy with social and biological value. We must face an unsettling fact. In some bizarre way, war works. But for whom? War is both social/cultural and biologically adaptive, and the riddle Why We War cannot be solved unless we accept this as the nucleus of our paradigm – especially now, when war has become far too destructive and potentially catastrophic for the human race. Humanity – or huge amounts of humanity – can be obliterated within seconds. Something must be done. The only salient questions are: What is war, why have we done it, and *Why do we do it?,* which are Historic queries; and, *What can we (or should we) do about it?,* a question that underlies the perennial anthropological controversy - nature versus nurture. In summary, we are looking at two things: the historic background of organized conflict, and the anthropological aspects of

humanity and war.   Therefore, each discipline –
history and anthropology – figures into this study.
The optimum result must be to move legitimately
toward an end to war.

Can we learn, or is it that we cannot help
ourselves? Is war always the result of economics, or
of nationality or ethnicity?   Can we change these
things? If too many people are too close does conflict
inevitably arise?   For Cold War baby-boomers who
dared believe in peace and love, can there be an end
to war?   And, for those who accept -- or even
advocate -- war as a price of the human condition,
should we stop?

But, can we stop?   Humans are the only
terrestrial fauna known to prey upon its own kind in
complex ritualized ways, and often for considerably
abstract reasons. Our own empirical sciences have
shown us that we are the sole species that kills
masses of its own kind for such things as doctrinal
differences *within* a religion, or for that ultimate
abstract creation of human society and culture –
money.

There has scarcely been a generation without
war. Yet, when no war is going, or when there are
those who cannot (*could not! would not!*) engage in
actual war, we nonetheless revel in our symbolic
warfare. I don't mean just the obvious examples such
as video games or professional football, but the more
subtle and pervasive varieties of ritual and symbolic
war. We have a competitive streak. Everything from
chess and pinochle all the way to the telling fact that
even our appreciation of so called "classical literature"
usually relies on the "central conflict", often between
protagonist and antagonist.

Why are all known cultures of all known history

so inevitably engaged with the potential for - if not the actual act of - organized physical conflict? To be so insidiously pervasive, so omnipresent, it seems that war must be relatively fundamental to some aspect of being human. Is that aspect biologic, historic, psycho-social, technological? Knowing the answer may allow us to outgrow mass murder.

Or, from another point of view, is it possible that the perception of the human obsession with war could just simply be an artifact of historiography, Western culture(s), and modern media? All of them deal heavily with war and socially acceptable violence. Undeniably such influences play out their roles on the stage of this greatest of human tragedies. Clearly, however, the active human preoccupation with homicide, fratricide, and genocide substantially predate the development of the aforementioned influences. Do movies make us violent, or do we make violent movies? Both are probably true. There was war before movies. There were stories about war told around many a fire in our preliterate past. Epic poems such as the Iliad were the movies of their times. Perhaps our "modern" progressive egocentrism fused with our modern technologic facility has simply bombarded us in film after book after film with the glorified vulgarity represented by war. Causation is an issue. But, we cannot escape that easily. We cannot simply blame the movies. No matter which came first, the chicken and the egg do exist. They are interdependent. We must consider that they exist for specific reasons. Ultimately, it really does not matter which is first. Chicken and egg will be followed by chicken and egg and chicken and egg. So it was, so it is, and so it has ever been with war. No, we cannot escape with a simple cause and effect statement.   What must be clear is not just causation, but also purpose. What are the benefits, and who are the beneficiaries of war?

"All Gaul is divided into (three) parts," wrote infamous warrior General Julius Caesar, and basically so is this work. Why we war is the central subject of an odyssey that will weave its way through disciplines of modern empiricism and ancient wisdoms (did you know that most grammar programs will not let you write "wisdoms" as a plural? The word and concept is considered as singular). The subject of war needs to be examined both anthropologically and historically. Anthropology will show the broadest possible range of the cross-cultural human experience of war. There are common aspects underlying cultural belief systems that motivate organized conflict. What is a "culture of conflict?"   Anthropology also offers glimpses of prehistoric cultural predispositions for war embedded in the archaeological record. History will show roots and social development of war. Comparative study of world history is testimonial to a consistent pattern of the development of social institutions that support war. The entrenchment of war in human social systems is an historical development. What is the "war system?" War is only possible as a collective response - a "group thing" that relies on re-channeling (limited) collective resources. The re-channeling is in fact a mal-distribution of wealth. But groups are made of differing individuals. The mal-distribution by definition favors some individuals and groups at the expense of others. Culture and society - the individual and the group - interact to reinforce a cycle of organized violence. And what is the cost? This assessment will be based on a concept of universal human rights. The concept of human rights is a historically recurrent idea of the relative responsibilities and obligations that should exist (ideally) between the individual and society. What does the war system do to the individual's ability to enjoy what human rights a society may offer? This is how we will judge war (UDHR).

This interdisciplinary effort serves to illuminate unifying threads in the bloody and baleful tapestry of organized human conflict. Far from a trite recitation of serial slaughter, what is hoped for is a methodology of social change. We have little time for idle speculation. War demands a certain intellectual and social activism. Success in making a change will rely on adopting a new perspective. That is what this book is about.

In the first section there will be an anthropological interpretation of war that is both cultural and physical. Is war solely a learned behavior – a by-product of all human social and cultural orientation? Can we thus unlearn war? Some ugly facts about human societies and cultures will emerge from questioning whether war is waged solely for social status, or economic exchange. War will be assessed as expansionist necessity and as ideological inevitability. We may be a species organized to aggressively challenge the environment. Unlike other species that reach equilibrium, culture and society may have allowed humans to continually exceed environmental – natural – restrictions. When social systems become our main environment, is war anthropologically inevitable? Or is it the nature of systems and relationships within human societies? War will also be discussed as a biologic mechanism of natural selection played out through culturally developed patterns. Patterns which - if we are to accept some sociobiological theories - may be unavoidable results of our genetic predisposition.

Also often evident will be the difference between ideal and real, or perhaps more precisely, between the intentions and the actual results faced by warfare's many participants. How does the soldier see war, and how does that view differ for others in society? What conditions do these beliefs produce? In this sense, this portion of the data presentation will take at least two forms - structure and function(s). Across time and space, war has a common structural development and purposeful function. No matter what, war exists and persists for some very good reasons. If our predilection for genocide is not to reign supreme, then the investigation of war must be far less cluttered with the rampant egoistic species-centricity that has thus far carried the day. We have to find a way to stop. We have to understand how to work against all war, not just the last one…or the next one… or, the final one.

Following anthropology, we will proceed to survey war in its various social historical manifestations. What is war, really? Investigating first an acceptable definition of what war actually means is essential to any reasoned discussion. Can it be defined in a way that all can accept? Are corporations waging economic war against the poor and working classes, for instance? Is rape gender war? And what about terrorism? According to the United Nations, there is little definitive difference between war and terrorism beyond the concept that war is state sponsored destruction, while terrorism is killing without the benefit of national sanction. Hmmm? What, for instance, is the earliest or most simple form of organized violence? What socially validates and justifies killing another human? How and why has conflict become more complex through time? This broad but brief historic survey explores the rationale behind traditions involving personal combat, through raiding societies, territorial skirmishes, and activities of feudal elite, all the way up to modern geo-political econo-nationalistic world war. Modern forms of terrorism (that post-colonial warfare of identity politics waged by the otherwise powerless) cannot be overlooked. Terrorism has created the conditions that are used to justify war, but war produces the conditions that justify terrorism. It is The Beast that consumes itself, and gives birth to itself. Already, youth gangs are being classified as urban terrorists. SWAT teams are training in urban warfare.

There are many guilty of war. Easy to define war crime as what *they* did. Leaders both current and historic regularly validate themselves through war. It is easy to list villains and heroes. Not so easy to see them as their foes saw them. For every hero, someone else saw villain. Every corpse – rich or poor – *was a family member.* Citizens become soldiers because it is in their cultural character. Soldiers fight because the leaders of society tell them to. Armies meet in war because society supports them. Both sides in war commit atrocities because culture allows it. And, civilization has reached so high only because we stand on a mountain of war dead. It is a horrific analogy. We will pick the bones of war, much as a forensic scientist dissects a corpse for the clues left by the murderer - a smooth criminal, a seductive slayer, a serial killer, a mass murderer. With each revelation we will realize that the original homicidal maniacs... are us.

1. ANTHROPOLOGY OF WAR

"In an anthropological spirit, then, I propose the following definition of the nation: it is an imagined political community...because, regardless of the actual inequality and exploitation that may prevail in each, the nation is always conceived as a deep, horizontal comradeship. Ultimately it is this fraternity that makes it possible, over the past two centuries, for so many millions of people, not so much to kill, as willingly to die for such limited imaginings.

These deaths bring us abruptly face to face with the central problem posed by nationalism: what makes the shrunken imaginings of recent history (scarcely more than two centuries) generate such colossal sacrifices? I believe that the beginnings of an answer lie in the cultural roots of nationalism."

-Benedict Anderson

Anthropologists investigate and compare cultures. We also examine the interfaces between the individual and society. Anthropologists also investigate the biological development – the evolution – of the human organism. These views give us a different definition of war than that of history which tends to investigate social and institutional events. Culture is the belief system motivating individual behavior, while society is a set of both positive and negative controls that are formed into institutions to govern group behavior. While culture (anthropology) and society (history) are inevitably intertwined, they must yet be distinct to be so. It may be useful to think of the relationship between society and culture as Einstein may have thought of light, and apply the imagery to history and anthropology. For example: while history is a laser beam of linear direct thought, anthropology is a sun of multidirectional light in which even the shadows tell stories. The prism of anthropology illuminates a rainbow of meaning about the complex reality of war. Anthropology demonstrates that war is a cultural and a social phenomenon that has biological consequences.

Like historians, anthropologists are human, and thus subject to both the influences of their own culture and society. However, anthropologists are also involved in a discipline that regularly makes them aware of cultural influences on objectivity. At the core of anthropological inquiry rests a multidisciplinary assumption. This is the idea – or theoretical orientation – that there are many valuable tools available from the diverse perspectives of human inquiry. War is far too complex to be evaluated on the basis of only one situation, motivation, or event. Anthropology fills that need to explain the "Why?" of the human social & cultural adventure. This theoretical orientation is comparative and integrative. But, what is shared and what is connected about the multi-linear aspects and avatars of war? Even the most cursory observations of war reveals a wide range of influences affecting culture and society. Apart from fairly overt particulars of historical events, there is an ever subtle and often more complex cultural dynamic to war. In some deep sense, humanity has come to believe in war. Not just the undeniable physical manifestations, but we believe in war as a concept which we assume must be played out. In short, we have a culture of conflict – a cult of war. The question is why? The answer to the question "why" in history is situational, singular, and unique. Why in anthropology is global. In history, war is a unique event specific in place and time, while in anthropology war is a phenomenon of the interaction between social systems and the cultural beliefs supporting them through time.

In anthropology, time is recognized differently. In anthropological thought, time is evolutionary and geologic. Why things happen is a big issue between history and anthropology, as disciplines. And, time is a key. The historical approach generally assumes cause and effect follow each other in time. Anthropological approaches assume that systems exist where multiple causes and effects continually interact with each other. Change occurs, but when it happened is less important than why it happened. History tends to be a line. Anthropology tends to be a web. Dr. Sydney Storey, one of my anthropology professors, called cultural anthropology "the squishies" because it deals with reconciling human motivation and behavior that often seems contradictory and unpredictable. This makes anthropology perfect for the study of both war, and the study of what can be done about war. This is so because war as simply a historical narrative becomes the serial tragedy of humanity getting better and better at killing people. Anthropology enriches and broadens the historical context beyond the "great man" approach. History frequently adopts this elite approach because of the dependency on documentation and research that is (still) usually done both by and about elite men. Anthropology embraces more of the human experience. More people are represented. History is originally of the humanities, while anthropology is a social and behavioral science.

> "Religious dogmas, economic practices
> and politics do not stay dammed up in
> neat separate little ponds but they overflow
> their supposed boundaries and their
> waters mingle inextricably one with the
> other. Because this is always true, the
> more a student has seemingly scattered
> his investigation among facts of economics
> and sex and religion and the care of the
> baby, the better he can follow what is
> happening in the society he studies. He
> can draw up his hypotheses and get his
> data in any area of life with profit. He can
> learn to see the demands any nation makes,
> whether they are phrased in political,
> economic, or moral terms, as expressions
> of habits and ways of thinking which are
> learned in their social experience."
>   - Ruth Benedict:12-13.

Anthropology is the multi-disciplinary study of human kind. It is a cultural, a linguistic, a physical, and an archaeological (artifact-based) study of why we are human, and of what that means. Many types of scientist participate in anthropological inquiry. This idea in the heart of anthropology – that the comparison of many theories in search of answers can help reveal more clues – is just as valid about war and how to stop war. Looking at the human being from the many perspectives of anthropology, conclusions can be made that may not be clearer in simplistic terms, but will certainly be truer of the complexity of the human experience. And war is one of the most complex human of experiences. In this section, we will look at culture, society, and biology as they relate to war.

An unfortunate reality is that Culture is always hard to absolutely define. As a term, it must cover virtually all of the diversity of human experience. Anything genuinely new that occurs requires culture to be re-defined to some degree. I can, however, establish a working definition for the purposes of investigating why we war. Culture is the set of conscious and unconscious fundamental beliefs and assumptions about the way in which world works that governs individual behavior. Culture is the ability to learn. And, a culture is made of what is learned. It is the primary human tool for dealing with our environment(s). The environment may be natural. But, with modern humans the environment is mostly social. The human being is a social animal that lives primarily in a social environment. People use culture as a map to navigate the social environment. As the word infers, culture can be the product of cultivation on the conscious level. This means that culture is plastic and changeable, organic and vital. There are many cultures. The smallest cultural unit is the individual.

My undergraduate advisor, Dr. Dirk van der Elst, used to speak of "Culture, with a big "C," writ large, and culture with a small "c." What he meant was that culture is the toolkit of the individual or of the group that faces a similar set of challenges from the environment, but that Culture (writ large) refers to the overall collection of human beliefs and responses to the environment. To mix another metaphor (a simile, actually) – this one drawn from author Peggy

McIntosh – culture is an invisible knapsack full of perceived options that an individual wears through her/his life. In this illustration, big "C" Culture is also the multi-level department store from which we fill our invisible knapsacks. Elements of culture are both shared and personal. Culture is always ahead of social institutions in adapting to the needs of individuals (until historically recently). Although culture is not fully proactive, culture remains the intimate and personal tool for individual day to day problem solving. As people confront the changing issues of life, they react through culture far more rapidly than either formal or informal social institutions can. They must. Society and culture are intimately related and interdependent.

Society is a set of formal and informal institutions governing group behavior. Human society acts to force regularity. In society, consistency is important. Among their most basic functions social institutions exist to provide people with regular, stable access to the critical necessities of live. For example, food, shelter, water and the like are essentials that cannot be done without. All social systems of all civilizations are first structured to make the necessities of human life dependable. Social systems tend to be conservative for that reason. Stable and predictable outcomes are what we usually organize for. Despite myths of progress, social institutions collaborate with stasis in the name of order. At the root, social institutions aspire to mediocrity. Any real progress usually occurs when things break down, or change too rapidly for institutions to cope. All too often, this is manipulated into war, instead of peaceful, political resolution. This is to the point that currently the term: "peaceful political solution" has become – culturally – a phrase indicating weakness. In a sense, it's as though not killing is a poor choice or that peace is a liability.

Culture changes whether we will it or not. But, the word culture also implies cultivation, as in a purposeful act. There can be a culture of peace. There certainly is a culture of conflict. It is a belief in organized violence that permeates human experience as we understand it. Currently, the cultural concepts that humanity share includes both war and peace. However, the culture of war is all too regularly the one that is institutionally supported and publicly endorsed. The institutions of war have networked themselves into human culture. In other words (and to align with this book's thesis), social organization and the institutions of society reinforce a culture of conflict. And, that the social organization of violence that war is results in an overall reduction in human rights.

Human society is largely an artificial construction. Artificial in the terms of artifice: "1. A clever trick; stratagem. 2. Trickery; guile. 3. Cleverness; ingenuity." And in the context of the definition of artificial itself: "1. Produced by humans and not by nature. 2. Not real; simulated. 3. Not natural; [but] forced or affected." (Webster 1993). As mentioned, society is a collection of both formal and informal institutions that together serve to organize and govern group behavior. It is our collective tool for dealing with each other and the natural environment. The smallest social unit is two people. There is kind of a stick and carrot (punishment and reward) aspect to social institutions. Informal (yet intimate) social institutions – like handshakes, bowing, jokes, and religious faith – help stabilize human relationships. For good or ill, informal social behavior is usually predictable and free of threat to those within the social group. Their power is largely influential. On the other hand, formal institutions – like the institution of marriage, the government, or the Catholic Church – strictly regulate groups. There is a hierarchy in formal institutions that has power not just to influence, but to control, compel, and enforce. The military and the police are formal institutions.

Clearly this is where we get into trouble. Because of the nature of authority, wealth and power become central in formal institutions. The coercive power of formal institutions in a society is mostly used to continue the relationships between concentrated power, and concentrated wealth. The group has social stability. But, there is a severe price to pay for the stability brought by formal institutions. At their best these social institutions, as instruments of order and control, seek to do the most good for the majority. This means that by their very nature – at their best – formal and informal social institutions mitigate, reject, or ignore minority concerns – however minority is defined (it is true that you can't please all of the people all of the time). This also means that social institutions are characteristically reactive. Proactive behavior in formal social institutions is most often limited by bureaucratic development.

Bureaucracies are the special wonders of modern social organization. They are central in the civilized ability to deny human rights and social justice. Administrative bureaucracies redistribute goods and services in a state. The reallocation is frequently unequal. Access to the wealth and opportunity in a state is disproportionate. A bureaucracy tends to set aside the responsibility features of formal social institutions. Bureaucratic authority is occasionally arbitrary or capricious, but this is usually rare. There are two major problems with bureaucratic authority. The first is that bureaucracies sacrifice flexibility for stability. The second problem with bureaucracies is that they can become prey for graft.

Bureaucracies maintain what we have come to call "institutional distance." People become objects lost to institutional distance. If you or your problem does not "fit" the institutional profile, then the institution will fail you by its very design. Any actual power the institution has to factually solve social problems gets lost in the bureaucratic distance. Someone may be "in charge," but no one is responsible – the institutional juggernaut shambles on, often crushing individual liberties as well as any collective opportunities to engage in radical (as in fundamental or "at the roots") social change. The more formal and bureaucratic the social institution, the more reactive to inevitable change it will be. In addition, more bureaucratic the social institution, the more its proactive potential will be focused on self-maintenance and defense. This appears to be a progressive feature of formal social institutions. The more bureaucratic an institution becomes, the more it tends to get set in its ways. The social institution gets better at developing only itself over time. It is the machine that takes care of itself.

The second problem with modern bureaucracies is that they are susceptible to corruption. In a social system favoring private property, concentrated wealth, and elite social status over the needs of people, bureaucrats cannot help but be swayed. Like politics and politicians, bureaucrats may have begun careers of starry-eyed optimism, but the longer one serves, the further one gets from understanding the lives of those they are to work for. Public servants in many areas of bureaucracy have succumbed to the temptations we are all bombarded with in a wealth dominated society. In a culture and society that places more value on wealth and material prosperity as prime indicators of happiness – and that at the same time has been becoming increasingly class restrictive – some people just take the money. A government contract being awarded to a corporation Halliburton) that a government official (Dick Cheney) once staffed is just the higher profile type of case. Local bureaucrats who exchange favors, under-the-table real estate deals between city council members and developers, even abusive and dysfunctional state unemployment department clerks arise from the climate of bureaucratic corruption.

Darwinism

Just as this book represents an obsession with "Why We War," the earliest modern investigators of the human experience were absolutely possessed by the need to define why we are, and how we came to be human. Perhaps the greatest of these obsessive individuals was Charles Darwin. The foundation upon which we all rest in this investigation was indeed set by him. Darwin's empirical epiphany and intellectual edifice is still either built on, or must be toppled, in order to proceed in any discussion of the courses of human development. It has not yet toppled. The omnipresent The Origin of Species (1859), and the only slightly less influential The Descent Of Man (1871) outline the biological development of organisms through processes of natural selection. But, what is included in the term natural selection? It is a complex interaction between genes and the environment that produces a change in biological types over time. The interactions include selection of partners for sexual reproduction, and competition for consistent access to critical resources. In the case of human beings (being social animals) groups – or *populations* – represent this fluctuating gene pool. These populations are organized into societies. As we have seen, culture is the set of beliefs about the way our world works that governs our behavior. That world – the environment that humans live in – is both natural and social. Our genetic adaptations to those environments are so continuous, subtle, and unrelenting that we are rarely conscious of them in any present sense. They are frequently a matter of geologic time – showing up after generations. But, if Darwin and all after him are right, these selective pressures have not ceased. Although we are not (as a race) always so aware of the details of natural selection that we let it guide our lives, we are aware of our (individual) need to survive and our will to thrive. We are aware through culture. Culture, then, ends up being a combination of what the individual learns through personal experience, and what the individual learns that is passed down through time via the mechanisms of society.

Modern social scientists have continued to develop understandings of the development of human culture. One of the most promising is a concept of cultural evolution currently employed by social activists such as Dr. Paul Ehrlich in his 2000 book Human Natures. What emerges is a fairly comprehensive look at humanity. Dr. Ehrlich suggests that history is a narrow scale of a more influential phenomenon he calls cultural evolution. He moves the human experience to the geological or evolutionary time scale.

Ehrlich, Early in his book, Paul Ehrlich poses what he calls his "favorite conjecture," stating that: ...human natures have been strongly shaped by multilevel human societies – families, bands, tribes, and so on – and by population pressures, all interacting in a positive feedback system." In the study of why war persists, we can read this as an organic model for the culture of conflict. War, then is not an artifact of a civilization as much as it is an artifact of civilization itself. War has become a "positive feedback system." That is to say, war is self-perpetuating in human culture because of social organization.

Since war seems so ever-present in the human experience, this cultural evolutionary concept allows a wider intellectual net to be cast in order to gather clues about how to understand and end the destructive social activity. A networks – or systems – approach to analyzing social and cultural organization for war that highlights how war came to be, and why it remains so integrated with the human being. By looking at war as an integrated part of social systems and human culture we can begin to disengage war from the other, more constructive aspects of social organization. This is the study of human culture and of war. It is the study of the systems of belief that condition human behavior for conflict. It is in part a search for central truths to humanity and human-ness. As with all Law, ignorance is no excuse. Partly, then, we are responsible for what we are and what we will become. We make war, but war makes us.

A. A Culture of Conflict – Proving Ground of Power

What cultural beliefs support the social complex of war? Why do all cultures seem to support war? And, how do these cultural beliefs that support war spread? What is the culture of conflict? Why do societies nurture war? How does a cultural belief become a social institution? How does culture affect the historian?

At some time in the past, I joined a cult. Not consciously, but thoroughly willing nonetheless, I joined the cult (ure) of the warrior. I became convinced that a warrior is somehow better and more honorable than a murderer or killer. In Code of the Warrior: Exploring Warrior Values Past and Present, author Shannon E. French defined why warriors need a code, what that code means, and ultimately how the code works to form the basis of a kind of masculine culture of conflict. If we are to accept French, this cult operates through a Code. The Code is as timeless as conflict itself, and is both cumulative and cross-cultural. Warrior societies from the Cheyenne Dog Soldiers to Knights Templar – from Samurai to Foreign Legion to Marine Corps – maintain a Brotherhood of War. French describes the Code of the Warrior as a necessary civilizing feature to the social organization of war. The Code is essential to the warrior's ability to successfully reintegrate into peacetime society. It is a chain that anchors the combat soldier to the vessel of civilization. I might agree. The moral and ethical aspects of the Code of the Warrior as outlined by French may well elevate the warrior above some aspects of the vulgar habitual atrocity that is war. But, this is where I part company from Shannon French and the others. Anthropologically speaking, the moral and ethical conditions are defined both from within and from outside of the cult of war (the old "emic and etic" approach). Ethical treatment and moral proscription is based on contemporary ideals of the greater society at large as much as on the "timeless" associations of the warrior hero as documented by French.

Professor French recounts the many myths that built the Code beginning with the Iliad. Noting that alliance leads to war, and that war leads to gain, she even admits the self-serving nature of the propaganda of this ancient war of aggression. But, her perspective prevents her from seeing a full modern parallel in the elite warrior propaganda she, herself, preaches earlier and later in the text. Indeed, she is under the spell of the Code – a true member of the Cult – or she would see that (as in the Chris Hedges title) war is the thing that gives her meaning. In the Iliad it was the machinations of the wealthy elite that draws all else into "the brutality of war." She cites Hector's nobility of character as the prime factor in his mythic immortality as a warrior hero. Alternatively, in my perspective the war system itself is the immortalizing agent. Instead of lamenting Hector, I lament the unsung nobility of character of the farmer of the Troad, or of the Achaean concubine. The Code may protect the psychology of the warrior, but it does nothing for the intentional and unintentional victims of war. Rape was honorable for the Viking and the Nazi saw himself as a warrior. This is because things like politics have dipped the warrior into the sewer as thoroughly as Achilles was dipped into the Styx. Nationalism is more recent than the Code, and nationalism has corrupted whatever part of the warrior and his code that does not serve nationalism. Functioning in service to nationalism transforms the warrior – no matter what his (or her) individual intent. No longer can Professor French's warrior serve only the abstract greater good. The result is the soldier. Despite their patriotic self-sacrifice, the reality is that the military specifically and soldiers generally are instruments of the state – they are means to the ends of the political and economic elite. Now the soldier in thrall to the state executes specific orders of distant politicians with equally different perspectives and goals. What cheapens the brotherhood of the warrior band is the expending of their lives for distant, ill-defined, or non-existent goals. Or, even worse, this nationalist transformation means the sacrifice of soldiers lives for goals that result in conditions far worse than prior to military intervention.

The warrior is supposed to serve the greater good – albeit with the point of a sword. The greater good is greater than any state. Even beyond concerns of humanity, life itself may be the greatest good. The soldier – however – serves the state. Patriotism poisons the warrior and reduces his/her Code to a kind of pragmatic utilitarianism. The state gets its soldiers, whose job it is to kill in the service of the goals and objectives of political and economic elite of the state. These leaders "conditionalize" the Code – massaging it to the aims of policy. In the hands of politicians, the Code becomes a tool used to dupe would-be warriors into instead becoming soldiers in service to the elite. The code emerges as a political tool for psychological motivation. The warrior in the service of the greatest good becomes the soldier in service to politics. Later, with the passing of the patriotic fog of war, the soldier is often left at best with depression, and a gnawing feeling of both betrayal, and of being betrayed. At worst, the soldier lives with social dislocation and post traumatic stress syndrome.

If the warrior seeks to redeem her/himself and the Code, s/he must frequently work against the aim of the state. Sometimes, this means s/he kills for a (supposedly) higher ideal than a flag. And sometimes it means that he does not kill at all. Nonetheless, the state with its political and economic elite manipulates the Code of the Warrior – tailoring it, and Taylorizing* it to fit the maintenance of concentrated wealth and power. Though frequently used, the Vietnam War is still a fine example. We see a conflict between the soldier and the warrior (as Shannon French defines him) in the James William Gibson book: <u>Warrior Dreams: Paramilitary Culture in Post Vietnam America</u>. It is a struggle between the killer for the state and the killer for higher ethical purposes. Gibson's dark approach highlights that this dissonance between warrior and soldier all too often occurs in the same individual. Gibson's book brings war full circle. He shows not only the implications of the failure of the Code for soldiers, but also the social and cultural trauma to (United States) society as a result of conflicts between the ideal and the real in Vietnam.

One of the reasons Shannon French wrote <u>The Code of the Warrior</u> was the post Vietnam War malaise that the American military establishment found itself in. French seeks (as with Gibson) to resurrect the ancient warrior and his Code to redeem the modern U.S. soldier from the shambles he was left with as a result of Vietnam. At the beginning of

Vietnam, American Cold War policy makers joined with corporate elite in promoting the conflict on grounds of public necessity. The people of Vietnam were to be liberated from foreign influence and dominance. Communism must be checked and capitalism freed. To this end, the warrior code was channeled. Films early in the Vietnam War like the classic John Wayne movie: "Green Berets," cloaked the war effort in the noblest of mantles. Valiant U.S. servicemen – soldiers – were warriors in a glorious redemptive struggle.

Then, something happened. As time marched on, the truth, battered and bruised, came with it. The turning point for civilian America was Tet of 1968. After that massive communist offensive against South Vietnam and their allies, public opinion changed. The war emerged as what it was. Vietnam became an interminable protracted conflict in which the aims and goals shifted with the political necessities of the moment. It was a conflict in which victory was a vague and ill-defined concept not fully understood by most leadership, military personnel, and the American public. The soldier on the ground was caught between warrior ethics and the rather less ethical, often immoral demands of political leaders, of their elite economic backers, and of war itself. In the U.S., the public increasingly turned against the Vietnam War. Even staunch conservatives and other traditional war-hawks advocated an end to the war. It was then that the hypocrisy began to show in films like: "The Deer Hunter," and "Apocalypse Now." These films and others since highlighted the ultimate futility of (the) war, as well as the twisted corruption by government of those men who sought to adhere to the Code of the Warrior while serving as a tool of state policy. Later news reports revealed that the movies were rarely fictional. Atrocities such as My Lai demonstrated the hypocrisy of war. This does not disparage the warrior or the soldier – or even the Code. Re-read it if you think it does. What this analysis does – as history has – is disparage the political and economic system of leadership that wasted so much human life on all sides. It was a leadership that then turned against the surviving soldiers who questioned the war system.

All the moral pretensions to a Code overlook the fact that soldier's "Warrior Code" is not a guarantee of more than following the moral values of the leaders of society. In that sense, the Warrior's Code is socially defined. After all, Nazis had the Code. The Huns of Attila had the Code. In fact, the character issue is moot. And, atrocity in war may be more consistently flagrant when the warrior's Code is used to join militarily effective behavior with social endorsement – when military morals are consistent with social ones. French makes the assumption that military values imbued in the Code of the Warrior elevate society, when instead it is the opposite. Political and economic leaders of society have twisted the Code for their own purposes. It can very well be said that social institutions have worked against the heroic values of the warrior. In this sense, it is the institutional manipulation of the Code that has made warrior's code moral values relative to the demands of concentrated wealth and power. If the moral behavior of the soldier is relative, not absolute, then there is no Code of the Warrior. Witness Abugraib prison. Strict adherence to the Code by military personnel did little good for the victims of race-based atrocity, such as Filipinos in the Philippine Insurrection, or Native

Americans at Wounded Knee, or Muslims at Guantanamo (Human Rights Watch).

When something is systemic, it allows that no individual (male) be held responsible. No villain (other than the profit motive) need be considered. That's "just the way it is," We are told. But there is a chain of events surrounding armed conflict that can readily be witnessed. Clearly wealth and power follow war. And, the wealthy and powerful are (usually) specifically identifiable people. War is an economy. Catastrophic loss for one side, volcanic gains for the other – you guess which side is usually the aggressor. Wealth in whatever concept is what organized conflict is all about - period. Conflict on the level of social organization that war represents is unthinkable without the idea of profit, status, and personal gain. However wealth has been configured – as position, as land, or natural resources, as cattle, or material goods, or as slaves – people have been willing to join together in order to dispossess others of wealth, or to defend their wealth from others. While it is unclear if groups with few categories of wealth show any dramatic reduction in organized violence, what is clearly inferred is that the concept of wealth, and especially personal property, promotes social organization and organized violence. In this concept, social status may also be considered as wealth. If not directly linked to wealth, social position is always translatable within any social system into material wealth. That is part of what a hierarchical society does – link social advantage to material culture. "He" who has wealth, has power, and "he" who has social power, can accumulate wealth. Money may not be the root of all evil, but the lack of money may be.

Historically, we may talk about class, and

honor, and religion as motivators to war, but the profit concept overrides and unifies them all. In search of wealth and the status that gives access to wealth in a society, people have marshaled whatever resources they have possessed. Protecting an economy, or expanding an economy, is among the top justifications for war. The other top justification is prestige. Call it honor, pride, social status, or whatever, if it can be made to be inspirational before and during the war, it can also be made profitable after the war. As will be outlined below (especially in C. *Raiding.*, D. *Territorial Skirmish*, J. *Imperial Expansion*, and P. *Modified Capitalism*), the social class that benefits from war historically seeks to promote the ongoing social structure.

A highly developed sense of material (economic) culture has become synonymous with human beings and civilization. We like our things. What this means is that we have let things give humankind social identity. What we have – in a material culture – defines who we are. This is the trap of capitalism and materialism, that a person's fundamental humanity becomes subordinated to the social concept of wealth. The ultimate reality that this cultural idea provides is one in which people and their experiences are less important than things and their accumulation. In fact, people *become* things under the social and cultural influences of the idea of private property. Thus, lives can be traded for territorial gain. People can die, "spent" for a "strategic objective," and, the end of war brings prosperity for the victor. Or, I should say, the prosperity from victory in war goes to the dominant class of the victorious state. It may be that the economic benefits of war "trickle down" to other classes of society – or it may not be so. In industrial and post-industrial contemporary nation-states, it has often been the case that war prosperity does indeed enhance the wealth of entire nations. The post-World War II U.S. economy combined with Cold War spending elevated the economic opportunities of most citizens – ethnic minorities and women (partly) excluded. For the bulk of the pre-industrial human experience with organized violence, however, mostly the elite classes financially benefited from war. In those days, war captives became valuable slaves and women were "booty" – profit. As always and in any era, human suffering was the widespread result of war. And, as ever, the motivations of the elite class outweighed the interests of the innocent dead. Collateral damages were within acceptable levels.

What this all means is that economics drives an interaction between the culture of war and the social institutions that make war – and the concentration of wealth – possible. Another way to say it is that war makes wealth possible. Or, more exactly, war makes concentrated wealth possible. And that concentrated wealth makes war probable. Economics, after all, is definable as the way in which resources are redistributed in a society. From the beginning of humanity, economics have been based on natural resources of the environment, and the social organization of labor that is the human ability to organize and extract those resources. Economics therefore, also means the ability to extract resources from the social environment. People become workers or soldiers in the service of obtaining resources. If they are soldiers, then the extraction is a violent exercise in economic exploitation of both the social and natural environments. Wealth for the victor is the result. War has been a (the) central method of both dominating the labor that extracts and creates wealth, and of "extracting" wealth from the social environment.

In the <u>Report From Iron Mountain</u>, Lewin (Navasky) relates a definition of the environmental imperative of the war system. All other species aside, the fictive panel of scientists in the prophetic project predictably settled on the balance between human populations and available environmental resources as the critical relationship. I would further define this in terms of the theory of carrying capacity – a geographic equation of the productive capability of particular ecosystems and of human ecology. Social institutions initially developed to increase the yield of nature's bounty to get more of what we need to live from the land we live on. This boosted carrying capacity means more people survive. More people *can* thrive. These same social systems that provide plenty can also create and maintain artificial disparities. We call these disparities wealth, but it really means poverty and want for most. It is instead, a concentration of wealth. What is most important in this view of war, society, and the environment are those who are poor and how they come to be poor in the environment of potential plenty. It is absolutely essential that the argument about why we war embrace the majority of people who are kept in a marginal status. While social organization has allowed humankind to dramatically boost the carrying capacity of the ecosystem, the fact of ongoing social poverty is also a product of social organization. The war system encourages a shift in focus away from issues of social class to an enemy (foreign or domestic) that can be blamed for disparity. Thus, the elite also use the war system to distracting advantage. Wealth remains concentrated, and the poor have someone else – someone foreign or domestic – to blame – and to fight.

Anthropological research has demonstrated that social, cultural (and biological) diversity may well provide for the widest range of opportunities for survival and prosperity. Culture especially offers the broadest possible base for positive social change. However, humankind's history of social intolerance to diversity has also become one of the single greatest potential reasons for war. So while many forms of cultural and biological diversity may be good for us, some forms of social diversity may not. In particular, economic diversity – especially to the point of disparity and denial of human rights may be adverse. And, the disparate social distribution of human rights encourages conflict when paired with concentrated wealth and power. Better understanding the link between society and culture may be the key to ending war (and perhaps key to human survival as a species). We have created social institutions first to ensure, and then to control our prosperity. Many of those institutions also have controlled the specific prosperity of select groups of our society as a whole. Institutions in the United States (for instance) treat diverse groups differently. There is institutional racism. Gender, race, class, ethnicity, nationality, ideology, and culture have all become reasons for formal and informal discrimination. Human potential to end conflict becomes limited when social institutions perpetuate social disparity based on diversity. The poor can be (and have been) politically motivated to conflict. Political leaders and the economic elite that would otherwise be responsible for the prosperity and well being of all instead use their control of social institutions to manipulate the poor to war. Instead of re-allocating or re-distributing wealth to end want, the political and economic elite maintain and enhance their concentrated wealth by turning the system and the poor to a culture of conflict – a culture of war.

This is another point at which war can begin to be disengaged from the equation. War serves a particular kind of human ecology. We can look at other ways to reinforce society and its ability to insure human survival and prosperity. It is not necessary to prey on one another in order to prosper. Environmentally, human social organization need not rely on war and the threat of war. It has just been the easy and natural response of the socially organized elite to turn to war as a solution to stabilizing the social environment we, ourselves, have created. It's time to choose another way.

1. Technologic patterns – The James Burke of War

In a landmark of original thinking, James Burke conceived and produced the <u>Connections</u> educational documentary series and books. These views into human cultural evolution centered on technology and society. In the first of them, Burke unfolds his "trigger effect" thesis. Humanity has developed as a technological species in the same sense as the punctuated evolution theory defined earlier in this book. Technology is the trigger. Although change is constant, we have a history of long periods of relative sameness and stability punctuated by watersheds of rapid techno-social change. An "invention" that usually is a reorganization of existing elements –

technological preconditions – changes the way we all live and think. These changes are inevitable and irrevocable, and they themselves precipitate more change, according to Burke. You cannot "un-invent" the gun, for instance.

The culmination of the first series of connections is a pinnacle of human social organization and technological ingenuity – A United States Strategic Air Command nuclear bomber. The final episode of the first series suggests that social and technological change is so rapid, and that the various means of self-destruction we have pioneered are so effective, that we must either choose a fate, or suffer one. And, even more than ever before, we must begin to see the World and our interconnections much differently as a consequence of both change and technology. Burke is thoroughly illuminating. The original madness of mutually assured destruction, and the continued post Cold War government emphasis on tactical nuclear, chemical, and biological warfare (and, other forms of terrorism) have made the words of Burke absolutely prophetic when it comes to why we war. He asserts that war is one of the most common and consistent triggers of change that humanity has ever known. As a social phenomenon and constant of human change, I assert that it is also one of the main reasons that human social organization has not progressed, as well.

Technology has provided the methods of human survival. But at each crest in historic waves of event, technologic advance has been punctuated by military conflict and technologic superiority has been defined by methods of destruction. Human history is a history of technologic conflict. The turning point was when tools became weapons and innovation was at the beck and call of destruction.

Other aspects of human technology, such as monumental architecture and civic design from "cyclopean walls" of Troy to the Great Wall of China, to the City of Quartz, give evidence of the deep investment in war. Also, metallurgy, chemistry, medicine, firearms, dynamite, the Gatling gun, radio, autos, planes, nuclear, space travel – all influenced by war. For example: Metallurgy & militarism – metal used for tools of war were originally bronze and copper. These metals (unlike iron and later steel) are not superior to obsidian or flint in cutting edge. But metals are easier for a central authority to control and mass produce for soldiery. Through these and more, humanity is intimately integrated with technology through culture and social organization. It has been an exceptionally useful symbiosis of sorts. While technology provides for medicine, shelter, superior crop yields, and other positive things, it also has been diverted to destruction. Simulators can help surgeons to perfect life-saving procedures, but they can also be used to train suicide bombers how to fly planes into buildings. This technological investment in destruction is discretionary. We need not choose to go to "the Dark Side of the Force."

	<The Great Wall of China
	< Nakhal Fort, one of the best-preserved forts in Oman Photographed by Andy Carvin, October 2003. .
	< Bourtange (http://www.bourtange.n l) fortification, restored to 1750 situation, Groningen, Netherlands

War impacts civic design. One way that the word civilization has been defined is: "settled populations living in cities." The way archaeologists and historians identify ancient cities is by their architecture. Civic design shows us much about the concerns of early civilization. Just as future archaeologists will be able to deduce our dependence on fossil fuels be looking at the remains of vast highway systems, so we can infer the dependant investment in war by the architecture and civic design of our near and distant ancestors.

< American Civil War surgeons using a casualty to train other surgeons in amputation. Civil War photographs, 1861-1865 / compiled by Hirst D. Milhollen and Donald H. Mugridge, Washington, D.C. : Library of Congress, 1977. No. 0866
Title from Milhollen and Mugridge.
Forms part of Selected Civil War photographs, 1861-1865 (Library of Congress)

< Modern land mines have caused traumatic amputations of many children. These victims have advanced the field of prosthetics. The late Princess Diana was one of many activists calling for an end to mass production and indiscriminate use of land mines.

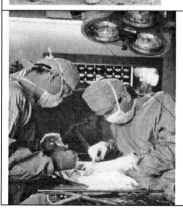

< Contemporary trauma medicine and many surgical techniques have evolved directly from war.

While health care and medical treatment has always been a subject of concern in human civilization, war has been a catalyst for advances in medical science. Many surgical techniques and chemical medicines advanced not when peaceful citizens were in need, but when the circumstances of casualties in war demanded it. War, and it's companion horsemen Famine and Pestilent disease, made conditions requiring rapid changes in medicine. On the surface, this may seem good – but this skewed investment gave humanity mustard gas and other chemical & biological weapons, like ricin.

	<Firearm inventor Samuel Colt was one of hundreds of weapons innovators who applied technology to efficient killing with the support of the business and governmental sectors.
	<The 1911 Colt .45 automatic pistol and the large "manstopping" cartridge perfected by gun inventor John M. Browning was adopted as the standard issue sidearm of the United States military at the insistence of another gun inventor, John Thompson – inventor of the "tommy gun" – a submachine gun. General and gun inventor, Thompson noted the lack of efficient killing power of previous military pistols in the American war against the Moros of the Philippines.
	< Gatling gun illustrated in an 1885 encyclopedia in Swedish http://www.lysator.liu.se/runeberg/nfai/0122

	< The modern incarnation of the Gatling gun the GAU-8 Gatling gun of an A-10 Thunderbolt II at Osan Air Base, Korea
	< Weapons to deter war? At each step of military weapons development, two things are in common; #1 The myth of deterrence through superior firepower, and #2 the tremendous corporate profit in arms sales once a government adopts the "new technology" for research and development. Atomic bomb inventor Robert Oppenheimer's Quote on seeing the technological achievement of the atomic bomb: "I am become death, the destroyer of worlds."

"God made men – Sam Colt made 'em equal." Under the influences of the war system, Springfield became the Nation's armory in 1789. Alfred Nobel made high explosive weapons possible. The DuPont family fortune was originally made in the manufacture of military explosives. The Gatling gun was created to make war so horrible that it would never occur again. Nuclear arms are supposed to also be "deterrents."

< Frederick Winslow Taylor was an early American efficiency expert who pioneered the ideas of production and motivation that made the United States the giant of industrial productivity in World War I and World War II. His method of "scientific management" caused workers at one Watertown munitions factory to strike in 1911, which resulted both in Congressional hearings and widespread adoption of his methods.

We Can Do it. Color poster by J. Howard Miller, World War II. National Archives and Records Administration.

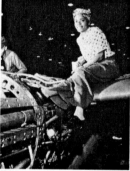

Riveter at Lockheed Aircraft Corp., Burbank, CA. World War II. National Archives and Records Administration.

< "Stars over Berlin and Tokyo will soon replace these factory lights reflected in the noses of planes at Douglas Aircraft's Long Beach, Calif., plant. Women workers groom lines of transparent noses for deadly A-20 attack bombers." Alfred Palmer, October 1942. 208-AA-352QQ-5. National Archives and Records Administration.

In the early 20th Century United States, Frederick Winslow Taylor – industrialist and entrepreneur – conceived of the maximum level of labor efficiency. His idea was to use the worker to do the most simple and repetitive task as rapidly as possible to produce as much "product" as possible in a given time period. This "Taylorization" led to abysmal working conditions, and equally high profits. But, that was O.K. because workers were as interchangeable as the parts they worked on. "Taylorization" in labor is never more evident than when a nation is occupied with war. And, in the modern era of the post industrial nation, Taylorization has been applied to warfare. F.W. Taylor was the first efficiency expert. His principles not only influenced war technology, but the efficient waging of modern war, itself. The most recent results are the Space Race – intercontinental ballistics, laser sighted "smart bombs," and star wars. And all are the products of the application of industrial technology to war. Another "product" of Taylorized war is that to many policy makers soldiers have become dispensable parts – means to achieve mission ends.

This image is licensed under the GNU Free Documentation License. It uses material from the Wikipedia article Nuclear power plant.

United States nuclear weapons test. USAFNS

B 52 nuclear Bomber. USAFNS

"Tactical" nuclear weapons. USAFNS

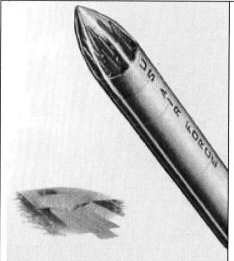

< The "Peacekeeper" was one of several types of multiple warhead nuclear missiles that were capable of independently targeting several objectives. Such MIRV's could contain ten or more nuclear warheads.

This image is licensed under the GNU Free Documentation License. It uses material from the Wikipedia article MIRV multi-warhead nuclear missile.

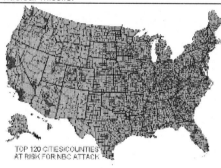

<FEMA NBC (nuclear, biological, chemical) attack risk map of the 21st Century United States.
http://www.alpinesurvival.com/ Homeland_Security_Fema.htm l

Now, in the era of the "Endless Energy" of the atom, we have nuclear reactors fashioned specifically to produce fissionable bomb material in countries around the globe. As well as the threat of the terrorist dirty bomb, we have 2500 nukes in the immediate command of President George W. Bush alone.

This image is licensed under the GNU Free Documentation License. It uses material from the Wikipedia article Archery.

Ricardo Domínguez *(left)* versus Rafael Ortíz. This image is licensed under the GNU Free Documentation License. It uses material from the Wikipedia article Boxing.

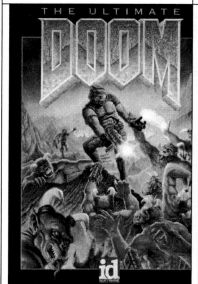

This image is licensed under the GNU Free Documentation License. It uses material from the Wikipedia article Doom.

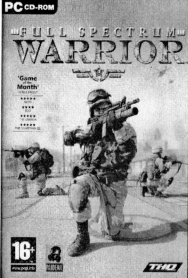

This image is licensed under the GNU Free Documentation License. It uses material from the Wikipedia article Full Spectrum Warrior.

Then, there are the "War Games. " These range from the pseudo war of sports (Olympics etc.) to Nintendo, PS2, and X-Box. In this category of human investment in war there are simply too many examples for this book to hold. Brand names of games like "Doom." And "Quake" are alongside of those that were developed with government funds, like "Full Spectrum Warrior." All are games that highlight the skills of war, and insensitivity to death; i.e., detachment and objectification.

2. War Games – War as a Video Game

"Children and adolescents are spending significant amounts of time playing video games, with little parental monitoring. The majority of these games contain some amount of violent content. Research suggests that repeated exposure to video games with violent content is associated with a constellation of negative outcomes for youth, including academic difficulties, aggression, trait hostility, and lower scores on measures of empathy." -Clinician's Research Digest. July, 2004, page 5.

Games like "Call of Duty: Big Red One" have found a way to commit two deadly sins simultaneously. The technologically heightened realism brings all the adrenaline rush and action-oriented exhilaration of fighting with none of the consequence. This techno-distance conditions players to seek perfection in systematic slaughter while removing any sense of risk, responsibility, or remorse. It is the thrill of the kill – "The courage of the knife, but not of the blood."

In the recent film: "What The Bleep do We Know?" producers William Arntz, Betsy Chasse, and Mark Vicente bring us to a new realization concerning behavior and thought that clarifies the results of video games in a less clinical way. The central revelation is that our habits "re-wire" our brains – brains that, in turn, control our future behaviors. It has long been known that how we think regulates our actions, but what has now been show down to the sub-atomic level, is that our actions condition how we think. Our reality is dependent partly on what we choose to experience. In fact, the chemical release in the brain as a result of many activities is addictive in itself. We seek the same thrill of that specific brain chemical release. We crave this action-release/response on a level far below the conscious level. In effect, we re-invent our brains for whatever behaviors and associated activities that we engage in repetitively enough. Normally this is called "learning." Although this is an automatic adaptive strategy, it is also clear that we enter into an addictive loop, here. Once systematic violence and insensitivity to human life becomes a game through technology, the addictive loop is war.

Humankind's symbiotic attachment to culture and its cold and impartial offspring technology has led to a relentless escalation in homicidal ability. Since the earliest hominid ancestor first clutched a jagged stone, our disposition to alter the environment instead of being altered by it has led to a horrific potential of self-destruction. Even our philosophy of physics – our very perception of the universe – reveals an objectified world where stable order (substance, matter, peace) and chaotic decay (energy, war) are in dynamic (kinetic) interplay. There is a disconnect between viewer and viewed. A kind if dispassionate dis-empathy develops from this coldly mechanistic brand of technology. Objectively, we impose our will over the environment as though we are elevated and independent. Even though physicists have long proven the subjective nature of the universe through the Heisenberg principle of uncertainty and its modifications, we still cling socially to the notion of objectivity. The objective social perspective has cased us to see each war as an incident, and not to see war as endemic to civilization. This false objectivity makes us think of a human being as an object, and to value one life above another.

If, as a species, we are to survive ourselves, it must be in recognition of the "lessons" of history. If the endless cycle of violence is to cease, we must realize that like our primitive ancestor, we carry in our hands the seed of life and the seed of death. We, perhaps, always have, and we certainly always will.

B. Words of War – War and the Language of Killing

"...the legitimacy of a state depended on linguistic unity..."
Kissinger: 145, A World Restored.

Language is the medium of shared culture and society. We define ourselves through language, giving ourselves both meaning and purpose. The way we talk to ourselves about war means a lot about why we war, and why there is no lasting peace. Words are used to define the enemy. Words are used to join "us" together against "them." Historians, who themselves are products of patriotic culture interpret events in an effort to create a single functional identity. Often the identity is national. Politicians make that history function by refining nationalistic history into political rhetoric. The average citizen grows up immersed in this linguistic environment. Words, phrases, and slogans of the linguistic environment of nationalism produce a particular social psychology. That social psychology is one which supports war.

For the example this time, I again select the United States. I have chosen personal experiences often in this book for reasons discussed form the start of this book. Some of these include the ambivalence of my life – being a pro-peace martial artist, for instance. Other reasons involve the current U.S status as sole superpower, and the creeping hegemony that has resulted. But, why I do so now is significant for some additional reasons worthy of mention. Firstly, as a native speaker, I am intimately familiar with American Standard English, as well as several sub-dialects. Secondly, I am a member of a designated minority group. Being of marginal social status means that I have a critically different view of language and national identity than those who have not had to be bi-cultural. So, while as a male born in the United States I am an insider, simultaneously, as a member of a racial group not in political or economic dominance, I am an outsider. Thirdly, I am from a social class that historically has little economic opportunity for advancement. I am poor. This means that I am from a social class that is usually recruited for war. Taken together, this all means that I see things differently. I see from the bottom up, not the top down. My father served more than three decades in the military. My uncle likewise spent over thirty years in law enforcement. In the neighborhoods (linguistic and otherwise) in which I grew up, military service was dangled as an ever-present opportunity to secure both economic stability, and increased social acceptance. The military was (and is) a way out of poverty – as the commercials say: "Be all that you can be – in the Army." I have always been aware of linguistic utility – especially the dissonance between life as I lived it, and as it has been portrayed in media – and of shifting dynamics of national unity. As such then, this is not a linguistic analysis as much as it is a look at how we talk to ourselves about war.

Historians from George Bancroft through the late Stephen E. Ambrose have woven with words a colorful nationalist history for the United States of America. It is a history, but it also is a rhetoric that supports war. Word choices they made in interpreting the facts of history enrich the rhetorical pool politicians use to motivate the nations' poorer people to war. But though I fault them, remember, these historians were themselves products of culture and cultivated awareness. Examine the way that nationalist historians have characterized the wars that the United States has participated in. The Revolutionary War, also called the War for Independence is offered as a brave, unique, and glorious struggle against the tyranny of England that allowed our Founding Fathers to "establish justice and secure the blessings of liberty to ourselves and our posterity." And, after the Constitution, the Bill of Rights insured liberty by guaranteeing Americans the right to keep and bear arms. The Civil War freed the nation of the evil of Black slavery and re-established the United States of America. The Spanish-American War was to liberate our "little brown brothers" from the yoke of oppressive European colonialism. World War I was a "war to end all wars," and a "war for democracy." World War II was a "war against fascism," and a "war against racism." During the Cold War, the U.S. continued as the "arsenal of democracy" protecting the world against "godless" communists. And even the failed Vietnam War was a struggle to protect the South Vietnamese from the "Red Menace" of the "domino principle." It was said that Vietnam was the conflict in which we won all the battles, but lost the war.

The word choices that historians make in recording war may either support war or inhibit the acceptance of war. Apart from the selection of words and their application to the interpretation of history, culture, or reality, the choice of whose voice is heard also promotes war. The victor always approves of war more than the victim. The rhetoric of the politician always differs from that of the draftee. Veteran Howard Zinn and other historians differ in the interpretation of the same events. They differ in some important ways that are fundamental to our understanding both of language and history, as well as war. Zinn, in his benchmark text: A People's History of the United States eloquently refers to history from the "bottom up" (pg 11, of the 1999 edition). By this he means history as has been experienced by those who make up the majority of the human race. Not the elite, but the average – if there is such. He and other historians feel what I see as a legitimate and pressing need to produce work which is both inclusive, and humanitarian. We know that history has been interpreted to serve war while it is more valuable – and valid – for history and civilization to serve peace. In Zinn, the brave struggles of the American Revolution are those of the Black slave who sided with the colonies only to find that promises to end forced servitude were not kept by recruiting Founding Fathers. Or the women who supported independence with their labor and lives, as well as with the lives of their sons, fathers, brothers, and husbands only to find that victory meant that women would continue to be politically powerless exploited workers for centuries afterwards. And, then there were the Native Americans. For them the American Revolution meant the beginning of the end of Indian liberty. American independence would mean Native genocide at the hands of the "free and the brave." If social reality is defined democratically as the most common experience, then the words of the "little brown brothers" about how their lives should be lived are more important to more people in Cuba, Hawaii, or the Philippines than those of Roosevelt, Taft, or either Mac Arthur. The voices of Black rebel David Fagin or Filipino leader Emilio Aguinaldo are as definitive as those of Frederick Funston. And, that the rhetoric of the political leaders of the four World Wars (One, Two, Cold, and On Terrorism) must be balanced against that of the dissident, or the peasant, or even the words of the simple soldier on *both sides* of each front. Ultimately, the words of a Vietnamese refugee may be more relevant than the experience of General William Westmoreland in defining war. This would be a democratic history. It is not (on bulk) the history we have in print.

It should begin to be clearer now that those terms by which we define ourselves and – perhaps as importantly – by which others define us, are quite important to how and why organized social conflict happens. Terms like race, ethnicity, and nationality are often used interchangeably in the media. But, word choices both represent and perpetuate cultural understandings. Every sub-term – like *Red* race, or *Black* race – has social and cultural meanings. Individual and collective identity hinges on what we assume those terms to mean. This assumption of meaning affects everyone's daily reality. It becomes essential to understanding ourselves socially and culturally to know what we call ourselves and why. War often predicates itself on words. There are the well-known derogatory and offensive stereotypes, but what is important here are the terms that are socially acceptable and politically correct. How a slur evolves, and becomes political rhetoric is at the root of why wars occur.

From RCA. NARA (NWDNS-44-PA-1795)	From General Motors. NARA (NWDNS-44-PA-2314)

In order to kill a human being, we must limit both their humanity, and our own. We use language to do this. War represents a social act of genocide for which the dimensions of humanity must reduce and contract to occur. The enemy must become objects that are less than human. We must become individual heroes that display characteristics that are more than human. They are craven, and we are righteous. They are demons, while we are gods. Or, at least we do the work of God. While they may (must) be dogged and implacable enemies in order to justify and validate our own determination, they are (must be) evil and misguided in their violence, while we are purposeful, honorable and just in our violence. They are offensive, while we are defensive. They aggress, but we intervene, respond or retaliate. Their attacks are vicious, while ours are strategic. We have victories, but our enemy perpetrates massacres. We are defending our freedom. They threaten liberty. We engage in police actions to counter their anarchy. This is the language of war, and of the rhetoric for organizing a society for war.

NARA ARC

NARA ARC

Language of this type is a necessary contrivance. It is hard to get a stranger to kill another stranger if common humanity alone is recognized between them. Knowing each other's childhood nicknames and sharing baby pictures may make non-combatants of us all. If "the enemy" can be made less than human through words, and images then killing is less of a problem. If the enemy can become a one-dimensional representative of evil, then killing becomes an essential duty. Adding nationalistic and/or religious language offers the soldier the chance for elevation to the social role of hero for doing his "duty" and killing the foreign heathen, idolater, or heretic. What language objectifies and dehumanizes within a social culture?

Political and economic leaders readily turn concepts embodied in the historical language of conflict to the service of war. The phrase "self-defense" and the concepts it embodies have been used as part of the linguistic basis for war. Self-defense is universally understood to make homicide justifiable – it justifies killing. I have written this before, but this is not redundant, it is emphatic. Law generally recognizes immediate threats to life and limb (and often property) as acceptable and appropriate reasons for the exercise of lethal force. The problem is that the language that I just used is regularly abstracted to endorse all manner of sustained organized mayhem. War is construed as a collective and continuous act of necessary self-defense. The concepts of immediate threat are transferred to a group of people – a race, a nation, or a religion for instance. The immediate act of self-defense becomes a protracted obligation. Lethal force becomes the only legitimate response for self-defense situations. The thought that there may be alternative approaches is discounted in the language of national self-defense. All other possible responses are predicated on lethal force. Instead of one option among many, lethal force becomes the central response. Killing, which would otherwise be the extreme reaction, evolves instead through language to be the primary social reaction, and a long-term reaction at that.

Personal combat is the term given to a fight between two supposedly equal belligerents. No two individuals are equal, or they would not be individuals - so too nations. Personal combat, then, is a term, a linguistic contrivance to rationalize establishing dominance. "Personal Combat" is elite and elevating. It is another way of using language to make warfare honorable and intimate. The usage of the term personal combat invokes social status, and moral content. That in turn inspires imitation. After all, the defeated was overwhelmed because they were "wrong," and the victor triumphed because they were "right." With the evolution of war came an expanded definition of personal combat. Through the use of language invoking personal combat, propaganda can swell the ranks of armies bent on "defending our honor." What was once either a sanctified trial between individuals (holmgang or einvigi), or a battle that was a series of combats between elite champions became a contest between elite military officers who used hundreds of men as their weapons of personal combat. Even later, we find the evolution of language whereby the opposing nations in a war are identified by the names of their (non-combatant) political leaders. On the evening news, the war was between Bush and Hussein – as though they were locked in personal combat. This language mitigates the loss of human rights of the many willing and unwilling participants of war.

As a motivator to war, the language of *want* can easily become the language of *need*. When this happens and want becomes seen as need, then an enemy becomes any who have what you need, or any who prevent you from getting what you need.

Wanting more food, or land, or resources of any kind is expressed as an absolute need. The linguistic distinction becomes blurred the more the words are shuffled politically. After all, a need is something that supposedly cannot be done without. A need is absolutely indispensable. A population that can be convinced that their needs are being withheld is one that is readily motivated to organize (perpetually) for war. The threat is as tangible as self-defense. The wants of the political and economic elite are regularly couched in terms of needs for the whole of the society. Certainly, plenty of genuine needs exist – and other fictive needs are manufactured when genuine ones do not exist. Since ancient times, the elite convinced the population that elite wants were the collective needs of the system. The common good would be best served if the common person accepted the needs (wants) of the elite as their own needs. Modern elite groups with controlling access to mass media maintain a war of words over "needs" that encourages systematic and fervent policies of national and international violence.

War can also become a moral imperative carrying with it the mandate of heaven and the will of god. The rhetoric of organized religion is almost always employed for the benefit of armed struggle. Few war efforts have long survived without the endorsement of some scripture or another. Usually the reduction is towards the simplest of literary constructions – a dichotomy of absolutes. The linguistic interplay between good and evil, sacred and profane, light and darkness are ever-present in the dialog of war. The enemy becomes a collective representation of villainy for which every negative religious metaphor is appropriate. Indeed, the identity of the enemy is often linguistically constructed out of the vilest and most degenerate images of religion. They become demons and imps out of hell who need to be cast back into the pit of their unholy origin. We, on the other hand, are the righteous in the service of Our Lord. Not professional killers slaughtering human enemies for personal and national gain, but holy warriors crusading in the service of God(s) and the church. The enemy murders as an emissary of chaos, we smite evil as representatives of holy order. All good killers go to heaven.

There is a language of singular nobility applied to armed struggle. The honorable combatant raises himself in war to the level of hero. Language surrounding this phenomenon gives us the terms of social and political leadership. Nearly all such elite titles (and offices) relate to the language of military leadership. King, Count, or Duke – Shogun, Daimyo, or Commander in Chief relate to an elevation in social status of things military. Members of the military leadership become the social elite. And, the social elite are the economic and political elite.

While soldier is a term of social distinction, the word warrior is separately elevated above that. Higher ranked still is the appellation "officer." The cultural association of such titles and meanings to peacetime leadership roles means a perpetuation of the control of society by military minded people for military objectives. While it has been seen as appropriate to elevate the warrior during war, to maintain the elite status of the warrior in peace can only invite more war.

The language of patriotism and nationalism is thus far the most convenient vehicle for war. Nationalist rhetoric is an umbrella under which shelters nearly all of the verbal justifications for war. It may be offered that war is the only way to protect the nation. Or, it may be that the nation must expand to claim its contrived birthright and fulfill its fictive "destiny." Perhaps domestic or foreign enemies threaten the "purity" of the nation ethnically, or culturally, or religiously. It may well be said that the concept embodied in the word *nation* creates opposition and invites struggle. Language that defines a nation establishes specific relationships between territory, citizen and leadership, to be sure. But, nationalistic language also establishes adversarial international relationships. Almost inevitably, the tone and content of language used to establish the uniqueness of the nation pointedly excludes and/or disparages other nations. Those other nations do likewise, and lines are literally drawn in the sand. For people within the nation to cross the lines of nationalist rhetoric is to invite often-violent reprisals from their own patriotic neighbors. To question the nationalist culture from outside of the nation becomes an insult worthy of war. To paraphrase an old adage: Them's fightin' words.

The written and spoken word – language – promotes a certain psychology within the culture of conflict. This psychology is expressed through language as ideological imperatives and political rhetoric.

Human psychology enables human culture and society in four principle ways. The mind associates, it also discriminates, projects, and reflects. We humans associate things that are alike, and we also discriminate. Things that are grouped together based on what is shared, while things that differ are separated and segregated. The mind also projects

94

possibilities into a non-existent future. We anticipate a time and series of events ahead of the time we live in. We plan. Human psychology is also reflective. That is to say that we consider passed events as forming a past. Human psychology defines a sense of time. Without these functions of the mind, both culture and society as we know it could not exist (Bobby Hutchison, personal communication, April 2003). If psychology makes society possible, then psychology also makes war possible.

War is like god to us – if He did not exist, we would have to create Him. If no enemy exists for us, we seem to find one, whether it be within our midst or from without. The social psychology of race, class, and gender – to name a few – has demonstrated amazing vitality as producers of conflict. Sides are chosen, and enemies identified, partly just because human psychology promotes such associations. However, people also associate a host of other usually intangible attributes to any primary distinction. Therefore, the enemy becomes associated with evil, with unreasoning aggression, with horrid cruelty. This occurs even as we associate our side with goodness and justice. If they kill, it is excessive, and predatory. When "we" kill, it was necessary and justified, if not honorable. These associations allow the psychologically arrived at "enemy" to be worthy, even needy, of death.

When we are forced to see the ultimate reality of our foe – that they are as human as we – then our Psychology even allows the gymnastics of associating the enemy (through language) with attributes of the honorable enemy. This allows the soldier to continue in his profession while postponing the psychological impacts of killing. Lieutenant Colonel Dave

Grossman has written a text on the psychological cost of learning to kill. He has noted that most people (even men) have a psychological avoidance to killing other people. Further, that specific training is both necessary and effective at producing people able and willing to kill others like themselves at progressively higher rates. This training is mostly psychological. It is physical only to the necessary degree that it produces the psychology of organized murder. The warrior becomes a soldier and part of a social unit. It is a new tribe for which he (usually he) will kill, or sacrifice himself. This type of training can be most effective if it is made part of the status quo of a society – part of the culture. The warrior-become-soldier usually figures prominently in the literature of nationalist mythology. Thus, the most effective killers come from a highly developed (stratified) social system.

In Grossman's book <u>On Killing</u>, he illuminates the world of combat from the perspective of those who must convince otherwise empathetic and altruistic people to willingly organize the murder of other groups of other ordinarily empathetic and altruistic types. The contradiction is not lost on Grossman, who even as an elite member of the warrior class still admits to the excessive amount of social and cultural pre-conditioning for war which now occurs in the United States and the world. Aggression, pride, honor, envy, insecurity – these are all psychological imperatives that can be socially channeled into cooperative violence. War leaders use this psychology to rally mass support for militarism. Grossman discusses in detail the most successful uses of psychological conditioning as relates to war. As would be expected, closeness plays perhaps the most telling role. The combat soldier has the most resistance to killing someone who is probably just like himself, while the resistance to committing murder generally decreases as you get to the class of officers not on the front. Distance helps. Finally, predictably, the wealthy and politicians who use their influence to promote and profit from war seem to qualm the least about the actual realities of violent death. It is a great and dangerous trick of modern society that the psychology of distance has become the major successful strategy of government in the effort to maintain popular support for war. People are seduced continuously with films and sports justifying violence even before political conflict. When political and economic necessity requires the mobilization of the people for a "war effort," the people are already pre-conditioned to patriotism, and to reactionary violence. War is the next predictable psychological state towards which leadership would agitate the population.

The enemy must be reduced to the simplest example of opposition. Politicians, the press, and military officials frequently refer to the enemy by the name of their thoroughly villain-ized leader, by a derogatory stereotype, or just as the enemy. Real people in the complex human tragedies of war become a faceless mass. Concepts like national, racial, religious, or cultural pride replace the truth of human commonality with the divisive rhetoric of war. To recognize the humanity of "the other" becomes un-patriotic or even traitorous. Jingoistic slogans replace dialogs of peace. Nationalism replaces humanism. The threat potential of the enemy must me maintained.

The psychology of war is predicated on the

idea that peace is always threatened. War is the absence of peace. Thus, war nurtures itself. What is peace threatened by, you may well ask. War is what threatens peace. The war leadership must convince the people that war will preserve peace. This can only be done through consistent conditioning of populations to the possibility of war. This means the establishment of difference, and of objectification. Human rights must be secondary to national concerns. Individual people who are just like the soldier must be made to be thought of as the "other" – as a representative of a group – as less than human. Even though the "other" is in all reality similar to the soldier – if not identical – the leaders who advocate war must be able to psychologically invest the "other" with subhuman or superhuman characteristics. The enemy must have no redeeming value other than antagonist. He (and *his kind*) must become worthy of destruction. It also means that the soldier's society and culture must be one that authorizes both personal and group violence as an acceptable solution to social problems. A psychology of war means that individual judgment is suspended, that human life is a commodity, and that the goals of the state are always more important than the needs of the individual.

To this end, a psychology of conflict must be culturally supported through language, and a warrior mentality must be continually developed. Images that evoke the soldier as righteous warrior justified by God or Country abound. The cultivation of the mindset of mayhem begins at birth for most men. Maleness is given social meaning by competitive aggression. Manhood is defined through the potential of dominance. Dominance is realized through violence. Authority becomes associated with all manner of things in order to motivate the soldier to allegiance and a determination to complete the mission. Just as the enemy must become the evil, so too must the war leadership become all that is good – mom and apple pie, the flag and the president – hometown, girlfriend, and nation all in one. To go to war becomes an affirmation of manhood. The greatest good becomes the willingness to sacrifice one's life in the effort to take the life of another…and enrich the life of even another.

Underlying all is the perennial cult of the warrior. In the book The Code of the Warrior: Exploring Warrior Values Past and Present, author Shannon French describes in detail why and how a warrior's code is necessary. Most of their lives, most people are taught that fighting and killing are wrong. However, the elite of society also needs to count on a ready source of killers from among the same population. The answer is a systematic support for the cult of the warrior in society through a warrior's code. Often in modern times the centerpiece is nationalism. Professor French teaches at the United States Naval Academy, and is part of that systematic effort to socialize and legitimize military behavior. She cultivates warriors by using literary, historical, and linguistic exercises. Killing in war becomes honorable necessity, and not wanton murder, through such training in rational warfare. To be fair, her efforts are to bring a code of morality and sense of rules to warfare for the men and women who must engage in it. Yet, making killing a moral act with social sanction cannot help but perpetuate war.

Another of the codes of warriors is that known as Bushido. The Japanese samurai were imbued from birth with concepts of honorable death and acceptable atrocity. The word *bushido* literally means soldier's way. Although interpreted in differing contexts to have differing meaning, bushido was first and foremost a philosophy of death I service to one's Lord. An interesting twist on this ancient warrior's stoic code was the emphasis not only on the death of opponents, but on the death of the samurai himself. In the book of the samurai Hagakure (Hidden or Shadowed Leaves), author/warrior Tsunetomo Yamamoto related that life is nothing, that all is insignificant compared to death. His philosophy was that resolute acceptance of death was the only true way to know life. For Yamamoto, the way of a man's death was the most important thing in life. To properly seek noble death, one must have war.

C. Physical Anthropology - Sociobiology and War

In 1986 a group of scientists met in Spain to make a definitive statement against any biological basis for war. The Seville Statement on Violence debunked five specific stereotypes or myths about innate human aggression and war in the effort to remove excuses that have kept people from working for peace. A lot of these pseudo-science stereotypes about the "innate savagery" of the "killer-ape" have been used to rationalize an apathetic resignation to war and thus a further commitment to war. The Seville Statement has provided guidelines for teaching peace (see appendix notes for full text). Here is a summary of the findings of the committee:

1) War is cultural and social, not animal. Other animals do not make war, the human animal does. Through culture we can

change.

2)   War is not human nature. There is no possible genetic basis for war, just a set of predispositions that are enhanced or mitigated in response to the social and cultural environment.

3)   War does not produce a better quality of life for the victors. War does not result in any scientifically measurable economic or biological benefits for its participants.

4)   Violence is not "hard-wired" into the human brain. The brain is an organ that can be used – like a hand – to create or destroy.

5)   War is not caused by human instinct. Such instincts which may exist are far more subordinated to learning and reason in human behavior.

These are admirable and timely findings that dispel many myths of human culture and war. They support education for peace, and as such are long overdue. It is also quite significant that the sciences are taking an international lead in promoting peace through education. However, what is the connection between human biology and war?

Anthropology is the multi-faceted, interdisciplinary analysis of the human being. Broadly, the anthropological paradigm has almost always been a dynamic blend of culture and biology. Two of the main branches of anthropology are cultural and physical (biological). In cultural evolution, the evolution of culture produces social changes, and the social environment effects culture. The human being is seen as unique due to possessing culture and society. Biological change is either considered negligible or insignificant, depending on the interpretation. This is not the paradigm of physical anthropology. In physical anthropology, biology becomes the primary environment that produces the basis of social and cultural change.

Physical anthropologists study the biological human being. They investigate the origins, evolution and development of humankind. Of course the physical nature of human beings can hardly be separated from behavior, and of course, through behavior biology may infer social and cultural propensities. The form and function of the human hand, for instance, can be traced in the physical record of evolution. The human hand also prescribes behavior. Humans carry and fashion tools. This is social behavior, and infers cooperative social behavior. Tools in standard types or styles used in standard ways strongly suggest culture. We may not see nuances of culture or refinements of social behavior, but we will know they existed from the physical record. Some scientists who specialize in investigating the connection between biology and social behavior are called sociobiologists. Although at the worst (like history and anthropology) some sociobiology theories have been used to perpetuate racism and sexism, still there are important questions about war that sociobiological theory can help us answer – even indirectly. Perhaps most important to those of us who wish to end war is the question of the nature of any biologic basis for human aggression and how society translates that biology into war.

Many anthropologists think that – through culture – human society has replaced the natural environment. That, by virtue of technology and social organization humankind has enveloped itself in a largely artificial social environment. Further, that the importance of this social environment is the stalling or re-directing biologic evolution. This made social evolution more significant. The assertion is at least partially indisputable. Technology as a product of culture has enabled humankind to substitute or modify some influences of the natural environment for social influences. But, culture has been proven to be subject to aspects of the greater natural environment. We still rightfully worry about epidemics, global warming, or next years' hurricanes or crops because we cannot control them. Aspects of geography and cultural ecology clearly demonstrate the historic subordination of culture to nature. Human to human, society and culture defines, but human to nature, nature defines. A sophistication of technology may allow a wider human potential for operating within the natural environment, but we will still be operating within that environment.

Social behavior acts upon the biologic state of humanity, but biology (nature) is the driving force. We may develop and distribute vaccines – for instance – but we need to sustain efforts at developing new ones because biology simultaneously evolves resistances to current drugs even as it evolves newer diseases. And, if we cannot beat a disease, then humanity changes its social behavior – bottled water or condoms, anyone? Either way, biology subordinates society. Social behavior has roots in biology, and biological change is the result of social behavior over time. This is the basic idea behind sociobiology. Human genes regulate, restrict, and influence the basis of relationships. As always, there is (at least) a second half. Many relationships become formalized as institutions. Social institutions create sets of conditions that influence gene flow in human populations. In this theory of human realities, we are far more bound to our biology than in the earlier orientations. There is a twist here. Humanity adapts to the social environments that we, ourselves, create. This is the critical conjunction between the varying interpretations of why we war. We are biologically aggressive, but war or peace can be selected outcomes of social institutions. Nature has given us nurture.

Thus far, we have selected war as a product of our social institutions. Do we need to? What does the data say? Can violence really be a biological need of the human species that absolutely must socially express itself as war? Specifically, is it a social or a biological imperative that we fight wars? To what degree is it both? Can we socially "guide" ourselves toward peace?

And, is war a biologic mechanism of natural selection? Is it inexorable, intractable, and absolute? What would replace war? Are the nations going to war those who possess biologically adaptive, or biologically non-adaptive traits? Are these traits being selected out of the evolutionary scene, or is war becoming more a part of the human being?

When humankind was not the top predator, did the other top predators make war? If not, then something special, something social exists about war. Or, are warring nations on the bottom, not the top of the evolutionary plan? Is war a symptom of a dying society?

First, there are some important basic elements to the idea that war is a biological adaptation. One problem is that there may not have been enough biological time passed for war to be an adaptation in a Darwinian sense. After all, Humanity may stretch back a few million years, but civilization as we know it is only twelve thousand years old or so. This is hardly evolutionary or geological time. Biological change usually takes awhile in most complex organisms. It would simply take longer for something as drastic and involved an adaptation as war to evolve as a feature of human biology. However, humanity is also a social animal. This changes everything. Social organization dramatically accelerates the effects, and rates – of change. A quick look at the rate of technological change as a result of social organization easily illustrates what could be happening to human biology.

The human use of fire (see "Fire and Stone'" below) may have happened as early as 1.6 million years ago, and was a dependable aspect of the human tool-kit as recently as 200,000 years ago. Fire as a technology not only encouraged people towards other technologies, but had immediate impact on the ways we hunted, the places we ventured, and the foods we ate.

The ways in which early humanity socially gathered around the fire was not unlike the social impact of radio in the former half of the 20th Century, or of television during the latter half of the 20th Century. Now, in the 21st Century, information technology allows us to socially isolate ourselves in front of computer screens. The digital age, the automobile, and fast food – among other social changes – have altered the ways in which we court, select mates, and reproduce.

These are clearly just a few examples. But, they help illustrate how technology can effect social change, and how, in turn, biology can be effected. Fire made foods and environments available that directly channeled human biological evolution. And the modern suite of sedentary diseases such as obesity and diabetes to liver disease to influenza epidemics are all the biological results of technologies. And, add to this the evolutionary theory of punctuated equilibrium. In this idea, evolution is usually imperceptibly slow for organisms, until a trigger sparks rapidly accelerating change. Already, we know that human biology changed as a result of agriculture, urbanization, and sedentary lifestyles that accompanied civilization. We also know that organized warfare was everywhere a symptom of this new thing called civilization. By all appearances, we may well be in a period of accelerated (punctuated) evolution with social organization as the trigger. If the thoughts of social thinkers like James Burke are correct, then how we deal with war in society is crucial to our development and survival as a species. Modern Warfare certainly makes sudden extinction possible.

Nurture Versus Nature: Human Instinct?

What human instinct there is could be another accelerator of change. Most animals display behaviors that are instinctive. That is, they respond to their environment in biologically pre-patterned and somewhat uniform ways. But what of human beings? We have long considered ourselves to be above animal instinct – far too sentient, self-conscious and spiritually unique to be at the mercy of instinctive behaviors that are often construed as base. By the way, this is also the heart of why racism can exist. Extreme concepts of the instinctive nature of humanity, as well as extreme concepts that place humanity at the mercy solely of cultural conditioning can both lead to racism, sexism, and class-ism. To take nature too far, or nurture too far as an explanation for human behavior has produced more confusion than sense. The idea of people as an elite species marks our interactions within our own species. Real humans are supposedly "above" animal instinct. Civilization makes us better, gives us dominion over the beast of the field...and the beast within us. The emotional distance and scientific objectivity (oxymoron) that we bring to bear on the study of instinct in the other animals is needed in the study of the human animal. For, we have instinct. We have both social instinct, and biological predisposition. Animal instinct is an adaptive strategy necessarily serving specific survival purposes, so too with humans. We respond in what may seem more complex ways, but this may also be an artifact of our singular dependence on society and culture. Both instinct and the potentials for social behavior have genetic basis in humans. Both culture and social instinct are the products of natural selection. How is it that societies seem to instinctively turn to war?

Be patient. This is how I see it. Experience triggers and enhances genetically prescribed responses. Nurture operates on nature opportunistically with humans. Instinct is triggered and modified by circumstance, giving humans wider behavioral adaptability. We try more things than other creatures, and have a collective storehouse of options called culture and history. Culture operates on the individuals' genetic predisposition. Responses to the environment fall within a plastic range. Our environment is mostly social. Through the social environment, we have continuously urged that the response to the environment be warfare.

Perpetuating such a cyclic environment has had an effect on cultural and biological evolution. People raised in war are likely to embrace war. While this in itself is not biological evolution, it does represent generations of social evolution. If war is on a gene, then each generation in recorded history has reduced the genetic potentials for peace.

Since our environment is mostly social, culture is central in understanding what can be done about war. And, as we have seen, culture evolves. It is what history is record of, according to Ehrlich and others. Human instinct is not rigid, but fluid, providing for a range of responses aimed at adaptability. Each individual's genetic make-up provides a package of variables. Society and culture add to the possibilities. Each package of variables makes us somewhat individual in possible response. Effective education must recognize and allow for this. Individuality means that flexible methods are essential if uniformly positive results are expected. This is due to the fact that individuality asserts itself over any human basic genetic uniformity. But society restricts the natural flexibility of an individual. When this means laws to maintain social conduct, then that restriction is labeled non-destructive, and we all go along. How then does mass murder become acceptable social behavior?

1. Sex and Violence

Sex and mating behavior offers us the other example of conditions potentially selecting for - in a Darwinian sense - the aggressive application of tools as weapons. Most animals and all mammals compete within the species for mating privileges. Although the relatively perennial sexual receptivity of the human female has been proposed by some scholars to reduce the intensity of male-male conflict and enhance peaceful monogamy, this is by no means a given. Male conflict and territoriality may well be heightened by the need to exclude sexual interlopers from sharing perennially receptive females and thus reducing the biological effectiveness of any single male. Socially, women actually behave in support of males displaying the desirable biological characteristics for insuring favorable conditions for the survival of offspring. What are these characteristics? Human male ideal body types favoring upper body strength, general health, paired with behaviors suggestive of compassion and fidelity. The ability assist in securing regular and abundant sources of food for a mate and offspring, and the ability to protect a mate and offspring come from these physical traits.

Chimpanzee studies by Goodall, Watts and others clearly demonstrate a surprising capacity for intra-species violence that is coldly calculated, organized to the point of ritual, and ultimately fatal. Such behavior in our biologically intimate cousins has quite jarring cultural implications. The Ngogo & Kibale chimpanzee studies suggest that early hominid ancestors of modern humans faced such competition, but stop short of answering the begged questions: How did our predecessors cope socially and culturally with the competition, and; what impacts did hominid coping strategies have on human evolution? We can and should speculate. Really, we cannot afford not to. The reasons for killing – the way humans do – are just that important. Did our predisposition to cultural and social behavior result in institutionalizing gender roles of both male dominance and male aggression? It certainly looks that way when viewed from a modern perspective. But, is it really so in an absolutely human sense? We know that the social formation of what it means to be male is the result of conditioning. That males are born biologically male, but that the meaning of manhood is nurtured into all of us by society and culture. Male is a sex, "man" is a gender role. Gender is social performance. The question remains one of degree as to how much of the killing potential is male by sex, or male by gender. Sexually – biologically – men are men, but "warrior," or "soldier" are social roles that are culturally defined. It may well be that the potential for murder and war are biologically part of the male sex. However, social conditioning and cultural belief may act on that perhaps limited natural aggression kind of like steroids. Killers are made, not born.

Both cultural anthropologists and sociobiologists infer that complex mating behaviors such as courtship displays, rituals, and taboos evolved from social procreative need. So too can war be explained. Biological determinants such as dimorphism also may be reasonably interpreted to indicate male on male aggression as in the models of many mammals. If male procreative success relied upon his ability to consistently provide supplies of excess food for female(s) and offspring, tool effectiveness would be essential. If male access depended upon the ability to prevent other male intrusions, then violence becomes another social tool. Sexual dimorphism (male body size and musculature relative to females) and aggression would be traits that would be selected for in the Darwinian sense. These are the results of rituals and roles defined and refined as culture, institutionalized in society, but derived from biology.

Dominance is key to this argument. Assertiveness, aggression, and violence are all just points on the same continuum. Males who were able to display aggression or apply violence at the site of a kill could retain more of that food resource relative to his peers. If a primate also manifested such behaviors within the social group, and consistently retained a larger portion of food or other critical resources, then such social behaviors would be drastically selected-for in the Darwinian sense.

Females would accept successful males as mating partners at a greater frequency, and for longer monogamous periods than their less successful - and more passive - peers would. Probably more numerous, certainly better fed and protected, offspring of these successful males would consistently survive to mating age more frequently than the offspring of less assertive individuals.

This is not to say those females of this ancestral primate lineage would themselves be passive socially and biologically. The popular view that solely males contributed the development of human aggression, while the egalitarian primate female peacefully organized stable complexities of early human society is driven more by present social trends than by direct evidence. Females who achieved reproductive success - and therefore passed on their genetic as well as social tendencies more often than their peers - could hardly do so without actively selecting mates. Dimorphism (size difference) does not prevent females from assertively denying non-successful males, vigorously defending procreative rights. In this arena, female (and all human) social behavior would even enhance female effectiveness at denying unsuccessful males. Sexual dimorphism may, however, not consistently allow females to successfully deny the most aggressive males or groups of males. Several females could cooperate, however, and resist any larger male. There is much evidence that primate females -- and presumably our ancestors as well -- can be quite selective on a number levels.

A female who asserted social dominance within the female group would retain more access to perhaps more consistent food sources than her counterparts or peers. Present concepts on the division of labor in early human populations notwithstanding, females (without children) could hunt and scavenge just as successfully as males. After all, scavenging is in most cases only slightly removed from gathering. It would only require violent physical strength when scavenged resources are "defended." Only then in this context would dimorphism be significant. Sexual dimorphism, the tendency for females of a species to be physically smaller than males, does not hold so strongly among human primates as among some other species. Large females can be and are frequently larger than males. Many females can successfully physically resist all but the most assertive, aggressive, or violent male attention. The most successfully reproducing males would frequently be among the most assertive, aggressive, or potentially violent type.

In any event, the assertive/aggressive female would more successfully rear more offspring - and thus pass along her own social genetic predisposition at a higher frequency than her peers.

Human culture and its evolutionary breakthrough quality - social cooperation - created the foundation for success. Edenic egalitarian altruism between all members of the human social group fostered our technologic dominance over the vagaries of the natural environment. Violence and aggression are merely the unfortunate by-products of our on-going evolutionary development toward world cooperation. Our problem with war and organized human conflict is actually a problem of perspective. We really only think that war is an endemic feature of human civilization. The truth is that humankind is suffering the growing pains of transition from nationalist economic systems to global community in which war will naturally become obsolete.

Well, tell it to the dead.

The diversity of organized human conflict as well as the historic (pre-historic) depth of such conflict tends to belie the cooperative view. At best, the historic evidence is that the larger the organized social group, the more possibilities for oppression and denial of self-determination produced for members in that social group. Also, as we will soon see, the frequency and intensity of war has grown as society has become more complex and presumably advanced (Noam Chomsky: personal communication, October 1999).

Sex as an example of biologic predisposition for war is one thing. However, gender – the social role and identity attached to biological differences – is much harder to fix in prehistoric societies. Gender is a social role. It is a complex set of postures, patterns of behavior and of thought that is learned. Social rewards and punishments result from how well a person performs, or "fits" their gender – their socially constructed role. Such artificial gender oriented schemas like those above are ludicrous in light of evidence from all known cultures of the plasticity of gender behaviors. Males and females groom with cosmetics to impress both their peers and their perspective mates – for instance. So what about organized social aggression? Why is it men who war? We attribute gender qualities to traits such as aggressiveness or altruism, to dominance or submission, and in reality such traits are not sexual. "Get in touch with your feminine nurturing, creative right brain" is a trendy phrase, not an anthropological observation. What the evidence of modern social systems infers, as well as what can be gleaned from prehistory is that war and the social construction of gender are linked. Males become men through socialization. Men become warriors through further socialization. This means biology is the basis, but that social and cultural development of maleness into manhood takes control in the area of war. So then, should we consider that this socialization for masculine combat conditions our biology? I would say so. If the human being responds to environmental conditions as a rule of their evolution as other organisms do, then war must affect human biology. Social behavior has influenced so much of human biology, why should it be different with men and war? As humanity evolved culturally, the social emphasis on aggression as a desirable aspect of manhood would naturally (if I can use that word) become an ever-increasing feature of human biology/genetics.

Patriarchy notwithstanding, men do not breed themselves. As socially important as we have made ourselves, men, after all, are biologically surplus. Among humans there are simply more males than are needed to maintain the biological (reproductive) viability of the species. Proportionally, there is more male genetic material than nature requires. It is the unbroken strain of mitochondrial (female) DNA that shows modern science what went on in human biological prehistory. It is the mother and child relationship that counts on the genetic level. All in all, it is a kind of feedback loop. The social success of warriors also provides them with biologic success. The biological success means that any predisposition for aggression and war will be passed on to the next generation. The nature of social organization created the conditions of recent human evolution. In a male, or female, or gender equal cultural development sequence, assertiveness, aggressiveness, and violent tendencies were invariably genetically enhanced and selected-for. Therefore the key is not biology, but the nature of social organization and culture.

Indeed, if the family unit is accepted as resulting from these biologic circumstances, then social aggression must be too. Consider the friction between rival juvenile males, or between suitor and patriarch, when mates are sought outside of the family group...what is a "Man" supposed to do?

As always, one can find examples where such violent conflict has been peacefully avoided. However, the corpus of data supporting these examples - sex and scavenging as loci for violence – is vast. Among humans, rituals are followed, displays made, and roles are assumed partially in order to reduce potential violence-causing social tensions and to provide meaning to human life. The wide range of solutions speaks to a central and fundamental problem. In a cultural system, lessons spread quickly. Those who possessed the technology of fire, who had the sharper tools, soon acquired more control over their environment. Socially, historically this has meant dominance over their neighbors, who were and out-reproduced, absorbed, or physically annihilated.

2. Men, Sex Drive, and Violence:

"Testosterone means that we have to either fuck it or kill it"

-Robin Williams.

Is war just the human version of natural selection and survival of the fit? Since culture and society have made humanity the top predator, do we prey on each other for dominance? War would then be part of the cultural evolution of societies. We war because our biology expresses itself socially. Males engage in combat because of their physical superiority. Men fight each other to affirm biological superiority over each other, and nations make war to prove economic and social superiority. Victory in war guarantees access to mates and a social level of prosperity that means greater numbers of the warrior's offspring are born and survive to pass on the war gene to successive generations. All is in masculine terms – all is patriarchy.

This male biological predisposition toward aggression enhances (and is enhanced by) masculine social role. Gender for most men is the social performance of a psychology rooted in patriarchy. Masculinity is not dominance any more than femininity is submission. Patriarchy is male dominance. Male dominance – patriarchy – means someone must be dominated. It is women within a patriarchy who are socially and physically dominated by men. And, men

116

of course seek dominance over each other. Yet, even with this background psychology of dominance, and the ability to construct the "other," or the "enemy," it is unnatural to kill. We must have social and psychological conditioning beyond masculinity to be good killers. But, masculinity is complex. It is a precondition for war, but also a precondition to fatherhood, or brotherhood, or being a son. As ever, conditions must be socially and culturally acceptable. This is another critical function of political science – making war and killing socially acceptable. There are – of course – always a few individuals produced by society who have truly socio-pathological tendencies. They are almost invariably men. The sociopath dysfunctions both biologically and socially. Such individuals are perhaps the accidental products of human society. But the sociopath is inevitable in social systems that endorse warfare. Most people (even men) find it quite difficult to kill other humans. There is a heavy psychological burden to bear when one kills. For war to be possible, society must promote the psychological conditions that enable and coerce killing. Good soldiers are trained psychologically to kill. Good citizens are conditioned politically to fear and hate the enemy. All of this invites chilling paradoxes between biological sex, and social gender performance. The expression of violence becomes gendered.

Funny thing about gender roles in films and society. Sex and violence have high priority but are (predictably) skewed. "Porn" films and intensely violent "Action" films have much in common. Women in porn films are portrayed as sexually insatiable. Men in action films are portrayed as insatiably violent. In the end of each film the actors display both intense

117

agitation and copious bodily fluids. Neither is intimate for all the contrived passion. There is a sense that dominant violence replaces mutual intimacy. And if the intimacy bond is evident something happens to the film and the viewer. Although not a connoisseur of porn, I am reminded of the extremely forceful killing scene in the film "Saving Private Ryan" in which a German soldier slowly stabs to death his American counterpart. The scene breaks a few of the regular action movie rules in its attempt at realism. In real life, knife fighting is classified by military experts as "intimate" (Grossman). This scene shows the hideously intimate reality of taking another persons life. It is chillingly sexualized. The heavier German trooper lies on top of the American and slowly thrusts his blade into the struggling American's body. All the while the German is whispering soothingly to the dying American – as he stabs the American to death.

Biologically men are unable to have unlimited sexual performances (erections, orgasms), while women are able to continuously perform. The cultural conditioning in most societies nonetheless promotes the fantasy that a "good man" is unlimited in prowess and access, but that a "good woman" is demure, limited and reserved sexually. Anyone who violates this gender conditioning is subject to all sorts of social sanctions and punishments. While this may be thought of as a kind of social balancing of biology, this still stops far short of conditioning women for war and men for nurturing. Because of their generally higher pain threshold and greater average endurance women may be better soldiers. Men because of their greater upper body strength and genetic redundancy may be better cast in the social role of burden bearing nurturers – fewer in number, kind of like the drones in

118

ant, bee and wasp nests. Instead, patriarchy means that women face institutionally supported abuse and domestic violence. Current numbers of men are biologically surplus as far as evolutionary principles are concerned. Surplus biologically, unless you consider the social institutions of patriarchy, and the social behavior called war.

After war, the victorious social system garners more resources from the losers for redistribution among the winners. Winners sometimes appropriate the labor of the defeated by enslaving them. Whether through colonization or through conquest, the resources of the vanquished becomes the wealth of the victors. And sometimes the victorious side dispossesses the losing side of a biological future. If no losers survive, then their "weaker" genes fail to be passed on. Genocide is the name for this type of war. The newer, trendy term, is ethnic cleansing. Bigots and racial separatists in the United States use the idea that they are biologically superior to justify hate crimes in preparation for race war. Skin-head, Militia, Klan, and Neo-Nazi of every type train relentlessly for a race war that will return them to social superiority to match their assumptions of biological superiority (Dees, Corcoran, and King). Ethnic and racial superiority is an underlying belief of many generations of people. Biological superiority is also one of the central underpinnings of that other justification for war – nationalism. The first ideas were put forward in the modern era by such notables as Herbert Spencer, and Alfred Russell Wallace who gave the world Social Darwinism. And, although this justification for racism and colonialism has been overturned long ago, the cultural hangover means that the belief that some races and societies are superior to others is still unfortunately basic to the thinking of quite a few people.

As with many things in war, the sending out of warriors would seem on the surface not to "fit" with anthropological ideas concerning natural selection, the environment, and evolution. This is - and is not - true. Apparently the social organization of killing possibly fills several needs in the evolutionary ecology of humanity. In natural selection in animal populations– free from human social modification – the weaker and non-adaptive individuals are victims of the environment and of situations that they cannot adapt to. This was one of the first problems of living in a natural environment that human society and culture conquered. We care for our old, and our young, for our disabled, and for our injured through social organization. We do this to a level that other creatures have not approached. Other creatures in the scheme of things seem to lose their weaker and sicker members to nature's contest. Instead, we Homo sapiens send (mostly) the young, strong, healthy males out to war. But, war is a human contest, not a natural one in a strict sense.

The actual purposes this may serve are quite sound evolutionary adaptive behavior, if one considers society to be our main environment. The benefits of social organization have made our male to female ratio artificially high compared with other primate species. This is the biological redundancy of "excess males" that was noted several times earlier. To reduce and channel the young strong warriors into war (and their deaths) serves four adaptive functions. First, war reduces the challenge to central authority. Second, war reinforces centralized power and wealth by instilling allegiances of young males to older leadership in times of "crisis," and by forming a "rite of passage" into the power group. After all, how many Presidents of the U.S., and high-ranking political figures were in the military? Third, rhetoric of war is used to re-affirm a social system in its function to care for those "less adaptable" types. Any non-combatant becomes dependant and somehow "less than" those who war. The reality that resorting to war is the threat to a thoroughly non-combatant "mom and apple pie" is lost in the rhetoric. Fourth, critical resources are redistributed by war. More resources are secured, and there are fewer people to share them. So, our leaders tell us, war functions to keep more people alive. The only real threat is to the lives of the soldiers and the collateral civilian "damage." But it is soldiers whose deaths buy the secure power and wealth of the elite. And it is the elite in society who claim the benefit of those resources.

Does this mean that war serves humanity? No, it does not. What it means is that it is social organization that serves humankind. And, in turn, that war serves social organization. But, war serves only a particular type of social organization. The fundamental institution of the family, for instance, is not served by war. The various educational systems are not war dependent. Institutions like marriage, etc. are not supported or enhanced by war. And, although war may have evolved as a response to the idea of wealth generated through agriculture and agricultural surplus, war is only by the most contrived abstraction in any way essential to growing food. Though these and many other institutions and elements of social organization are not war dependant, they are prey for war. War diverts social resources away from other aspects of society. Only certain types of political and economical social organization are served by organizing conflict into the mass murder of war. What this means is that war is perpetuated by the class it serves. The war system ravages the ecosystem. Far from being an imperative of the environment, war actually allows the redistribution of natural resources only into the control for profit of a few. This exclusive quest for profit means a disparity of human rights and economic justice. The physical reality of war encourages an exhaustive and consumptive relationship between society and natural resources.

Natural selection does mean that species and individuals within species compete for access to resources. With humans, our main environment is social. But that is about where it ends. The access to resources and biological reproductive fitness does not rely on fighting in war. Otherwise, our social systems would be totally warrior dominated and each returning soldier would have multiple sexual partners whose job it would be to pass warrior genes on to the next generation. As it is, our social systems favor elite rule. So, we must look at war as it biologically favors the social elite. In this context, for biology to play a role in war it must advantage not the soldier, but those who send the soldiers out to fight. Otherwise our present social systems would reorganize either away from the elite class, or away from war, or away from both.

On the one hand, the social and biological benefits of war would go to another social group. The current elite would not be economically and politically ascendant if war did not serve. On the other hand, peace allows the maximum amount of genes to persist, and biological diversity is the true health of a species. War restricts diversity, and it does so not on any sound evolutionary ground, but on the grounds of social advantage. Poorer, working class young men are the ones who make up the front lines units of virtually every modern military force. They die to preserve the privilege of the class that can (economically) escape war. It is the progressively more advantaged classes that can avoid war, prosper from war, and pass their genes to the next generation. It is the poorer (ethnically diverse) males that are encouraged to seek social advantage from joining the military. If this were as simplistically true as it sounds, then the rich would have out-produced the poor by now. However, the social nature of wealth and power are such that they must ever concentrate in fewer and fewer hands. Working class and working poor always grow in numbers. But the elite always retain control of social mobility. This cycle works because of war, and in it lay the need to perpetuate war.

The G.I. Bill for the U.S. military following World War II is a prime example of social advantage becoming biological advantage. Returning veterans got housing, employment, education, and healthcare opportunities denied to non-military poor, and unneeded by the wealthy. Institutional racism meant that the ethnic poor veteran resumed life as an ethnic poor citizen. Sexism meant that "Rosie the Riveter" lost the job that gave her some measure of independence from the patriarchy. After the War "Rosie the Riveter" was fired to make jobs for "G.I Joe." And, "G.I. Joe was White. The baby-boom began as veterans and newly unemployed women were encouraged to get married and have children. If they were White, poorer draftees and enlisted men could become middle class after the war. Most middle class military returned to middle class lives. Only a few veterans from wealthier families were able by virtue of that elite status to convert their military experience into larger gains in status, power and access within the private sector. The Kennedy and Bush families are perhaps two of the most famous. John F. Kennedy's father converted an illegal bootlegging fortune amassed during prohibition into the legal political capital necessary to fund the Kennedy political empire. And, George Bush senior capitalized on his WWII combat pilot experience to move into both business and politics – making the Kennedy dream even more real by leaving behind his own dynasty of Bush politicians as a legacy.

D. Archaeological Evidence - Fire and Stone

One of the best methods for evaluating human experience before the written word of history is archaeology. Human activity of every kind leaves material evidence in the soil. This material evidence is what we call artifacts. The science of collecting and interpreting artifacts and other evidence of human and pre-human activity shows how deeply ingrained are our potentials and tendencies for aggression, violence and war. Human history, as we will see, is frequently and initially a documentation of war, but what about prehistory?

Most human artifacts are examples of technology – or the way we use tools to modify the natural environment. But, this can still tell something about culture, and social organization. Prehistoric human technology meant mostly lithic – or stone – tools, and fire. Premier perhaps in the human toolkit is fire. The recorded use of fire goes back nearly two million years to early Homo erectus. Control of fire meant that people could live comfortably in a wider range of natural settings by creating an artificial climate. Fire can modify aspects of the environment. Cooking brings more foods into the human menu. Fire can be used to frighten animals for defense or the hunt. And eventually, of course, fire leads to a host of other technologies such as metallurgy, steam, and chemistry. In reality it is unknown and unknowable exactly when human beings first began fully controlling fire. Most anthropologists believe that lithic or stone tool use came earlier, perhaps preceded by wood and bone tools. Fire can be used to harden and sharpen wood as well for stiffening hides or hardening bone. Thus while fire enabled human populations to stabilize and expand the livable range of human environment, it also provided reliable tools of the hunt, and eventually those of war.

Although probably not the first among hominid (early human) tools, stone is the most durable in the archaeological record. Stone – and stone tools – lasts. No doubt tools were also made of other material than stone. However, most wood, sinew, horn, and bone that once was, is now dust. But, enough non-lithic material to be suggestive has survived by sheer luck. And, forensic anthropologists as well as experimental archaeologists have produced reports confirming the use of stone tools on all sorts of other materials. Preserved bone shows cut marks made by stone tools. Stone-tipped weapons have been found in burials. Stone tips have been found in preserved bone. Not all such bone is animal bone. Many human remains show signs of trauma that could only be caused by other humans. All of this evidence is grist for the interpretive mills of the collective social sciences. How could we interpret the data? Does any or all of it relate to war?

The standardization of tool types associated with populations widely distributed over space and time leaves no doubt that very early in human experience there were broadly dispersed cultures that were proving socially adapted for environmental success. There were also sets of fundamental patterns of social organization that were beneficial to survival. What this means is that people were collectively organized around doing things together that were successful. These things involved tools. Doing things together was important, as was doing things consistently. Predictability resulted in survival. This requires tools that are standard in type – or nearly identical in form and function(s). Standardized tool types reveal two things. First, human beings were using specific tools for specific jobs, and that meant technology. Second, the same tools occurring over territory through time meant social organization and culture. Ideas and skills were being remembered and shared through time. Early humans modified their environment and taught their offspring to do the same. It is the key to human success as a species. This success was measured against the demands of the environment. Successful behaviors and technologies were repeated as long as they worked. This does not mean an absence of variation or flexibility. Certainly, different conditions existed geographically and through time. Change may be the only human constant. If conditions changed, then human culture and social organization changed as well. If not, we would not be here to discuss it today. This initial conclusion is supported by the bulk of both the data and current interpretations. Human success was based on culture, cooperative social behavior and technology /tool use. Technology, then, is basically the modification of the environment by humans in reaction to change. All of this before what we call war.

Environmental modification is also associated with the earliest examples of hominid/human behaviors. This means that early humans (like all creatures to some degree) changed their immediate surroundings for their own benefit. It has nothing to do with being a conscious or an unconscious act, it is a fact of existence. Technology, tools (fire, stone), and cooperative social behavior are the hallmarks of the human being. In time, humans would become so successful at using culture, social organization, and technology that these things would themselves together form a modified environment, partly insulating the species from the natural environment. Always searching for the predictable tried-and-true consistent success meant that social behavior became ritualized and institutionalized. Quite early, the evolving set of human social institutions became as intimate an environment as the ecological or natural environment. Part of that intimate modified social environment that humankind has since created is war. Apart from ants and a few other highly social insects, war does not exist in nature – we invented it.

But, if the idea of success and survival for our ancestors was based on consistent behaviors from which were expected predictable results, then why the apparent risk and unpredictability of war? There is a common set of indicators of human success and well being. Food, water, shelter are among the needs that all humans face. Other indicators of success involve a sense of freedom. Free association, a sense of worth and potential, a feeling of belonging, and a sense of security are among the social needs that, when present in a society, indicate success. Nowadays, these social success criteria are collectively called human rights. But, in the ancient times as early social civilization evolved, institutions developed. These indicators – these needs that we now call human rights – became integrated with systems of exchange. Economics was born.

Work has always been the basis of economic exchange. Productive labor appears to perhaps have always been divided between genders. As society evolved, labor became abstracted. Wealth was no longer to be simply what labor produced. Now, work had a social value, also many non-materially productive social roles acquired additional social value of their own. These roles began with leadership in times of crisis, and with religion. (Later, of course, these two social roles diversified into many. And, all expanded with the addition of "support staff" that were usually family - support staff that we now call administrative bureaucracy.) The evolution of class followed from the development of economics. The social and cultural environment developed so that wealth and social status could be exchanged for the needs that one could not personally secure directly from the natural environment. Social organization allowed our ancestors to succeed in many varied and challenging natural environments. As society necessarily became more and more complex, wealth and status became ends to themselves. After all, if all the needs and most of the wants of humankind could be satisfied through the social system, then why preoccupy oneself with anything else?

As economics evolved and became more

complex, so did class. Social status requires social reinforcement. Wealth is the foundation of the ability to reinforce status. Wealth came to require protection either from outsiders who sought to take it from the "group," or from those classes within the group who came to feel that their survival and prosperity were threatened. Social organization for survival and success in the environment became modified. The new environment created by social organizations was an institutional environment. This new environment evolved institutions not just dealing with the vagaries of a natural geography, but instead for the protection of wealth and social status. One of the institutions was (is) the police. Another older institution is war. These changes show up in the prehistoric record of evidence at the point when tools become weapons. It is genuinely a point when plowshares become swords.

Tools as Weapons

Tools linked to culture and social behavior secured the place of humanity in evolutionary history. However, the consistent use of tools and the cultural trend to survive by modification of the environment has also led to a uniquely human ability for self-destruction. Other animals kill their own kind, but none are as devoted to it as humans. Along with cultures of all types and environmental adaptations too numerous to describe has come the manifold methods of mayhem and murder. Through culture we have learned to prey upon any other species. Moreover, we have learned to prey upon one another more consistently and effectively than any other known species. When did tools become weapons?

Probably when killing had to become dependable.

Improving the effectiveness of tools is certainly connected to human survival. There are many types of tools that humanity has used to thrive. Hunting, gathering, farming, and building tools are what have formed human life. Tools for the hunt are in essence killing tools. This combination of technologies that is human culture means that one thing led to another. In the text of <u>The Origin of the Work of Art</u>, by the philosopher Martin Heidegger, a piece of equipment (a tool) is defined by its form, its composition, and its intended use. At one point the need for reliable survival meant reliable killing. Tools became weapons when this threshold was crossed. This is change, but may it not be progress.

It is generally conceded anthropologically that the earliest known lifeways of our remotest ancestors centered on nomadic or semi-nomadic movement. Those who came before us subsisted by hunting small game, fishing, and gathering of seeds, fruits, nuts, vegetables and herbs. They moved to the best place possible each season. Always, our ancestors were going to where wild game was most plentiful, and the fruits of the field most bountiful. Farming and animal herding came later. Infrequent outright big game kills probably augmented opportunistic scavenging. Vegetable and fruit resources would be regularly sought out as they seasonally ripened. As with even the largest predatory scavengers today, the sheer physical inability to exclusively dominate environmental resources like water holes would – for ages – maintain such areas generally under unspoken bonds of peace. At best (worst) a contentious territoriality would evolve between species - or within species - over such natural resources for millennia to come. A natural equilibrium was established between each species and the natural environment. As with many species, low population densities might preclude the need for much conflict between early human bands (Donald Johanson: Lecture, April 1998).

The idea that the environment and geography have provided determining factors in human development is not new. Most scientists of the human condition have suggested that at least parts of both human biology and culture have in some ways been geographically determined.

Marginal environments like those described in the so-called "hilly flanks" type of scenario would definitely increase adaptive pressures on species in relation to any type of marginality of essential resources. If this was true at the onset of plant and animal domestication, then it would also hold true in the millennia leading up to settled life. When and where things are scarce, peoples' relationships get critical. How they deal with the environment gets critical, and how they deal with each other gets critical. By critical, I mean specific, structured and crucial. Water holes are but a meager example of natural conditions which, when blended with the existing human adaptations, would become powerful perpetual stimuli for potential slaughter. Marginal environments and resources - geographic or temporal - may actually concentrate selection processes for organized aggression. Inter and intra species violence may well result from cooperative behavior – behavior that we arrogantly consider to be our "saving grace". Cooperative success could quite easily result in adaptive advantages for calculated violence.

In every natural history film, class, or study the

savage pecking order at the carcass of any large dead thing gives us our first detailed examples of why and how tools could have become weapons. Necessity, invention, and culture may well have come together for our remotest ancestors at the prehistoric kill site. The kill site as a nexus for the foundations of human culture is not a new theory (Eherenreich et al.). But the application of this idea in this book blends hitherto mutually exclusive theories of biological and cultural determinism into a single co-complimentary hypothesis. This is a case of culture influencing biology, and biology influencing social-cultural development in a kind of Dao of social science in which both yin and yang continually emerge from one another.

Examining humans without technology in a natural ecosystem leaves little doubt that we were probably not at the top of the food chain in the early circle of life. Though it is unsure where early humans fit, some pre-historians and anthropologists have placed our ancestors below big cats, bears or hyenas, but above jackals and coyotes. There are implications that prehistorically we share eco-niche affinities with wild dogs and we have historically shared this niche with them.

At any rate, the "kill site" is a locus of violent conflict between man and beast, or between man and man. Our predisposition to cooperate does not exclude violence. Indeed the opposite is true. Cooperative behavior implies the need to manage desperate situations. Combine cooperative social behavior in tool using species with desperate situations over marginal resources and the product could quite logically be violent inter or intra species activity. There is both inferential and archaeological evidence for this theory.

By the time humanity begins to settle in agricultural communities the idea that other people may be as great or greater a threat to survival and prosperity was entrenched. By the time history is first written down, it was already taken for granted that people needed protection from other people.

Now a sampling of archaeological record...

A fairly thorough overview of the archaeological record of war was printed in the magazine Natural History, July/August, 2003. Anthropologist/author R. Brian Ferguson of Rutgers University in New Jersey gathered together the findings of many key colleagues in the investigation of organized human conflict in the article "The Birth of War." It is interesting in the extreme that the anthropologists differ so much in the interpretations of the data in the Natural History article, while the scientists contributing to the Seville Statement on Violence express such unanimity.

Concluding that warfare has not always been the human condition, Ferguson begins by screening data that may challenge his view. Napoleon A. Chagnon's Yanomamo: The Fierce People had been a staple in the study of organized human conflict. In the 1968 book, Chagnon presented warfare as central to the human condition well prior to what we call civilization. Marvin Harris produced work in 1974 that placed population pressures at the root of Yanomami warfare. But this ecological approach failed to explain war because resources of the natural environment are not scarce or limited. (If we make analogy to other Native Indigenous American groups, such as the

Indians of pre-contact California, this environmental balance is wholly plausible. Indians of California found that their food resource base was so plentiful that inter and intra tribal warfare was rare). Ferguson's 1995 book: Yanomami Warfare: A Political History, showed that the Yanomami war was not over natural resources such as food, or human resources like women, but over social resources – outside resources of European manufacture like steel knives, pots, and other goods.

In 1996, a new pessimism emerged with works like War Before Civilization, by Lawrence H. Keeley. This archaeological review assembled the most violent evidence from prehistory to support the idea that war is just a natural part of what people do – of who we are. Harvard archaeologist Steven A. LeBlanc asserted that wherever you find people (in the archaeological record) you find warfare. In the book written with Katherine Register, LeBlanc compiled impressive evidence of pre-historic violence. In Constant Battles: The myth of the Peaceful, Noble Savage, signs of war included defensive skeletal fractures (signs of attempts to block blows), mass burials, missing skulls, trophy skulls, bone-embedded projectile points, paintings, and specialized weapons. Site 117 from the Nile valley is an ancient graveyard of 59 skeletons. Of the 59, twenty-four were found in close association with projectile points. The inference is that these were victims of social patterns of organized violence. Site 117 is 12,000 to 14,000 years old. Rock paintings from Australia dated at 10,000 years ago show what appear to be duels. Other archaeological signs such as defensive settlement patterns strongly suggest the type of systematic organization around war that also had implications for other aspects of the distribution of wealth and power within early human societies. Though some walled settlements (Jericho) seem to have been walled initially for flood control, the bulk of such architecture dating from 6000+ years ago are structured for military defense.

Although Ferguson and I disagree as to the existence of evidence of a direct causal connection between agriculture and war, he does see five preconditions for war. First, he noted the shift from nomadic lifestyle to a sedentary settled lifestyle – protection of local resources that allowed the people to settle down in one location was worth fighting to retain. His second precondition for war was the population growth and the pressure that puts on resource availability. Ferguson's third was the development of hierarchy – elite classes and the internecine rivalries that social class can produce. The fourth precondition was trade and long distance commerce. Trade especially in status and luxury items are considered worth organizing to fight for, according to Ferguson. The fifth precondition for war is given as severe ecological disruption. Drought, flood, or any interruption in the natural environment could produce struggle over the resulting shortages and military social organization to control social crises. (The five Ferguson preconditions in summary are: permanent settlements, population increase, social class, commerce, ecology).

Ferguson, then examines fundamental patterns of social organization and war. War occurs in hunter-gatherer groups when social organization is complex enough to include groups greater in size than the extended family. Clans, bands, and other such groups require retribution and are of a size and structure to allow what we would call war. Of course, social scarcity and war itself may have been reasons for the growth in complexity of social organization. In other words: organized aggression may just as well have required groups to get bigger, and not the other way around.

Once a group becomes dependant on organized force to preserve its structural integrity, it also becomes dependant on the industries that supply the materials of war. Once the society is organized around war and the perpetual threat of war, the resources of society are allocated for militarism. The result is that there is less to go around within the society. Because of the mal-distribution of resources allocated to the war system, and the concentrations of wealth and power that are part of any war system, human rights cannot help but be misallocated as well. The nature of wealth is distinction. Wealth manifests distinction through poverty. Power manifests itself through powerlessness.

While Ferguson does not accept some of the common theories for the origin of war – like cultural ecology – he does find that social scarcity is usually caused by political and economic conditions within the society. But this artificial "civilized" scarcity itself is also a result of the disease of social organization for war. As such, it is itself a cause of conflict. In turn, the desire of the few to hold on to power and wealth requires more force, and further scarcity is the result.

Ferguson's final interpretation is that war is the result (usually) of self-interest on the part of the elite. To use his apt words: "...leaders often favor war because war favors leaders." It is natural that self-interested act through self-justification.

2. PREHISTORY

Before any examination of the historic patterns of human experience that define our concepts of both history and war, an examination of the development of human potential is in order. Prior to history, and a definition of war, is prehistory, and predisposition for war. What is the prehistory of war?

It is nearly impossible to adequately put into words the unimaginably vast stretch of time before written history. We existed long before we were literate. What we call History is dependent on documents – written documents of human society. But, human experience far pre-dates the written record of historical events. It is admittedly an old analogy, but if the time of humanity on this planet were a yardstick, then what we call history would only be the last black line at the end. Most of what it means to be human was developed during that huge prehistoric period. That, of course, includes the formation of culture, society, and war. Human prehistory is a matter of geological time. Origins of human social organization span not tens of centuries like history does, but thousands of centuries. Geological time may be the case with human prehistory, but many otherwise very good social scientists tend to dismiss the importance of this period with comments like that of Ehrlich on 159 of his book, Human Natures. There may have been "long periods of apparent cultural stasis," as he wrote, but this does not mean that nothing important was going on. Indeed, long periods of stability indicate that we may be able to produce a culture and a society that is not centered on the destruction of the species.

How did we get to be who we are? How did

humanity become top predator? We have no claws or fangs. We are not tough skinned, or armored. Naked and alone in the wild, we are lunch for any predator. We cannot naturally travel fast, swim far, or fly. We cannot eat most wild foods. We cannot be away from water for long. We are not well endowed, yet (for good or ill) we dominate the planet. We have a mind, and we have each other. Those are our major tools. The human mind is unique among the animals. We communicate abstractly and make culture. We appear to be the only creatures that associate, discriminate, reflect and project in such complex ways. What makes us human is the ability to note similarities (associate like things), to consider differences (discriminate, separate, & isolate), to rationalize a cause (reflect on why), and to predict an outcome of our actions (to project plans into the future). Our minds and the ability to share them with others is why we are human beings. Humans are the thinking, planning, and sharing animals. Human beings, being human, create culture and society to offset the physical deficits. Now, culture is our main tool for dealing with the natural environment. It was not always so.

What exactly is "Civilization?" It is not well defined. That is also a challenge. We know that being civilized – despite the connotation of the word – means more than living in cities. We have no clear line that says this is and this is not civilized. Yet, we consider ourselves civilized despite any current trend for ever increasing amounts of organized violence. The best we can do is set conditions that all civilizations seem to share. War is one thing civilizations share.

Civilization is complex social organization,

division of labor, and the integrated institutions that allow humans to settle in one area. Civilization seeks to provide equilibrium for the essentials of human life in view of environmental change. Human beings have certain universal needs. Food availability, among other things, is not assured by nature. To make sure that there is a steady supply of essential conditions and items, we organize. Labor is divided, specialized, and institutionalized. We become Civilized.

Just as we can identify universal conditions of human need – allowing us a working definition of civilization, so the environment sets the conditions of civilization. This is called environmental or geographic determinism. It should really be read plural - determinisms - because it is always more complex than we seem to make it. Regardless of what civilization, or of where in time we look, all humanity is dependant on the geography and natural environment. All civilizations are essentially agricultural/pastoral (aquatic venues included) - relying for food on plants and animals. Therefore the way that people organize into civilizations is always reflective at the core of geography and environmental specifics. But, that is not all that determines the character of a civilization. At a certain point in human social organization, we become a problem to ourselves. We pollute, we oppress, wealth and power become concentrated in the hands of a few – in brief we make war. These other kinds of determinisms are social and cultural. They are the result of institutional behavior and beliefs. Sometimes we are our own worst enemy. This has sparked global controversy about human rights. Race, gender, class, political economy, and human rights become prime factors in evaluating the health of a (civilized) social system.

What is politics? What is economy? What is production, or consumption, or labor? What makes a society stable? What is culture? Why have civilizations ended? And, why do we spend so much energy and time killing each other – in short why do we war? These are things that are matters of social and cultural evolution. In other words, they are constants. Who we were is not who we are, or who we may yet become. But, all human experience can be wrapped up in the constants of social institutions, culture, and biology. There is no tree without roots. Food and water are universal biological needs of all humans. We have further identified social rights as universal in many doctrines of human rights. These have become constants no matter which civilization you examine. It is these constants – the biological and the social/cultural – that give us a basis for comparison throughout time and place. Because the search for answers to why we war and why we are who we are may mean preventing our own extinction, the subject of how we look at ourselves is critically important. Everything is important. Everything we examine must be clearly defined, and compared. Comparison is key.

The earliest beginnings of civilization also evidence the beginnings of war. This is the Neolithic period, circa 10,000 years before the Christian era began. The Neolithic, or "new stone" Age, is not so much an age of stone as it is an age of nascent civilization. Along with civilized society came organized war. Civilization is basically a complex level of human social organization in response to the environment. Humanity needs a degree of stability to thrive. Human lives are short. Human bodies are fragile. The natural environment fluctuates. Seasons change. Disasters big and small occur. A drought is small to nature, but droughts have heralded the end of early civilizations. Civilization allows groups of people to better deal with the changes nature throws at them. Civilized society aims at stabilizing the human condition in the face of the perceived disequilibrium of nature. Early human civilization developed through one of two circumstances, and perhaps through both. About twelve thousand years ago humans began to domesticate plants and animals. Human manipulation of flora and fauna allowed our ancestors to break the older and more marginal Paleolithic dependence on hunting/scavenging and gathering.

The raw resources of modern war lay in these two new expressions of human culture. The domestication of plants, and of animals – agriculture and pastoralism – promoted a less nomadic existence that eventually resulted in larger populations, and in a more settled and sedentary lifestyle. This trend toward new ways of interaction with the environment meant new ways of interaction with each other. Despite the opportunities for a prosperous peace of plenty, one of these new interactions was invariably war. Probably the two most catalytic features of newly emerging agricultural societies were surplus and private property.

Among other things, more regular sources of abundant food encouraged relatively dramatic population increases within these new societies. Agricultural and pastoral social systems can produce more than they consume. This often necessitated storage of surpluses. These surpluses are wealth.

Value of such wealth was (and is) calculated as equivalent to the labor involved in producing it and by virtue of need. We call it supply and demand in modern capitalist terms. The storage and control of surplus for distribution in times of need would be best managed at a centralized location, and by a centralized leadership. Both the land that produced surplus, and the centers for storage and distribution became linked to individuals and families as possessions – as property. A sense of belonging between people and things developed into exclusive relationships of private property. Administrators, be they priests or kings, came to represent the central control of agricultural surplus (wealth) and its distribution (economy). Social class was born. Social status was born. Then, social value became more than labor value. The work and the lives of some were more valued than others. Each of these features also demanded the evolution of additional new social structures. Surplus food, surplus time, and surplus people eventually generated cities. Wandering gave way to the concept of a seasonal range of travel, then to a territory, finally to settlements, towns, cities, and, eventually to nations.

The organization, storage, and distribution of surpluses generated by herding and farming urged our Neolithic kin to new heights of cultural ingenuity. The diverse evolutions of new social structures are limitless. Religion, science, technology, literacy, and government are but a few of the early developments of ancestral humankind. Soon, specialization of task and new levels of the social division of labor became central features of civilized (city) life. Increasingly free from the need to personally tend to daily dietary demands, people soon found other ways to productively spend their time. With each cultural refinement, and each social evolution, systems of human destruction are also evident. Members of early farming communities now could spend all or part of the year generating pottery, or shoes...or spears. These new specializations of labor and the surplus items they produced added to the economy. New forms of wealth and status were defined by these items and the specialists who made them.

Civilization(s) bred war. Increasingly larger populations generated (and still generate) increased need for surplus and for the stability of the flow of resources. Why then war? With all of the diversity of human possibility, why does each society develop an organized capacity for homicide? Of all the potential solutions to these new challenges, why retain war?

Maybe because we maintain scarcity. Humanity – especially civilization – also creates the conditions of human want. Human history is a history of social organizational variety bordering on the artistic. This creative diversity of artificial social behaviors has meant that a diversity of natural environments is open to humanity. Artificial, as in the sense of artifice, or natural, like the environment, humans do not simply prosper, we over-prosper. Either we use everything the environment has to offer, or we keep others of our kind from using what is there to be used. The resulting human created human want has produced the conditions that have increasingly resulted in us turning our social skills to the organization of violence that is war.

All things have their limits. The dynamics of geographic or environmental interaction with socially organized, culturally savvy humans has meant that a peak of efficient ecosystem use is reached. We use everything we can and spread to everywhere we can to use up more. This appears to be true of all organisms and environments. This law of ecosystems is often called the carrying capacity of an environment. When the line is crossed, and the organism exceeds the carrying capacity of the environment, both suffer. Despite our ability to use culture and social organization to temporarily insulate us from these evolutionary relationships, it would be sheer egotism to think of humans as above this law. Our collective history shows the results of this type of species centered view: ecosystem or social system collapse. The Fall of Rome, or the dispersal of the populations of Ankhor. And, regardless of the seeming stability in any given system of human organization, the environment will inevitably change over time. As ever, environmental hardship can create marginal social situations that, in turn, can trigger violence.

Ultimately, the more property, wealth, or status within a society, the more motivation there is in that society for the formation of opposing groups. In short, the nature of war is not - and never has been - limited to nationalist politics and interstate economics. War is just as frequently civil as it is international. Much of the history of war is class war – outlined by Karl Marx, and others. Groups or individuals within a culture or social system come into conflict over real or perceived deficits in resource allocation. It is the few against the many. Someone or some group feels slighted, or is genuinely missing out on something critical – like food. Wealth or status is limited or denied to people who believe they should have access. Those who do the most work are denied social mobility. They are the working "many," who are dominated politically by a "few" economic elite in control of production in an industrial society. To the "few" who control the flow of wealth and resources, too much social mobility of the "many" means social instability. All are factors that historically generate and perpetuate war both within and between nation states. Group size is not irrelevant, and a global community may be inevitable. However, the size of the human tribe by its inherent complexity may contribute to war. Without doubt, war has persisted.

As soon as physical conflict within the species became related to resource access, then, almost immediately, such a general genetic tendency for violence as existed within that population would socially assert itself. Social systems that adapted to conditions by using organized violence ensured that other adaptations would fall by the wayside. The killers out reproduced the non-killers. The deadly new strategy for success demands imitation – its potential not only excludes other strategies, but physically extinguishes them.

At each level of social development, private property and ownership became a new and increasingly divisive dynamic to human relationships. Private ownership on a collective scale generates an abstract social concept of wealth. Human relations become governed by the profit motive. The shadow of wealth and ownership is want, and envy. Property led to wealth, and wealth led to poverty. For one to be rich, many others must be poor. Disparity is the motivating influence of this type of social organization.

The new potential to control resources not of ones own planting and herding generated new types of social specialization. Just as some were scribes, or artisans some became politicians, raiders, warriors, and soldiers.   Labor became another commodity, as did humans themselves.   Individuals and groups of people control wealth to keep themselves wealthy. Those without (or with less) property, wealth, and power remain poor. Such social distinctions led to political behaviors that limit both the redistribution of wealth away from the wealthy, and that diffuse the various types of resistance of the poor to their poverty. When such political methods fail, we see organized violence.   Modern police and military operate to maintain a certain status quo.   The status quo is that of property, wealth, and power. Modern social justice movements, protests, and marches are organized to change the status quo of privilege. Riots, and revolutions become the violent resistances to poverty and powerlessness by the poor.

For glimpses of social organization, civilization, and war prior to the systematic recording of history, we can turn to legend, fable, and myth. Already in these early oral histories, matriarchies are mythological, and war is joined to patriarchy. Even as these oral histories of myth became written history, war was central to civilization.

One of the earliest pieces of literature in human civilization is the Epic of Gilgamesh. It is, among other things, the story of the struggle for power between the two wealthy classes of ancient Mesopotamian civilization – the priest and the warrior. Both have power based on their wealth. Initially, the priest class ruled. Called *Ensi*, the chief priest(ess) held power in the civilization because they administered the land, collected and distributed its wealth (in the form of food) in the name of the gods. The class of private property owners beyond the reach of religious fiefdoms was at odds with each other over prime locations which offered the best opportunities to amass more surplus – more wealth. This class was called *Lugal*. They were themselves, as Gilgamesh, a warrior elite. Originally, they would win status and wealth through personal military enterprise, like Gilgamesh. Later in Mesopotamian history the Lugal was the king who would sponsor the warrior aristocracy that would be used to concentrate royal wealth through force of arms. Eventually, they would become true Royalty – hereditary rulers – elevating themselves over the priesthood and concentrating great wealth and power as absolute emperors with the mandate of the gods. Later still, these violent war-bent figures became considered as demi-gods, or gods themselves. John Wayne in *Iwo Jima* is an archetype of the half-god warrior Achilles. Achilles modeled himself on Heracles. And, Hercules is but an echo of Gilgamesh.

A. Myths and mythology as Historiography

History is supposed to be about written documents, their origin and interpretations. Yet, the earliest human histories are pre-literate, unwritten, and thus prehistoric in a strict sense. Oral traditions of these times that were later set down as myth are our sole documents. Our first glimpses of organized human endeavor come through the mirror of myth. Joseph Campbell – among others – has demonstrated the centrality of myth in human culture as a primary tool for understanding ourselves and our role in the universe. Our myths make sense because they make sense of the world. Myths give us a place in the world and myths give us peace of mind when there is no peace. In his landmark work A Hero With

A Thousand Faces, Campbell showed us that myths are metaphors about the (essential) transformations of the human spirit that are the necessary and shared heritage of humankind. Mythology in this sense may actually tell us more about ourselves than the documents of history. A myth may tell us not just what occurred, but by showing us what was important, may show us why things occurred.

Examining myth as metaphor for human history brings us fresh understandings of the human psyche and its capacity to commit war. In our myriad mythos we see the many faces of god, but also the many, many faces of war. Throughout it all, we can find and follow the thread of truth about war as a central feature of human culture. War emerges as an essential part of our historical identity as human beings and as part of our fundamental link with god, however god is conceived. War cannot be stopped if the links between historical identity and religion go unexplored. This is one reason why the Judeo-Christian-Islamic texts are so important in the understanding of why we war. They are both historical and mythic. Modern culture has ancient myth embedded within it. In modern society, organized religions are among the most powerful and influential institutions. Myth and religion are cornerstones of identity and behavior across cultures. In many cases, one cultures myth is another cultures' religion. Culture is the set of beliefs that govern human behavior. Religious systems are motivators of mass human activity and are ethical justifications for what people do. Many aspects of myth and religion justify, moralize and even glorify war.

Myth becomes ritualized in religion. Ritualizing our behavior in religion has also meant that war has come to have a ritualized content and ritual meaning. The ethics and morals of a religion permeate a culture and influence social organization. Under the influences of organized religion the complexities of life are reduced to simplistic and absolute terms. Social behavior becomes fundamentalist and reactionary. Through religion, overtones of absoluteness, such as a "good side," and an "evil side" have become part of war. This has occurred through the close association between war and myth – between myth and religion. A group of people organized in a tribe or a nation is rallied around the war effort by leaders invoking the heroic metaphors of rightness for their side, while condemning the evil enemy. Drawing on the religious metaphor has allowed leaders to simplify the otherwise irrational act of mass killing into a grand and noble struggle between light and darkness. No matter where ultimate evil may actually exist, the leadership of each side in war always casts the other side as darkness personified. Invoking religion helps them do this. The enemy is no longer human, or capable of good, like we are. The foe is a representative of evil, and "...our mission is clear..." as George W. Bush said, shortly before his usual ending of "God bless America."

Before scrutinizing the ubiquitous conflicts from Torah, the Holy Bible, and the Qur'an in the next section, let us investigate some of the other great traditions of the human search for the ultimate meaning of life and death. What does myth say of war?

In the Greco-Roman cycle of myths the gods made war on their parents, the Titans, in order to secure heavenly power. They continued to make war on each other as well as any other supernatural being of the general pantheon. They even had a god of war – Ares/Mars – who sought to create war among gods and humans alike. Perhaps the most famous ancient Greek myths are the Illiad and the Odyssey. Both are probably fairly true accounts of war in Mycenean (ancient Greek) times that have been interpreted by the later Greeks as heroic warrior epics full of cultural metaphors of mythic proportions. Such myths justify warrior aristocracy and militant nationalism.

Another example of mythology giving character to institutionalized militarism is the origin myth of the Roman Republic. Two brothers locked in mythic struggle – Romulus and Remus – fight until one is dead. The prize for killing his brother is that Romulus founds Rome. Rome further legitimized its militant nationalism by tracing its founding warrior hero's bloodline back to refugees from the Trojan War of the Greek Illiad.

Japanese creation myths revolve around weapons. The deity Izanagi uses a spear to create the islands of Japan. This father of the gods uses a sword to dispatch the fire god, whose birth caused the death of Izanagi's wife, Izanami. Thus, as with the Greek Titans, Izanagi kills his own offspring. Amaterasu, the daughter of the first god Izanagi, gives the first Emperor, Jimmu Tenno, the first of Japans crown jewels – a sword. Thus, all political and religious authority derived from weapons. It was on this mythology that the warlords, or Daimyo, and the Samurai warrior class rose to the top of the social order in Japan under the Bakufu, or military government. The Shogun – a kind of general of generals – reigned through "protecting" the Emperor, who was the holy descendant of Amaterasu. Religion was used in support of military social organization and war. The sword became the soul of the samurai – military servants of the Daimyo whose sole cultivation was war.

Other non-Judeo/Christian traditions are not much different. To the pagan Norse, heaven was itself a hall of immortal heroes slain in war. Their only heavenly job was to fight and drink in preparation for the Great War at the end of the world – Ragnarok. Beautiful women in Valhalla were Valkyries – choosers of the slain.

At the birth of African mythology the principle deity, Osiris, is murdered by his jealous brother, Seth. Isis, and Horus, wife and son of Osiris, reclaim and reassemble his dismembered corpse making him into the first mummy. The red-handed Irish war icon Chuchulain was considered to be blessed by the Gods when he entered his violent blood-madness. The Azteca Mexica made war for the purposes of obtaining captives for sacrificial religious observances.

Each of these mythologies is cast in anthropomorphic terms – in human shapes and thoughts. They serve as models for emulation. Each of these myths was central to both national identity and political authority. These myths were central to the cultural character for each of these peoples. They were not myths as we think of them now. They were the religious orthodoxy of their times. And, as such, were the unquestioned foundations for human behavior. Remember: In God We Trust.

B. Historic Method & Development - Historiography and War –

History is the incomplete written record or oral

152

tradition of the experiences of humans through the contexts of time. Incomplete, because not everything that occurred was deemed worthy of recording, and because not all that was written has survived. Someone had to decide what was worth recording as history, and why it was worth being history. These people called historians typically write from their own perspective. The history they produce reflects the interests of their class, their gender, their culture and society. There are facts in history, but also huge gaps – especially in the areas of motivation and causation. Facts tell (part of) what happened, but not always why. Causes are most likely multiple, not singular. Contrary to many popular perceptions, one thing does not always and inevitably lead to another and another. What historians do is interpret the facts of history. We make sense of events. Historians are often well aware of multiple causes for events. But, historians use analytic theory to argue for the primacy of one cause over others. In a way, we reduce the complexity of reality into the convenience of simplicity.

Historiography is the study of how historians interpret(ed) history.

The discipline of writing history is itself another of those specializations of labor made possible by civilization and social organization. While there are many types of history – such as political, economic, technological, or social history – all are dependant on documents and their interpretation. Documents mean writing, and literacy means social advantage. Interpreting historical writing means leisure time. And, again, leisure time is connected to social advantage. For most of human history, those who have been able to gain both the level of literacy and the free time to assess history have been men of the privileged classes. Class has a major impact on history and historiography.

History, like language, is very plastic. War history is said to have been: "written by the winners." Or, in other words, history is written to justify winning. And history has usually been written to validate social position. Although this is not always a conscious goal, it is always an unconscious fact of culture, society, and human nature(s). This does not mean that historians have not been critical of their own societies and cultures, not at all. It is simply that we all bring our cultural baggage to the task of the historical critique. It also means that historians may sit down to examine historical events, and may do quite a good job. But, it means that historians rarely sit down and attack the class from which they come, or the patrons that employ them. Napoleon Bonaparte went as far as to say "History is set of lies agreed upon." This may well be true, but what is also true is that (until very recently) history has been totally endorsed by the elite and commissioned by elite, if not written by an elite member of society, himself. Thus upper class (male) individuals interpreted the facts of history in service to – if not an individual patrons goals – then in service to the elite in general. Historians have been both under the spell and have cast the spell of history for various reasons and diverse ends. Until the modern era, however, history has been made to serve to the wealthy and powerful.

History has been the result of class privilege and the continuing advantage of privileged class. This is why so much of history is political, military, and nationalist. This is also why so much supportive rhetoric used in continuing to organize society for conflict comes from historic interpretation.

154

Historiography mostly serves power, concentrated wealth and war. Qin Shi Huangdi was the first Emperor of China. When he wanted to consolidate his political authority, he changed history. He did this by commissioning his own version, and burning any dissenting books – reportedly burying alive any dissenting historians. The Greek historian Thucydides of Athens compiled his history in order to justify the hegemony of the Athenian League.

Think for a moment about only two wars that the United States was involved in, and the historical rhetoric surrounding and supporting them. In this case I write of the 1898 Spanish-American War and the Iraqi-American Wars of a century later. In both cases, the U.S. projected military force half-way around the world in order to secure positions of self-interest. In each case, there was domestic dissent – anti-war organizations that were public and vocal. In both situations, the pro-war administration invoked history as a support for their policies of aggression.

The Spanish-American War rhetoric was that the United States had a Manifest Destiny to become a global power as the other European powers had. Also high in the echelon of political justifications for war with Spain was the assertion that the U.S. had an obligation (a God given duty) to liberate the Cuban and Filipino people from oppressive domination. Later, this grew into what has been called "Big Stick" diplomacy. The Monroe Doctrine Corollary asserted the right of U.S. military intervention anywhere in the Americas. Compare this to the Iraqi-American Wars in which the administration invoked justifications of an American duty as the sole super-power to intervene first in the oppression of Kuwait, and then for the security of the World. The Kuwaiti people, and then the Iraqi people were to be liberated. Wars of "liberation" are popular. In each case, God was on "our side."

In the Spanish-American War, the United States used the success of its history of brushing aside Mexican claims to much of North America, and the outright genocide of the Indigenous Americans to legitimize war. In the case of Iraq, the U.S. used the history of success at being the "Big Stick" as legitimization for war with Iraq. In both cases, the United States economically benefited by securing foreign resources, and by further validating itself as a (or the) global military power. Each is also a case in which the local people the U.S. "liberated" came to quickly accuse the American Government of becoming the new masters of exploitation.

Interpretation of history provides cultural identity to a people. The American Revolutionary War is used to establish an identity for the culture and government of the United States as champions of freedom, and eventually as the "Arsenal of Democracy" for the world (forget for a moment that the U.S. is not a democracy). Although a cultural identity of freedom need not translate into social institutions which promote war, the self-image of an "Arsenal of Democracy" is indisputably warlike (Franklin Roosevelt: Speech, 1940).

As a critical historian it is impossible to overlook alternative interpretations of the Revolutionary War. The very name presupposes drastic change. But the interpretation that the Revolutionary War resulted in revolutionary change has been questioned. Other nations call the American Revolution the War for Independence, for instance. To many thoughtful and diligent historians, the American Revolutionary War simply resulted in a change in elite control from foreign to domestic leadership. To these historians (among whom I stand) United States history since the Revolution has been a history of the struggle for inclusion, or the systematic exclusion of those people who fought in the war(s) but never got the freedom promised by the socially elite leadership of the Revolution. These differences of interpretation over the Revolutionary War are inextricably linked to the existing cultural, social, and economic differences in modern American identities. It may be clear which historical interpretation above is endorsed by the institutions of political and economic leadership. It may even be clear why they endorse and support the interpretation that is supportive of their elite identity. What needs clarification is how the elite interpretation results in war. And, these are just a few examples from United States history. What about further back in human history? What if we go back to "In God We Trust?"

The key to historic study, as noted above, is in documents and their interpretation. What is the purpose of history? The contributions to the discipline of history and the value to this project of differences in historical interpretation rest in looking at how the early documents characterize war. One of the earliest historic documents is the Hebrew Torah. It is essentially what was amended to later create the Christian Old Testament, or the earliest part of the Judeo-Christian-Islamic bible. This text is unique, and perfect for the study of why we war. First, the Torah is a religious text that uses history to confer cultural identity and political legitimacy on an ethnic group. This sense of religious nationalism is the root of many tenacious military conflicts, not the least of which plagues Palestine and Israel even now. Second, it is a work of interpretation, and as any historic document is open to re-interpretation. Third, the Torah is the foundation of culture for the Western part of Asia (through the Qur'an), and the foundation of culture in much of Western civilization (through the Bible). Fourth, the Hebrew Torah, the Judeo-Christian Bible, and the Qur'an of Islam are among the documents most historically cited as validations for war. They have evolved as a kind of triad that lends moral justification and institutional endorsement to war.

 The Hebrew God of the Old Testament advised the chosen to raze cites, and to put entire populations to the sword. War against the non-believer, the idolater, and the foreigner became the distinguishing act of faith of many Old Testament heroes. This militant pattern of behavior led to the Kingdom of Israel and the fabled wealth of Solomon.

 The Roman Catholic Church first became the Church of the Empire because of the image of victory in battle seen by Constantine. Later, the Pope organized the Crusades. A set of "Holy Wars" that at one point saw the churches of Jerusalem awash in human blood "ankle-deep," according to one crusader. Holy Crusades that generated merchant class wealth and that stabilized nationalist European political power. And then there are the Catholic pogroms – wars of extermination –

against Jews and other non-Catholic Christians. Pogroms against Jews allowed European political leaders to confiscate Jewish wealth.

 Then there are the Christians. Those who saw their link to God as so exclusive that entire populations of "heathens" could be enslaved for profit, or massacred. Colonialism was good for the heathen. If they resist, they must be forced. Indigenous peoples of the world were "not industrious," and their lands were seized – their human rights voided by the Christians. It was protestant Christians that could rationalize slavery and god. And, it was the protestant Christian faiths that considered that they had a "Manifest Destiny" to eliminate Native America.

 In Islam, war was seminal to the foundation of the Caliphate. The Prophet Muhammad was made to flee from Mecca, and had to organize for war in order to survive. This led to traditions of religiously legitimate warfare such as fatwa, and jihad. Expansionist Islam under the Umayyads and Abbasids used religion and the institutions of religion to legitimize military conquest. The resulting conquered lands made the vast wealth (and disparities of wealth) of the "Thousand and One Nights" possible.

None of these conflicts are simple acts of faith. They are the result of institutionalized religion. Faith, when it becomes a socially organized institution, can be turned to war. Simple faith in supernatural intervention did (does) not make war. Social institutions organize the faithful for war. One may ask: what is in it for them?

Scholars of the western world are all too familiar with some of the more sanguine aspects of Judeo-Christian-Islamic religion. Beyond spiritualism and philosophy, these three linked religious traditions are historic. This triad (Old Testament, New Testament, and Qur'an) is unique among religious texts and holy books in it's assertion of ethnic, historic and political significance. However, it is not exceptional among sacred traditions in its emphatic evidence of religious obsession with homicide, fratricide and genocide. Quite the contrary, one of the truths that link the Bible and Qur'an to all other major religious traditions is the central role of battle and war.

Like war, the institutional edifice of organized religion(s) has tentacles in virtually every aspect of a society and culture. Thus war and religion give each other a mutual stamp of approval.

Be mindful of the hypocrisy. At least with the religions of Homer, Xenophon, Herodotus, and in the Heike Monogatari, etc, war was part of the pantheon. In the Hebrew/Christian/Muslim traditions, the God was supposed to be one of hope, of life, and of (eventual) peace – at least for the chosen. In these religions, the difference between God and humankind is the difference between peace and war. For all the religious histories to be obsessed with peace, war was the ever-present problem. Whatever the obsession with peace in Judaism, Catholicism, Islam,

Hinduism, Buddhism, Confucianism, and Taoism - all are simply implications of war. The history of organized institutional religion is a history of war.

Christianity, with its "Prince of Peace'" is no different. It is simply what happens when myths become the property of the state. It is what institutions of civilized religion do to peace. The civilization of myth into religion brings revelations about war. When the Catholic faith became the religion of Rome, it was due to a vision Constantine had concerning victory in battle. It is no wonder that one of the first acts of the new institution of faith under emperor Theodosius became the systematic destruction of rival Christian sects. Becoming a formal institution allowed the Roman Catholic Church to make war. While this should seem incongruous it is by no means untrue. The Crusades at the end of the European Middle Ages was a Catholic war of aggression engineered and supported by a religious institutional orthodoxy bent on social power and on material gain.

The ultimate results of these types of religious history are institutions of war. Since the very beginning of Islam (despite the Umma) it was Sunni versus Shi'ite. And to that we can now add fundamentalist fanatics like Osama Bin Ladin and secular fascists like Saddam Hussein. Then the Hebrew covenant with the chosen – a territorial imperative of fire and brimstone. The Jehovah who razed cities is invoked to compliment the Zionist religious nationalism of the likes of Ariel Sharon. And, finally, George W. Bush anoints the War on Terrorism with the eerie invocation that is by now both ominous and nauseating: "God is on our side."

3. HISTORY OF WAR

"War is the health of the State. It automatically sets in motion throughout society these irresistible forces for uniformity, for passionate cooperation with the government in coercing into obedience the minority groups and individuals which lack the larger herd sense."

-Randolph Bourne

What is war, really? Is it to be found purely in the physical manifestation of organized purposeful slaughter of our own kind? Is war a political description of social interactions that have exceeded diplomatic resolution? Or is war the logical extension of diplomacy? Without the threat of war, would other diplomacy be ineffective or impossible? Most would consider war to be both psychological and physical. Is war, then, a psychological expression of human relations brought into tangible reality? Is war a kind of vulgar realization of one or more aspects of human potential? An ancient Asian martial aphorism relates that to conquer your enemy, you must know him [sic]. Historical observation supports the conclusion that we have never been without the threat of unified, armed aggression. If war is truly in some tragically human way genetically unavoidable, then the human race must face the biologic threat with the universal human tool of culture. On the other hand, if it is human social institutions that breed war, then we must find the ways to refine them into breeders of peace. After all, we make our social institutions to meet our needs. Can we decide to need peace? Just as we have met the other natural challenges of our environment, human culture through technology must adapt to the human caused environment of endemic conflict. If humankind is to realistically end war, then we must know all we can about it. That means history.

However, history is not sacred fact. Human history is an incomplete written record or oral tradition (see *Historic Method & Development* above). The written record may be factual within the understanding and intent of whoever recorded events, but what history yet remains is the human interpretation of fact – not the fact itself. True objectivity is mere illusion. What historians do is make connections. Historians join facts together through interpretation of them. Historians join the past to the present, always determining what is important based on current interpretations of importance. While there are many types of history – such as political, economic, technological, or social history – all are dependant on documents *and their interpretation*. History, like language, is very plastic. Historians have been both under the spell <u>and have cast</u> the spell of history for various reasons and diverse ends. As we have seen, many histories support and endorse war. An important anthropological fact here is that individual historians are products of their cultures. They are themselves the result of unique interactions between their predisposition and historic context (cultural evolution). Historians (me included) are products of their social systems as well as of their cultures.

Here is where definitions become important. Not the least, of course, is: *what is war?* If we take war to be a struggle of good and evil – of heroes and villains – then we make war willingly and forever. Our "good" is always someone else's "evil," and no peace can be had. Unfortunately, this definition is the point of view of the nations' leaders whenever they turn to war. It is the point pushed by George W. Bush, and the current U.S. leadership. It is the point pushed by those who oppose American corporate and government influence in their regions. It was the point of Theodore Roosevelt, and later, it was the point of Hideki Tojo. It was the point of the Caesars and of the emperors of China, and of Shaka Zulu. Each side uses moral and religious "rightness" to support moves to war.

But is war right? The meaning of the word defines much about who will support it. In this era of mass culture and mass media, the link between a word and subjective reality are crucial. A political campaign urging a war that is also supported by corporations and media can use a lot of institutional clout to convince you of a particular definition for a word like war. Instead of killing, war becomes an act of liberation, or a police action, or preemptive necessity, or humanitarian intervention. We should not have to each be personally in a war zone to set aside false assumptions about what war means. There is a critical difference between war as portrayed in a Rambo-type film, or a video-game, or an adventure novel, and war as lived by real people. If when you hear politicians talk of war, you envision an Arnold Swartzenegger movie, then you are a lot more likely to support, or a lot less liable to resist, war. If you define war as the route to peace, then you are under an illusion unsupported by historic fact. Let me introduce you to some textbook definitions of war and the new vogue – terrorism – ending with my own definition of war.

Some Definitions of War:

1) Act of War - any act occurring in the course of declared war; armed conflict, whether or not war has been declared, between two or more nations; or armed conflict between military forces of any origin (U.S. Code, Title 18).

2) Main Entry: 1war
Pronunciation: 'wor
Function: noun
Usage: often attributive
Etymology: Middle English werre, from Old North French, of Germanic origin; akin to Old High German werra strife; akin to Old High German werran to confuse
Date: 12th century
1 a (1) : a state of usually open and declared armed hostile conflict between states or nations (2) : a period of such armed conflict (3) : STATE OF WAR b : the art or science of warfare c (1) obsolete : weapons and equipment for war (2) archaic : soldiers armed and equipped for war
2 a : a state of hostility, conflict, or antagonism b : a struggle or competition between opposing forces or for a particular end <a class war> <a war against disease> c : VARIANCE, ODDS (Merriam-Webster).

3) LET IT BE RESOLVED BY THE UNITED NATIONS THAT:
A comprehensive definition of terrorism and terrorism will be accepted.
This definition will be as follows:
A TERRORIST is any person who, acting independently of the specific recognition of a country,

or as a single person, or as part of a group not recognized as an official part of division of a nation, acts to destroy or to injure civilians or destroy or damage property belonging to civilians or to governments in order to effect some political goal. TERRORISM is the act of destroying or injuring civilian lives or the act of destroying or damaging civilian or government property without the expressly chartered permission of a specific government, thus, by individuals or groups acting independently or governments on their own accord and belief, in the attempt to effect some political goal (Definition of terrorism adopted by Gateway Model United Nations, Spring, 1995).

4) War: Organized purposeful murder of your own species (Al Smith).

Genocide is the term we use for the systematic and purposeful extermination of a race. Be mindful that biologically there is only one race – human. War therefore, is genocide. Many of humanity's most developed systems are aimed at the purposeful extermination of ourselves. Perhaps the defining human characteristic is the inherent act of war. No other species has been documented making war on itself. Even the most socially organized insect populations do not kill tens of thousands of its own kind simply because of politics, or a different religion, or creed. As specialized as some creatures' natural weapons get, none invest as intensely as humans in the variety of tools for destruction. No animal makes an economy of war. No beast spends its life training and strategizing on the best methods of killing like we humans. The historic human obsession with armed mortal combat goes far beyond the surface of any individual or ethnic culture.

We identify ourselves by our history. We document and preserve not everything in human experience, but those things which define ourselves to ourselves. Weapons show up in graves. It is then that weapons (that were once tools) became decorative as well as deadly. Such embellishments are examples of social status. There was (is) a warrior aristocracy. If war shows up so much in our collective history, then it is because we selected to record it, to interpret it, and to reproduce it time and time again. We define war, but war also defines us.

War has left its bloody-taloned imprint on all of human history. There are many methods of premeditated organized murder to be used in fixing necessary definition to the curiously human activity called war. There is a progressive chain – a cultural evolution – of human behavior showing the historic justifications for aggression, violence, and war. Each link anchors social organization to war. Trending from simple to complex, the historical foundations of war are cumulative. Like a comprehensive examination, war tends to embrace all aspects of its history. Human culture has a long memory. Justifications for killing one are transferred to justifications for killing many. The life and death authority of leadership becomes unassailable through tradition. The tradition underpinning authority is war. War becomes a fixture.

A. Self-Defense?

All around the world, self-defense is a licensing philosophy for systems of "justifiable homicide." Self-defense is the most universally fundamental rationale for taking life. An oxymoron for some, justifiable homicide is still legally accepted as a defense plea in nearly every judicial system known now and in the human record. Self-defense is the most widely acceptable reason for the extinguishing of the life of one human being by another (Ironically, a close statistical occurrence U.S. courts is a plea of "diminished capacity"). What this means is that in nearly every level of human history (behavior), the prospect of human to human violence to the point of extermination was (and is) taken as a given. It also means that part of our cultural evolution has been an acceptance of killing others of our species as a necessary part of fundamental survival. Among all the other threats to life and limb, we rank ourselves as a primary threat.

On top of the legal sanction on killing that self-defense represents, there is also the state sponsored murder called the death penalty. When governments authorize killing and social institutions support death as a punishment, war is also more easily rationalized. But, just as the death penalty has been misapplied to some who have later proven to have been innocent, there are always collateral innocent victims in war.

There is a question mark in the title heading this section. Is it really necessary that self-defense be violent? This is not the place to debate whether an individual has a right or a need to engage in violent self-defense. It misses the point, entirely. What must be understood is that _nations need not produce the conditions where war occurs as self-defense_. If we assume that killing another person is sometimes the only way to defend oneself (a big assumption), then it seems important when those "sometimes" are that justify homicide. Here we are not asking _if_ self-defense is necessary, but _why_ it is necessary. The needs of a society are different than those of the individual. The resources of an individual are not those of a social system. If a person does indeed resort to lethal violence in self-defense, it is usually because the social system failed to guarantee the human right of security. Remember the statistically high plea of "diminished capacity?" This is why self-defense is legally justified unto homicide. The social system justifies it because it realizes the failure of the system, not the individual. In this case, it is the capacity of the system to provide for the safety and security of the individual that is diminished. This is also why national leaders bent on policies of war attempt to cloak themselves and their militant policies in the guise of self-defense. The societies involved have failed to guarantee peace. Very soon defending the self becomes more. Soon defending the "Nation" or a "Way of Life" becomes justified as self-defense. Politicians invoke this most ancient of sanctions and link it to the concept and practice of war. Religious leaders join in with their similar versions. War becomes defending the moral rightness of the nation. One question: If the system fails when an individual has to resort to violent self-defense, then has not the same system failed when leaders urge war?

What does the law say about when it is O.K. to kill? Author and military educator Shannon French invoked Saint Thomas Aquinas' principles of Natural Law to justify killing. In the book Code of the Warrior, two doctrines are identified that transfer self defense into war. The doctrine of forfeiture allows killing in defense of others. The doctrine of double effect justifies killing of innocents – if they are accidentally killed in an action meant to save others from harm.

These principles of Natural Law inform our ideas about killing in self defense. And these same principles mitigate the death of innocents in war.

B.   Personal Combat

One of, if not the oldest form of warfare is personal combat. It retains a strange mystique even now. Action movies nearly always end with the hero confronting the villain in one long last fight to the finish. How do we know the hero? He is the one who wins. All through the film, the (lone) hero struggles and wins against always enormous odds. His enemy is powerful in evil, and forces the violence on the hero. When the hero can morally take no more, he erupts into righteous anger and violence. It is a perennial rite of passage. One man against all odds wins again and again until the final violent confrontation with his enemy. Our hero finally makes things right by his victory. Personal combat is part of a "heroic" tradition, and has been both a legal and a religious formula for deciding right. In what was known as "Trial by Combat," the winner was seen to be the victor in the eyes of both society, and the deity. Justice was in the hands of the God(s). In this concept, might really was right in the absolute religious sense. But, of course, the winner of personal combat also brought social prestige and influence to himself, and to his group. His point was made – publicly – and to him went the spoils.

Among the ancient Norse, Saxons, and Germans single combat was meant to reduce the tendency among warrior classes to feud. In lands where the gods warred and heaven was seen to be a hall of slain warriors, feuding could escalate with devastating results to society. The tradition of fighting over honor called *einvigi* evolved out of what could be described as an anything-goes brawl. Later, a more structured public contest called *holmgang* developed. The *holmgang* law was explicit as to the duties and rights of the contestants. If the accused was slain, only half-blood-price was paid. If the accuser was killed, then his claim was held to be false and no blood-price was paid.

Another area or the social sanction of violence lies in the institution of the duel. This is a social trial by combat. Although ancient mythology is full of one-on-one conflicts, the first recorded duel in the modern West happened in Europe about 501 CE. The duel took many forms, but became institutionalized as a legal confrontation fought "in cold blood," with witnesses and ceremony in accordance with codes of honor and chivalry. Courts of Honor controlled dueling among upper classes, but lower classes dueled as well. Class and class struggle permeate dueling in the history of the United States since the time of the fatal encounter between Aaron Burr and Alexander Hamilton. By that time, the duel was embedded in upper class male society. Although to be male of any class meant to be involved in what was called "rough and tumble," the formal duel became a way for aristocratic planters to distinguish themselves from the "gouge and bite, pull hair and scratch" that was the custom of less affluent men. Modern high-income exhibition sports like boxing and wrestling thrive as entertainment because they echo the duel and the ancient trial by combat.

Is war a gender-based expression? Men historically engage in war. Warrior is a male profession in all but a few historic societies. In those few societies where women warriors existed, women were on a more equal social footing with men. If war is the failure of politically reasonable or equitable resolutions to social problems, then war is an expression of dominance through violence. Since men carry out the activities of war almost exclusively, is social dominance through violence part of being male? War being a broad example of dominance by way of violent means would indicate that there must be a historic root to both the social construction of maleness and of violent dominance. As we have come to practice it, male dominance leads directly to war.

Aside from religion, the other intangible quality called honor is the main reason historically leading to war (according to war historian John Keegan honor is the #1 cause). As a phenomenon, honor rates its own section in this book. Here, there is a different connection to be explored – the link between war, gender and honor. Honor is an eerily male concept. Honor, status, social power, ethnic nationalism, patriotism are all sides of the same sphere. The sphere is that of dominant social status, and historically since the time of single combat, the sphere is that of male dominance.

It is also a dominance play. The hero will not accept being dominated. He must, instead dominate. To do less is not "manly." To be dominated is be less than.

The winner of such a single combat situation typically secured his dominance even if no property was claimed, or no life was lost. He is honored. Notice the use of the male pronoun. This concept of the rightness of dominance through acts of violence seems historically male. There has apparently always been a hideous link between gender, sex, and violence. Gender is a social role that is learned from birth. Sex is a biological description of organisms, or their potential acts. When violence becomes part of the social description of being male, sex becomes another potential weapon. As an act of violence and dominance, none – perhaps not even death – is as widespread a part of war as rape. Rape is an act of violence. It is not sexual, except mechanically, or in the case of obsessive-compulsive psychological imbalance. The penis becomes the sword – a weapon to be used in ritual ways. In its essence, rape is an act of violent dominance. Male dominance in a social system is war against women.

Rape and the threat of rape is the central aspect of this dominance and honor. Rape is a hideously violent act of dominance. Men, like the nations they represent, turn their aggression to violence when other avenues fail. Often, of course, it is the same men and nations that have convinced themselves of the failure of alternatives. Their honor is threatened. When that happens, aggression becomes violence. War or rape – nation or man – dominance and honor are re-established through violence. And, when nations go to war, rape is always another weapon in the arsenal.

Rape is used as an act of dominance over males as well. Long hushed in male dominated society, even as much as the rape of women seems almost celebrated in titillating detail, the rape of men has recently been shown to be not an uncommon phenomenon. Movies like American History X, or Shawshank Redemption have played out this scenario of dominance, but the life experience of T.E. Lawrence (of Arabia) and others shows that men too are victims of sexual torture and violence to secure dominance. The horrifying stigma that rape is somehow a failure and loss of honor for the victim, and the even more frightening linking of victory to rightness have meant that modern societies rarely support the victim of rape. The winner of war or personal combat is right. Winning is honorable. The loser in war must have been wrong. Losing is dishonorable. The assaulted victim of a rape must often prove her/his lack of "wrong-ness" in the damning public forum while the rapist has the benefit of the assumption of innocence. Under male dominance, rapists and war have flourished, and the victims have the burden of proof to bear along with the condemnation of being defeated. Women through history and around the world are constantly under the threat of rape. It is said that: "her honor is at stake." The central premise of male dominance is that women are seen as a form of property and source of honor and prestige. War and violence to avenge rape or to protect women from rape makes the man a hero to his group – and sometimes makes him a rapist to the other group.

C. Raiding

It is at this point of social organization – the raiding party – that certain forms of manhood become even more particularly violent and dangerous to society. A raid is usually a quick vicious mobile incursion by one group into territory claimed by another. Although the modern guerrilla raider may have political objectives, the reason is usually to acquire some resource. The real or imagined scarcity of a particular resource can motivate a raiding party to form. However wealth is calculated, the raiding group are not militarily strong enough or sufficiently organized to hold territory that they raid into, but they can expect to seize and remove wealth. Food, women as brides or concubines, slaves, ponies, or any forms of portable wealth are targets. As with all wealth based social systems, the valuables taken by the raiders makes them rise in their own societies. Returning raiders are richer. This can motivate other raids. Of course, defense is a reason to raid. And, retaliation for earlier raids is also a reason to raid in return. Social systems evolved to specialize in raiding, or in resisting raids.

At this place in history, civilization rears its ugly head. War is systematic state sponsored violence. It could take the form of the organization of a raid or of a set of defensive walls and regularly trained troops to defend against raiders. Violence is older than civilization, but it is with the advances of social organization that we call civilization that the mass killing really begins. Raiding in history means a concentration of social and political power built around the prospect of violence. It means fortifications and specialized workers in violence – elite warriors, common soldiers, and domestic police. It means organizing society around a broader definition of wealth. And, it means fewer wealthy, and more poor. Wealth is concentrated. Resources that could lessen poverty within a society are instead allocated for defense. In order to offset inadequate resources in a society, raiding of others is regularized – institutionalized. We think of civilization as progress, and see modern life as the apex of civilization. Modern humanity is indeed civilized. All things flow to the city, and the state. But wealth and power have also produced the conditions for organized violence.   Power begets wealth begets power, and the power of the state is used to insure that all things flow to the wealthy.   Currently, all rural and non-industrial areas give labor, and resources to the health and protection of the state.   All urban laboring classes likewise render unto the state the benefits of their work.   The benefits of the city and state (supposedly) flow out to the people.   The wealth is protected from the raiders outside.   The reality of civilization is that only a few have full benefit.   The rich raid the poor as habit.   The poor raid the rich out of desperation.

These benefits have all proven questionable, as has the idea of progress.   Pollution and other forms of environmental degradation, disease, political and economic oppressions are among the questionable benefits of our present level of civilization. The human rights that civilization was to guarantee have often become denied.   Deforestation and waste strangle the planet in the name of a high quality of material life for a few.   Pandemics spread when the technology and distribution networks capable of providing a cure are not used because there is no profit in it.   A Third World (with all of the Third World want and strife) is maintained by the First World, so that the benefits of resources, labor, and markets of the many can be hoarded by the few.   And now there is the generation of a Fourth World that is never meant to "catch-up."   Self determination and human rights become largely economic rights that are set at a price that few can ever expect to meet. No one wakes up wanting to be powerless and poor, and virtually no one who is rich and relatively powerful questions (or fails to maintain) a system that privileges them.   Perhaps the oldest of the questionable gifts of progress and civilization is war. The complex form of social organization that "civilized" behavior represents has also meant that conflict has become organized. The investment in this organization for conflict maintains social disparity. The military raid is one of the earliest examples. The corporate raid is one of the latest examples.

Raiding demands that a group become organized for predictable success. Raiding also became historically possible when there were predictable resources to raid. These predictable resources came from organized, civilized centers. Resistance to raids also requires different levels of social organization. It should be noted that the word "different" was used instead of "better" or "more complex." War may have changed human society, but it would be rash to presume that war has made us better. There is an intimate connection between civilized humanity and war. In many ways, modern war is a sophisticated form of the ancient raid (see the definition of war). The economic relationship between first world and third world countries is also a modern form of the raid. Resources are scooped up by (corporate) raiders for use in their own territories, and military force is there to protect the interests of the raiders.

Objectification of human beings is part of the raiding mentality. Women become objects in such chauvinistic societies. Valued as property for their labor, women become the objects of the raiders. Group mentality implies leadership, but in reality the members of the group surrender responsibility for their individual acts. It is at this point in history, and at this level of civilization, that leadership evolved.

As with most aspects of war, the raid is immortalized in myth and legend. In Homer's Iliad, Helen of Troy and her women (important in Mycenaean textile industry) are kidnapped by raiding Trojans under the command of Paris, Prince of Troy. The kidnapping allows King Menelaus of Sparta to unite the warring Mycenaean's in the mutually beneficial war against their trade rival, Troy. A war of elite heroes began over a raid made possible by the fact that women were considered as an economic resource of private property. What does this say about power and gender in a society? When this is a central cultural history of a people, what type of social institutions may develop?

The Huns, and later the Mongols were initially raiding societies. Although they eventually formed semi-permanent ruling castes over lands fully conquered, in the early aspects of their histories the raid was their specialty. Essential to the raid was the ability to quickly subdue a larger population through brutality and terror. Frequently, local populations were agricultural, sedentary, and hierarchical. Settled peoples have a tendency to acknowledge central authority. Their method of achieving social organization was usually through surrendering autonomy to authority. In these cases the raiders would take advantage of the social organization of their victims. By exploiting the local deference to authority raiders could identify and eliminate local leadership, replacing it with their own. Raiders could also round up the population, isolating it into segregated groups for further exploitation or destruction. Swift, sudden, and ruthless, the raiders of the steppes of Central Asia are still the subjects of military study in modern colleges of war alongside modern masters of guerrilla raiding like Mao or Che.

The European slave trade of the early colonial periods (ca. 1400-1800 CE) was frequently based on raiding. Either the European parties themselves would conduct slave raids for profitable captives, or they would encourage Africans to raid other Africans for slaves. Either way, the result was a vast resource and wealth reallocation-through-force away from Africa and into Europe. Raiding for slaves destroyed African social economy even as it shattered African cultures. The other devastating result of the slave raiding centuries was interminable wars between Africans. Stepping into the political void caused be the destabilizing raids, many European nations established colonies in Africa. Colonization in Africa perpetuated poverty, social strife and militarism. Although officially ended in the early twentieth century, European colonization and other after affects of slave raiding continue to create contemporary ripples of warfare and revolution.

In both the wars of modern Africa, and in the wars of Bosnia, etc., rape gangs were the product of the raiding mentality. Institutionalized through the military, rape and the threat of rape became standard operating procedure aimed at subduing the population. Unofficially, rape was also used as a form of genocide. Rape as military torture guaranteed that a level of damage would be done that would perpetually instill a climate of fear and intimidation in an occupied area. Rape as genocidal practice focused instead on changing the make-up of the next generation. In raids such as this, the captured and defeated men are typically slaughtered outright. Then the women and girls are systematically raped by soldiers with the specific intent on making the women pregnant with the children of the murderers of their fathers, brothers, sons, and husbands. In raiding, the militarist force is typically too weak to occupy territory for any extended period of time. They instead concentrate on removing resources to their own territory or, as above, they concentrate on despoiling and depopulating raided territories.

Other concepts, like private property, male dominance, and the divine right of the winner of single combat all blend in the rhetoric of the raiding leader. All things being equal between groups, raid begets raid. Often, self defense is invoked as rationale for raiding in reprisal for having been the victim of a raid. If either of the now opposing forces is convinced of their own military superiority, then war may "officially" be declared.

D. Territorial skirmish

If a people occupying one area seek the resources of another people occupying another area, then one group may go to war in an attempt to permanently take the territory of the other. Acquiring the resource means dispossessing the people of their land. Typically it is a natural resource or geographic advantage that is being sought by the aggressor. Today, we can hardly forget oil. But, historically it may well be a choice location astride a lucrative trade route. There may be deposits of precious metals or jewels. Territories may contain vital resources such as water or arable farm land. Access to ports on rivers and oceans may be the issue. Such resources are not as portable as those mentioned earlier. A raid is not enough.

Covetous concepts of personal property generate an inability to compromise and thereby prevent warfare. We prove what is ours by our ability to keep others from having it. Sharing denies ownership. It is ours or not – there is no in between. "We" need what "they" have. "They" will not share. Often the population is motivated to go to war because their leaders tell them that the security of their tribe, nation or way of life is threatened. In times like this, the only choice is to take over the control of a territory and to either dominate or destroy the indigenous people. Of course, the loss of territory by the defeated becomes justification for more war. Before World War Two, Adolph Hitler cried out for "lebensraum." His visceral argument was that his chosen people needed more living space – that Germans needed more Germany. In fact, he wanted Germany to have access to the sea for maritime trade, and to secure land resources stripped from Germany as a result of the Treaty of Versailles. The new wars would be either to take back what was lost, to seize the territories of others, or to resist colonization.

Although the resource that the territorial war will gain is often something – like water, or arable land, or natural/mineral resource – that will benefit the tribe, the distribution within the tribe is always uneven. The ruling class of the conquerors will retain the main economic advantages of territories gained through conquest. The more organized the practice of territorial expansion, the more consolidated the wealth will become in the hands of the elite. Even high-ranking military leaders at this stage of social organization do not profit as much as government and merchant classes. The social flow of leadership means that retired military men often go into government or commerce in societies that feature territorial expansion as a civilized means to an end.

The price of goods and the cost of living to the general population stays relatively the same. Gas prices remain high, as do oil company profits. Government contracts go out to favored corporations. Consumers must be kept consuming, as the resources gained in territorial expansion become products on the market. Those who have been defeated – who have lost their land – also lose human rights. They become pushed aside, subjugated as minorities, enslaved as a commodity, or killed.

The destruction during war, the subjugation and sometimes genocide of the defeated is partly possible because the winner sees themselves as morally right and superior. Their rhetoric and mythos have made them that way.

E. Religion &"Holy" War

"It's interesting that God is brought into the picture when the government is doing great violence. Maybe it's when you are doing great violence that you desperately need some support. You're not going to get any moral support from any thinking person, but since God isn't thinking at the moment, maybe you can pull out God to support you. He certainly isn't around to contradict you." -Howard Zinn, page 94 of Terrorism and War.

While the idea of God – however you see it – may seem in the modern sense of religion to be opposed to war, still next to honor, more war has been righteously waged in the name of some deity or the other than any other cause. Looking back on the divine right of both self-defense and of personal combat that have already been discussed shows that religion may indeed be the main motivation to the madness of war. Our enemy is "godless," and "heathen." They (only they) engage in "unholy" acts on and off of the battlefield. And "God is on our side." Most leaders use God. The current American president, George W. Bush, has been unceasing in invoking God. Whose God is he calling on? In a land of the supposed separation of church and state, who knows? All of the world's religions are represented in the United States. There is the nationalist assumption that the God of George W. Bush – the Judeo-Christian-Islamic one – is the foremost, or one true God. Perhaps more accurately, the God of Bush is the Calvinist version who loves private property. Or maybe his God is the Old Testament Lord of Hosts who advocated razing cities and putting entire populations to the sword.

In any event, the joining of religion to nationalism comes from making faith a formal social institution. Religious nationalism becomes orthodoxy, a dogma that leads to war. Most often the dogma of religious nationalists is the hymn to the ritual of war. It is a rhetoric that links morality to political cause and categorically sets aside any ethical qualms. If the enemy is outside the realm of "God," then they be guilty of any evil, and can expect no mercy. As potent a tool as religion can be in uniting people in a sense of a least spiritual commonality, organized religion is just as powerful a tool for fixing a broad category of those to be excluded. It is no different for the U.S. president to invoke God than it is for the Ayatollah to invoke Allah in uniting the nation in war.

The Jihad is a struggle that is the obligation of every Muslim. It is a foundation principle of Islam. Although the struggle may be spiritual, the historical link in the Muslim world between church and state has meant that Jihad has almost always meant war. This is the effect of nationalism joined to religion. In Islam, religious leaders are policy makers. War becomes holy. Since before the first Caliphate, war has been the solution to any threat to the faith. Before Jihad was taken up against outsiders, there was Jihad of Sunni against Shi'ite and Shi'ite against Sunni.

While the political model in Islam unashamedly united the civil leadership with the religious leadership, the monarchs of Europe saw civil political leadership and the spiritual leadership of the Catholic Church as being separate offices. Politically the power of the Catholic Church was that of a kind of separate government that united Europe in one faith. But, since the time of Charlemagne the Catholic Church had also confirmed political orthodoxy as well. To remain King, one must have the support of the Pope. The Crusades were a series of wars initiated by Catholic Pope Urban II in 1095 CE. The wars lasted for more than a century – far longer than Urban II. However, the final victors were the Muslims of the region called the "Holy Land" – roughly present-day Palestine/Israel. Originally, Pope Urban II stated a desire to unite Christendom in a holy effort to save the land of the birth of the faith from the infidel. Never mind that the "Holy Land" was holy to Jews, Christians and Muslims.

Then there were the internal Crusades of the Catholic government of Europe. Called "Crusades," these were frequently bloody wars to maintain control and wealth of the Catholic Church and its political partners. Any challenge to Catholic Church behavior was a threat to Catholic power. A threat to Catholic power was also a threat to political orthodoxy that the Church confirmed and legitimized. While the Church's power was restored and reinforced by each Crusade, the political players in support of the "Crusade" gained the material wealth of the defeated infidel, heretic or apostate. The pogroms against Jews that were sporadic and endemic to Christian Europe found broad murderous play in the Inquisitions of Spain and elsewhere. While Jews were targeted for the economic power that they had traditionally been placed in charge of, other Christians had not been exempt since the time of Augustine. The Albigensian Crusade of the beginning of the Thirteenth Century saw the Catholic Pope Innocent III urge a wholesale slaughter of the Cathars – A Christian sect otherwise generally known for the social well being of the area of France they inhabited. The pope offered to nobles joining the Crusade the rich confiscated the land of Albigensian Southern France. It was during this war that a papal envoy leading the Crusade massacring fellow Christians is purported to have said (paraphrased): "Kill them all, Let god sort them." It was a time of "holy war," a time of "just war."

European central government with the papacy as its head would benefit immensely from many of the Crusades, as would the countries of feudal Europe. The warrior aristocracy had grown large and contentious over power and wealth. The Crusades allowed that the potentially profitless instability of a factious warrior elite to be channeled into a vehicle that would profit and stabilize society – war. Of those

Europeans who participated in the Crusades, virtually only the Catholic Church, the nobility and the merchant classes benefited. The Church was able to stave off change for another three centuries, before it was to be successfully challenged by protestant reforms. The merchants – first in Italy, then elsewhere – became a class as powerful and influential as princes and kings. For Europe it would herald not just a renaissance of Greco-Roman culture, but also would give rise to a period of capitalism, nationalism, and colonial expansion that has not yet ended. And then there were the wars of the Protestant Reformation and bloody Catholic Counter Reformation when Christian again killed Christian using religion to support the new nationalisms of Europe.

Now we see the advent of modern religious warfare. It is religious nationalism that keeps Hamass, Hezbollah and Israel at each other over land that is still held holy by (at least) three of the world's major faiths. The *Ikhwan* of Wahhabi fundamentalists are behind Osama Bin Laden. In Iraq, Sunni still battles Shi'ite. In the United States, they argue whether or not to further link religion to nationalism by having prayer in schools. The American press has frequently followed the lead of the White House by using such phrases as: "Islamic terrorist," as though the terms are inseparable. All the while the Pledge of Allegiance already makes the U.S. into "One Nation, under God..."

F. Occupation of the Social Elite

War is a history of social status achieved through violence. Out of the social organization for carnage that is the early history of war, there emerged a profession of murder. The rise of social distinction based on social role (or job) is as old as humanity, or older. Because political dominance, the gathering of wealth, and religious justification are tied to war, "warrior" soon became a specific class in most societies. Later, warrior became a full-time occupation in most societies. In time, those who organized the raids, those who motivated the territorial conquests became elite in the societies where they lived. In most civilizations, the warrior class became the leaders. In many societies, religion and war went hand in hand. Even when he is not an active warrior/soldier the leader is often a former warrior. How many American presidents have *not* been in the military? Killing, or the willingness to do so, is part of what is considered leadership. But the warriors' leadership status in society is not simplistic, or clear-cut. A warrior is not leadership material simply because he is able and willing to kill. He (gender is significant) is of leadership status because he kills for abstract reasons. The warrior goes into the service of death to defend his country, for national pride and honor, for patriotism. The reward from the social system is status. Finally, none of these things is as tangible as the death a warrior or soldier leaves in his wake.

Historian Barbara Tuchman, in her book <u>A Distant Mirror</u>, recounts the life and times of Sir Enguerrand de Coucy VII, member of the 14th Century Second Estate – the warrior class of France – a professional killer. Tuchman notes the central contradictions of the warrior class. They were supposed to adhere to the codes of Arthurian chivalry mandating piety, service, defense of the weak, and humility – to name a few. However, it was the warrior class that was the threat. It was their struggles for power and greater wealth that caused people to need protection. Proud, egotistical, and bellicose, the warrior class produced war but no food. To train, feed, clothe, and equip a Knight like de Coucy required the dedicated labor of a score of serfs whose lives the warrior controlled. Each warrior knight took years of rigorous training to produce. All the while, the warrior-to-be was fed the best meats, drank good wine, and was liveried in the best – all without his labor. The social investment in the knighthood and their men-at-arms reallocated vast resources into warrior class and away from the poorer class. This relationship proportionally would continue to follow war. Labor and resources would be channeled out of society and into war. Society supported the warrior class that preyed upon it.

Sometimes the warrior reaches highest status. And, be mindful that the warrior elite can and have found ways to totally dominate societies. Male dominance means they do still. This total warrior dominance in a society is not always achieved through force. Most often the military establishment that the warrior class represents becomes fundamental to culture. People surrender power to the warrior because they believe killing to be an absolute necessity under certain circumstances, like "self-defense" mentioned above. Your nation has been plundered by outsiders. Raids have rendered the integrity of the borders of the land to be in doubt. Property has been carried off or destroyed. The economy is in shambles, and there have been atrocities. Security and honor are threatened by the outsiders. Since war is the only answer, then the warrior must lead the people. These are the most plausible and accepted reasons to turn control of society over to the reddened hands of the warrior elite. In some societies, such as the feudal Japanese, or the Europeans of the Middle Ages, the warrior elite refused to hand the power of government back to the people.

Tournament, joust, holmgang, samurai, and chivalry have the same root. Knights of chivalry were charming killers. Edward, the Black Prince at Limoges slaughtered over 3000 non-combatants. They were a parasitic class. They fed off of all below them in the social structure, even as they, themselves were bled by those few above them. Knights, retainers, and samurai ruled by force of tradition, and by a tradition of force (The Columbia Encyclopedia, Sixth Edition. 2001).

Only a few in a society can become warrior elite. It takes dedication and wealth to become a full-time killer. Not every man is able to murder for a living. The concentration of resources in a society that allows for an elite class of men dedicated to war to exist is unique. Weapons cost money. Training as a warrior requires free time not devoted to growing food. This, in turn, requires that someone else grow the food for the full-time killer class. There is an infrastructure of war that supports the warrior – or soldier. It is a war system. Society is organized around the elite, and war was (is) key to keeping a social system focused on the goals of the elite. Concentrating wealth and political power in as few hands as possible was and is a prime goal.

War functions well for the social elite, but what about the bulk of the human population? Except for plunder, and a vague (false) sense of security, the warrior produces nothing except corpses. Thus the elite occupation of war is at best symbiotic, and is usually parasitic. With this understanding can come a genuine look at alternatives to war. But, there is as yet no way to dislodge the tick of militarism from the body of society. Through association with the elite of society, war has become an extremely entrenched and powerful set of behaviors and institutions. To seriously engage in social changes that omit war requires the separation of the elite political and economic power groups from their reliance on and commitment to war as a way of maintaining dominance. It would be a fundamental change in the way social power is constructed. This change is difficult if not impossible to entertain for the elite, but it is perhaps more difficult and impossible for the poorer classes that make up the bulk of society.

Warrior elite classes often became objects of fear and resentment by the rest of society. For an example, this time, lets examine Shakespeare's Henry V – Branaugh version. Opening scene: Archbishop of Canterbury is concerned over church power. He urges and legitimizes the claim of England on France. War over land, wealth, and power is given orthodox religious sanction. The famous "Once more unto the breach" appeal to savagery "as a tiger," and to "manhood." Dishonor not your mothers and fathers, he continues, invoking social pride, and national patriotism. "Cry God for Harry, for England, and for Saint George!" After the melee, King Harry threatens the residents with rape and murder, if they do not yield. Later, around the campfire the troubled night before the decisive Battle of Agincourt, King Harry in disguise converses with his soldiers on duty. Finally, after the men at arms chew on duty and death, they agree that "we know enough if the King's cause be right." Then on the day of battle, there is the "upon Saint Crispin's Day" speech, King Harry urges his outnumbered men – common and elite – with the stirring announcement that his company will share the "greater share of honor..." personal fame, and glory. Llewellyn's fanatical grip on the "rules of war," and "laws of arms" leaves him confounded again and again as such rules are violated.

In the end, all of King Harry's poor friends from early life are dead or laid low. But, to Henry V it is "a royal fellowship of death" that attracts his attention. The accounting of the dead after the English victory at Agincourt was of those of "note," – of the nobility – and not of those other thousands mired in mud and their own blood.

The warrior occupation in most societies became hereditary. The wealth accumulated in support of war and warriors also became hereditary. Status, wealth and occupation blended. Wealth and power tended to be handed down father to son even in non-European systems that did not feature primogeniture as a rule. Male dominance is enough. In fact, male dominance in a social system is enhanced and refined in a war system. Leadership was the result. But a new kind of leadership, one consumed with the exercise of power and the wielding of weapons. From father to son passed wealth, title, and occupation. If the right to rule was challenged from within or from outside the land, then force was the only answer. What was to be expected from a warrior?

G. Honor

Honor is socially defined as what you do. Honor is behavior. Honor is social behavior. Honor is exemplary as a matter of its sheer existence. How, then, can war be honorable? Look back in history to what is still current. War is "honorable" if it is a matter of… "Self-defense"…for instance. Once, conflict brought potential survival. Then social status and influence were the capital of violence. To win in battle meant prestige and honor. Mayhem and murder became the influential stock and trade of the elite. At a certain point, only the elite could financially afford to devote their full time to war and it became the foundation not only of their prestige, but also of their continued wealth. And, as time went, money became more important than human life. Those with both life and wealth found decreasing need to risk both on the field of war. Business and politics were safer, surer methods of concentrating power and wealth. Having become elite through war, now new tools could be wielded, and people could become weapons. The soldier was born. Those who had been a warrior elite class became aristocrats in control of standing armies composed of poorer people called soldiers. How does an elite class motivate the poorer classes – those who suffer their wealth – to fight and die to maintain their status? The poorer classes are motivated through honor.

As soon as civilized states existed, the ideal of collective pride called honor became a political tool to be used in service of war. Honor and its identity symbols were examples that the social organization –

the state or the nation – had become more important than any individual human life. Unless, of course, we count religious and political leaders who are said to embody national honor. In that case, if the President, or Pope is threatened and thus the honor of the nation is at stake, millions may be sacrificed to that honor. As stated earlier, honor, status, social power, ethnic nationalism, and patriotism are all sides of the same sphere. Personal pride and national honor are perhaps the most irrational reasons for violence. As children, we are taught that words cannot hurt us, but as adults we are armed by the state to protect the honor of the nation to the point of the legal murder called war.

A cult of honor emanated from the leadership and their symbols. The level of identification with the cult of honor was in direct proportion to a person's ability to associate personal fortunes with those of the nation-state. This is why nationalistic enthusiasm during peacetime is not evenly spread throughout a society, and also why war and honor are closely tied. Those with property, wealth, and power are always more prone to the cult of honor. They have a tangible vested interest in protecting a system (nation or state) that insures their power and privilege. Honor in the form of nationalism became a tool of the social elite. If the people of a nation – those with varying to no fortune – can be made to project themselves into the position of the elite through the vehicle of honor, then the patriotic poor become the military fodder of war.

This initiation into the cult of honor that is nationalism is surprisingly easy to accomplish. The poor who always shoulder the burden of death in war must simply be convinced of a threat. Since such an extreme personal threat is quite rare in the lives of most, the psychology of peril can substitute. Through the symbolism of national honor – the flag, the border, the anthem, the holy icon – a leader can invoke war. Self-defense and national defense become interchangeable through the prism and mirrors of honor. The greatest and most honorable death is that suffered in defense of national honor. No greater martyrs exist (politically) than the patriotic dead. The cult of honor is perpetuated in the eternal flame flickering over the hero's grave of the Unknown Soldier. The second most nationally honored are those who kill – and win – for the country. Do not expect to be so honored if you fail. Vietnam veterans, who became expert killers, failed to receive the same national honors as other death-dealers because they failed to win. What was to be won? Not honor, the Vietnamese posed no real threat to the United States. However, corporations, political careers, and power bases were rocked. Men were sent to kill in service of elite seats of power. These men were sent with the symbols of the cult of national honor as their icons. No draftee or volunteer went to protect power and privilege of the few who maintained the war, yet that is what they did. That is the power of honor in war. Honor and nationalism are the tools that distance those with property, wealth and privilege from the actual killing.

H. Class and war

Class is the stratified level of economic opportunity and status within a culture or society. Class differences – differences in opportunity, in access, and in social status – may be based on racism, ethnicity, gender, education, age, disability or a host of other recognized group classifications. Since Marx, class struggle has been interpreted through social organization to mean armed struggle. Karl Marx did not specifically state that class struggle needed to mean actual warfare in the military sense, however, the Leninist expression has clearly given the industrial and post industrial world an example of organized violence in the service of class leveling. Since then class had been the banner in the forefront of many a "hot" conflict during the "Cold War." This is not untrue of the so-called post Cold War world. What is often not properly discussed is that maintaining class power, privilege, and distinction has been the violent militant banner in front of the capitalist opposition to class struggle. Power and concentrated wealth ever seeks to preserve itself. Those with money and those with power work through the system to continue their positions of social control. Political economy has become the science of constructing society to serve the interests of the few over the objections of the many. Social systems protect class advantages by making war – warfare to protect a standard of living, or "way of life." This may be war on "foreign" societies, but can also be war on "domestic" classes. Usually this means a (sometimes armed) conflict between the haves and the have-nots in a society. The "have-nots" lack human rights and economic justice. What the "haves" have is social and economic power. Social and economic power means the ability to influence the system to react to protect class advantage, and to control, retard, or prevent class mobility. Institutions in the system, under the influences of the elite, react to keep the have-nots from having. This is the inevitable result of class. We may call these institutions the legislative and judicial systems. Sometimes we call it the criminal justice system. Law and social order equals class. The elite class also has at its disposal an armed and trained domestic paramilitary force whose aim is to maintain the wealth and power of the elite. We call this military force the police.

Since the beginnings of civilization (which means since the beginning of war), humanity has relied on two things for success in war. Those two things have been manpower and weapons. Whichever side could put the most men, and best-armed and trained men in the field would usually win any conflict. There are clear economic relationships between war and winning. No more important and insidious economic relationship exists than the one between weapons and men in war. The amount of money it took (and takes) to arm, train, equip, maintain, and deploy a professional fighting force became a primary burden to most societies. This military burden usually, of course, prevented the redistribution of wealth for the general benefit of all. And as a general consequence people also suffered reduction or denial of human rights. Since so many of the resources in civilized social systems were (and are) allocated to war, the profession of killing in service of that system gained in status.

Warrior became a class in society from which many political leaders emerged. In the history of practically all civilizations, there have been times when the military formed the only political leadership. In some, citizenship itself was purchased through military service. You would only have full citizenship in the ancient Greek "democracies" if you served as a warrior in defense of the city-state. Women, craftspeople, farmers, traders, slaves, etc. had no genuine political rights at all. The thing (aside from gender) that limited access to the exclusive club of the political killer was money. The economic resources in time and materials that had to be reserved for the perfection of the many methods of death and destruction were (and are) considerable. And, of course, the political and economic power brought by war tended to bring more of the same to the warrior class. A military elite existed in virtually all societies. Virtually all of them exercised considerable money and political power to keep the warrior class distinct and exclusive. It was a men's club that few could join. Relatively low technology societies like the Cheyenne of the American Great Plains had associations like the Dog Soldiers, whose status came from their pledge to die in defense of the tribe. In social systems more invested in technology, such as Iron Age Greece, the class separation of the warrior was far more evident.

Political control over a society by military elite is usually called feudalism. This system of military aristocracy required near constant conflict. Always the rationalizations for war were to secure borders, or prevent the aggression of a neighbor, or to preserve a "balance of power." In other words, the warrior could always find a reason to fight.

Firearms changed war. Now, everyone could play. Starting with the longbow, in Europe and the crossbow in most of Asia, average members of society could now take the burden of killing (and dying) out of the hands of the elite. A new class was born – the common soldier. Leaders and warrior types had almost always conscripted elements of the general population into their forces. Imperial Rome and China had their professional military, and the

Ottomans raised slaves to be professional fighting forces, but for most of history to be a "common" soldier was a part-time occupation. Cheap easy to use projectile weapons changed that. The political economy of the warrior elite class allowed them to invest in both the development of the institution of soldier/conscript and in the technology to make this new class profitable and insular. Effective yet inexpensive to manufacture weapons in the hands of the poorer and more numerous classes meant that war could exponentially expand in scope. The death toll would rise. Business and merchant classes would benefit economically from political support for development and production. Political leadership would benefit from democratized war because through it, they would become generally more distant from personal threat, but still receive maximum benefit from the success of war. The military leadership from which the political and economic elite classes emerge would gain in social status, economic opportunity, and political legitimacy in war. It was the start of what we now call a "military-industrial complex."

The above mentioned Kenneth Brannaugh film Henry V, interprets the William Shakespeare play about the battle of Agincourt in France. In it we see peasant class English and Welsh responsible for King Henry's victory sacrificed to the system in the course of the war. There is a difference between warrior class and soldier class. Soldiers are poorer. The yeoman archer of England of this period could tip the scales of battle by virtue of archery skills that were mandated by law to be developed year-round. Whenever and wherever this happened in history, armies grew in size. The traditional warrior elite could now become an officer's corps by dint of class. Now it was the amount of soldiers in the field that would offer the best chances for victory. Soldiers were (and are) more expendable than the elite. Soldier's deaths are more frequent and less important than the deaths of warrior elite. Soldiers must be fed, clothed, and trained at the expense of the state, and thus are bound to the service of the elite in charge of the state. Warriors retire to careers in government or business. Soldiers retire to farms and jobs.

By the time humanity invested in guns, the soldier was already a fixed part of the organization of society and war. Lower class energy mobilized for upper class purposes was what firearms brought to war. These new developments in the war system created the political conditions that institutionalized war in the form of what is called a "standing military." Instead of investing social capital into institutions of conflict resolution, we created things like the draft. Conscription – or coerced and compulsory military service – was an institution of the war system that directly deprived people of human rights. It and other such institutional "adjustments" further intensified class divisions in society. The poor conscript during the American Civil War was compelled to military service under legal penalty, while a man of wealth could buy himself out of service by purchasing a substitute. A man of means who wanted to fight, could ensure an officers commission by virtue of wealth and position. This would put him in a position – if he wished – to be out of the genocidal carnage of the front line fighting, yet still in prestigious enough proximity to reap the major social benefits of military service. This is not to disparage officers as a group (more than the average soldier already does), but to point out that it is the poorer, lower-ranked soldier who does the bulk of the fighting and dying. In this new landscape of firearms and the soldier, the social investment was not toward popular political policies of peace, but instead toward democratizing war.

Democracy meant that your equal place in the front lines of battle could be assured. Mass produced guns in the hands of masses of soldiers made modern war possible. Napoleonic war was the term for the type of mass killing that involved huge numbers of "citizen soldiers" with guns coming as close as possible and firing directly into the tightly grouped ranks of their adversaries. It meant horrific slaughter. It was this type of war that made the United States Civil War the most costly in terms of American lives of all other U.S. wars combined. Since the advent of "democratic war," the body count has gone into the millions. It became central to the system to convince individual men in society to set aside class differences and to sacrifice themselves for the benefit of aristocrats and elite. Political rhetoric and nationalistic harangue, usually bonded by fundamentalist religious dogma were (and are) the devices of the state in its effort to maintain power through drawing all classes into war.

An interesting and revealing irony of social organization and war is the contemporary condition of gun ownership in the United States. A citizen's ability to keep and bear arms in the support of a well regulated militia is a well known privilege granted in the Bill of Rights. This is indeed institutionalized militarism. The initial inference is that the right to keep arms is a check against the tyranny of government. And government abuse of rights is the historical context of the original document. However, there was a fear of the "tyranny of the masses" that made guns in the hands of citizens a threat to the newly formed central government. Episodes such as the Whiskey Rebellion or Dorr's Rebellion highlight the potential for conditions of instability and continuous revolution that men like James Madison feared. Out of the two-edged sword that private gun ownership was emerged a solution for government. Focus on Nationalism and expansion instead of internal political and social problems. Historians like James Beard built a new national identity to infuse otherwise disparate classes and ethnicities with a sense of common purpose if not opportunity. The early and persistent commitment to Westward expansion that the United States reaffirmed under Thomas Jefferson provided a convenient direction for those armed citizens to point the weapons of democracy. Citizens with guns became an informal army effective in enforcing expansionist policies and Native genocide under the prescription of Manifest Destiny. The more contemporary outgrowth has been organizations such as the National Rifle Association (NRA) which support both militarism and "conservative" – i.e. militarist – government. This cannot be mentioned without also noting the high incidence of gun-related violence in all of U.S. history today included.

I. Nationalist Activity/Patriotic Activity

"War evolved with the state...war made the state and the state makes war.

–John Keegan

Nationality is a political description of place of birth or naturalization. This is the most modern expression of the state. Although frequently based on geography, it is a wholly artificial social construction of identity. Consider the many ethnically, economically, and culturally diverse nations. The only unifying feature is often a national concept. The social power of this national concept is nationalism. Diverse groups brought together under a single set of images, and ideas. Often this mostly fictitious panoply of historic metaphors and icons is used solely to legitimize geographic dominance. Nationalism is a set of concepts that rationalizes war in protection of the control of a set of natural resources. Since the era of colonialism, those resources have not had to be local. Nationalism can be exported through war. European colonialism and the Manifest Destiny of the United States are two of the most useful examples of nationalism being exported. Both rely on the use of force or the threat of force to be effective. Nationalism is a social system that relies on war. A nation must defend its borders. A nation must expand its borders. The economic connection between a nation and all available resources is crucial to the maintenance of the society. By the maintenance of society, I mean the continuation of a social structure dominated by the elite of the nation.

Patriotism is the rhetoric of inclusion in a nationalist system. Patriotic paraphernalia like monuments, flags, anthems, slogans and such are tools of nationalist inclusion. In many ways they are no different than ethnic slurs or religious fanaticism. To form inclusion on a nationalistic level means that all others must be excluded. The bulk of the population can be rallied to the service of the nation –

which means the interests of the nation's elite – by using jingoistic and patriotic slogans and such. The choice for war becomes more than a simple one, it is simplistic. In nationalistic terms: "we are defending our country and our way of life." Kind of rings a bell, does it not?

Us versus them. You are with us, or you are against us. Alongside god, country is the most popular reason for mass destruction. Country – nationalism – allows honor to blanket groups with differing interests into one single simplistic mass. Creating a nation means war. Defining the nation-state has almost always meant war. And international war can be bigger. Nationalism as an institution equals military conscription – mostly, of course, from among the poorer and working class of the society. More people, and more bodies. The nation-state is the level of social organization and human civilization in which we see warfare become the business of bureaucracy. Fully institutionalized war. It is a cultural evolution in political economy. War gone both corporate, and government. It is at this stage (if that term can be granted) that patriotism became a construct of the state. It was the voice of a war system aimed at the goals of manipulating existing cultural features. Nationalism is a militant idea that was always to the service of concentrated wealth and elite groups in a society. It is worth repeating that by now people in these elite groups rarely (if ever) actually fight in the forefront of wars that they promote and perpetuate, yet those in elite groups, nonetheless, are the primary beneficiaries of conflict. The elite are also the center of the promotion and expression of nationalism.

War had previously been the exclusive activity of the elite (section F, above). Yet, through the growth of specialized labor and the increasing control of the productive capacities of a society by wealthy elite groups, the class of concentrated wealth had transformed into political ruling classes. These elite economic groups used (use) their social control as political control. The elite no longer needed to personally risk themselves for ever-increasing power and wealth. They could now rely on nationalism. They could rely on the cultural concepts of uniqueness that are a part of any human society and exploit the human tendency toward xenophobia to recruit the poorer, more powerless to fight and die for them. Jingoism replaced the dialog of peace. The country must ever be prepared for defense against those who would threaten "our way of life." This, of course, means that an ever-increasing amount of time, energy, and money be put toward the planned aggression that military spending is.

This combination of feelings of a shared culture and fear of the "other" (however the other is identified), is what we call patriotic nationalism. Nationalism is one of the most obscene aspects of human civilization. It serves no one but the elite. Nationalist patriotism is one of the most artificial of concepts. There are no national boundaries if the Earth is viewed from above. Boundaries on maps are created by politicians and power-brokers in order to protect their own wealth and power. In the bulk of recorded history, humankind would be better served by a sense of unity based on shared elements of human need instead of the sense of separateness that is nationalism. The history of any nation-state shows this, if we who look at history do so without the foggy lens of nationalism. Each "national history" is the story of the artificial inclusion, or equally artificial exclusion of groups of people. Who can be part of the "National" experience and identity is often based on who will accept the political leadership of the elite economic group, or who can be useful to the elite in either an economic or political sense. This is especially true of the national history of industrial and post-industrial nations, such as the United States. If you are not infected with the "America, love it, or leave it" virus, then even a cursory glance at American history shows the selective inclusion, or exclusion of varying ethnic and cultural groups based on this model of political economic utility. This is not unnatural. It is the predictable result of a social system that is dependent on war.

Provocative and patriotic "with us or against us," and "in order to preserve civilization and our freedoms" statements take the place of the dialog of peace. And, as ever, ethnic and racial lines have been drawn. Nationalism feeds such division and inflames hatred and violence.

J. Imperial Expansion and Colonialism

"...The methods by which this continent has been stolen have been contemptible and dishonest beyond expression. Lying treaties, rivers of rum, murder, assassination, mutilation, rape, and torture have marked the progress of Englishman, German, Frenchman, and Belgian on the Dark Continent. The only way in which the world has been able to endure the horrible tale is by deliberately stopping its ears and changing the subject of conversation while the deviltry went on...Whence comes this new wealth and on what does its accumulation depend? It comes primarily from the darker nations of the world -- Asia and Africa, South and Central America, the West Indies and the islands of the South Seas..."

-W.E.B DuBois

Empires and imperialist expansion occurs when the needs of a nation's elite can no longer be met by the traditional exploitation of local resources. Land and people claimed politically and militarily by that nation are not as profitable as they once were. The resources, markets and labor forces of the nation no longer generate the spiraling increases in wealth the elite have come to expect. Resources must be sought outside of the territorial boundaries enforced by the nation. This is kind of like Territorial Skirmish (D above) on steroids. The result is an empire made of colonized peoples. *(Colonies may be an internal feature of a nation, or they may be external).* There is a point in the cultural evolution of any capital intensive nation-state when the needs of the social elite to increase prestige, power, and wealth become so pervasive that they come into conflict with the remainder of the social system. The poor are getting poorer, the rich getting richer, the economic markets are saturated, labor costs can be forced no lower. Also, national and/or geographic barriers inhibit the continuing nationalist expansion that characterized the earlier evolution of the state. Countries run into the (artificial) borders of other potentially equally destructive nations. Often this will lead directly to war, if one or both nations are convinced of superiority. The losing nation becomes a client of the winner. This occurred in many places in history. Early Imperial China, Imperial Rome, the various

Mesopotamian empires, the Mongols, the Azteca Mexica, for instance, all resorted to war when faced by such challenges.

Governments of old had never been structured around the validation of general social equality and human rights. However, the rise of the (military) Empire parallels an even more dramatic systematic suppression of human rights. An excellent illustration is Imperial Rome. Rome was built through bloody militant expansion. In the earlier republican period, the Romans were ruthlessly successful in gaining control of the Italian peninsula through aggressing against their neighbors. Rome continued to invest in institutional militancy by offering mutually beneficial political partnerships with those they had defeated. These republican partnerships guaranteed that Roman military support would be cumulative. The defeated would be offered a package of political and civil rights in exchange for military support and non-interference in Roman policy. Eventually those who were the Italian foes of Rome during the republican period would be able to gain full Roman citizenship – if they were men, and if they served seasonal military service.

As a consequence of success against the Carthaginians in the Punic Wars for economic control of the Western Mediterranean, Roman political economy changed. The Roman Republic began to expand far beyond the Italian peninsula. The act of military conquest required longer stints of military service. Maintaining control of far-flung provinces also demanded larger numbers of troops who were military specialists and not the seasonal soldier/farmers of the earlier wars of Italian expansion. Also, the social economics of Roman military conquest were such that the gap between rich and poor grew steadily. Eventually, the small landholdings of poor individual soldier/farmers ended up in the hands of an economic elite class that relied on enslaved workers to generate profits from vast plantations. All of these trends caused the further cultural evolution of military professionalism. Through the military reforms of leaders such as Gaius Marius, an Imperial War machine was born. Roman soldier became a career. The poor flooded the military in search of wealth gained as plunder. Local mercenaries or auxiliaries were contracted. Armies became corporate political units for which killing was business. No longer would the conquered be offered any concessions as in the Republican period. All the wealth of the defeated peoples became tribute for the Romans. Legions swore loyalty not to Rome, but to commanders such as Julius Caesar, who paid themselves and their soldiers from the lands and plunder of war. Victory in war equaled profit. Success in war was then translated into political position for ambitious professional soldier/politicians. The Roman Empire was born. It was an empire supported by the most successful professional killing machine that Europe had known – the Imperial Legions (wikipedia.org).

With the coming of the professional standing army grew a kind of acquisitive military expansion that we now call Old World colonialism, after its place of origin. Europe at the end of the Middle Ages was in this sort of level of cultural evolution. European nations began looking outward, first at the other nations of Europe, then at the world. New nations warred on each other with little visible gain, except for the solidification of elite ruling class families, the growth of military professionalism, and the entrenchment of capitalist economics. Soon, the political economy of the Catholic Church – the central trans-national religious/political bureaucracy of the times – required a social reorganization that first meant the Crusades, then later, the so-called "Age of Discovery" that was in reality another type of war. European colonial expansion was military. War was for the acquisition of territory, resources, labor and markets that would insure the national (now imperial) elite their positions of political and economic power. The Spanish called it "God, Gold, and Glory."

This earliest type of modern colonial imperialism required the expansion of the war system because the colonized territories would require a continuous oppressive military presence. A territory colonized by force in which the indigenous people frequently were denied human rights by the colonizers resulted in political unrest, uprisings and guerrilla war against the colonizers. The local population must be disarmed, except for those who can be recruited into military or paramilitary colonial police forces, or the colonial administrative bureaucracy. The benefits of labor of the colonized were reserved for the foreign colonizers, and to a lesser degree to their indigenous supporters. These indigenous supporters of the foreign colonial elite became a new class. This further increased social tensions and potential violence. Of course, motivated by personal gain and class enmity, soldiers made especially effective and excessively brutal police.

Colonialism meant the suppression – by force or threat of force – of human rights. Conversely, the suppression and denial of human rights guaranteed the formation of equally militant anti-colonialist movements among indigenous populations. This would often mean guerrilla war – the war of the weak against the strong.

One result of Old World colonialism was the American colonies that eventually became the United States. Even while still a colony of England, the future U.S., in turn, would develop its own colonies. These internal colonies came first from among the indigenous American Indian populations, but were quickly followed by imported colonies of African Slaves. These two groups set the foundation for what has been termed "internally colonized minorities." Institutional racism was born as an elder brother to the United States. Groups of people whose very humanity was in question by the Europeans, and whose human rights were out of the question could therefore be exploited for maximum profit. A series of Indian wars, the genocidal wars of transatlantic slave trade, and the American Civil War were results, not to mention ongoing social strife caused by the concentration of poverty in Indian and Black groups. This is a social strife that inevitably grew from the systematic denial of human rights that is racism.

In a little over a century since achieving independence from being a colony, the United States had formed its own nationalistic rhetoric. Writers like Alfred Thayer Mahan strategized how the U.S. was to dominate the globe. Imperial expansionists like Albert Beveridge and Theodore Roosevelt eagerly endorsed the "acquisition" of U.S. colonies abroad. The United States forced a policy of expansion on the grounds that the U.S. was liberating primitive peoples (Hawaiians, Filipinos, Cubans, etc.) from tyranny. American politicians and businessmen argued that war would protect the American way of life by sharing the blessings of liberty with those less fortunate than ourselves – one nation under god. The Spanish colonial empire was corrupt, restricting human rights, and even pursuing genocidal policies with its colonized peoples. The United States had an obligation – a Manifest Destiny, it had been called – to shoulder the "white man's burden," and to liberate "our little brown brothers" from foreign domination. Soon after the U.S. defeated this evil enemy, in the wake of the "liberation," Filipino rights of self-determination were denied by the U.S. and the Philippines became a colony in all but name. Within months, native Hawaiians saw the bulk of their remaining rights taken as genocidal economic policies denied them opportunity by virtue of their race. Sugar and pineapple barons from the U.S. had made Hawaii into a plantation for corporate profit. In Cuba, the United States expressed nationalism by amending the Cuban constitution, by installing a permanent military presence, and by encouraging widespread corruption of the Cuban economy by U.S. business interests.

Again the pay off of war is greater power and privilege for a few, at the expense of many, and the further investment in the war system. This new colonialism of the U.S. would become the imperialistic way of the future. Neo colonialism dominated the remainder of the twentieth-century. Bringing in sources of cheap labor and allowing foreign resources and markets to be exploited at relatively low cost made perfect sense. Now, more than ever, the military would be needed to protect U.S. interests abroad. In the wake of the Spanish American War, the Philippine Insurrection, and the Moro Wars, the U.S. military expanded to reflect its importance in the new imperial politics of the time. And, as a result of

"Great White Fleet/Big Stick" diplomacy of Theodore Roosevelt, the American imperial war system became the custodian of human rights enforcing Third World economies everywhere in its influence. A toothsome wolf was now set to guard the hen-house.
From the Philadelphia Public Ledger, the American Anti-Imperialist League quoted this account:

> "Our men have been relentless; have
> killed to exterminate men, women,
> children, prisoners and captives,
> active insurgents and suspected people,
> from lads of ten up, an idea prevailing
> that the Filipino, as such, was little better
> than a dog.... Our soldiers have pumped
> salt water into men to "make them talk,"
> have taken prisoners people who held up
> their hands and peacefully surrendered,
> and an hour later, without an atom of
> evidence to show that they were
> even insurrectos, stood them on a
> bridge and shot them down one by one,
> to drop into the water below and float down,
> as examples to those who found their
> bullet-loaded corpses. It is not civilized
> warfare; but we are not dealing with a
> civilized people. The only thing they know
> and fear is force, violence, and brutality,
> and we give it to them."

At the beginning of the twentieth century, the U.S. government presented the world with [neo-colonial imperialism, manifest destiny). The Corollary to the Monroe Doctrine had legitimized U.S. military intervention ("projection of force," in the jargon) anywhere in the North American continent. In the next two decades, The United States "intervened" in nearly every Central American country. Political stability, human rights, and the sense of economic justice have been problems there ever since. At the end of those decades was World War I, and then World War II, and after that, a Universal Declaration of Human Rights. Then there was World War III – a Cold War. At the start of the twenty-first century, the U.S. government (under G. W. Bush) has put the same rhetoric to the same purpose. U.S. projection of force is the hope of a few, and the fear of many. It is World War IV.

K. Race, Ethnic Nationalism & Ethnic Cleansing

Ethnicity refers to heritage or culture expressed over time. The history – the cultural evolution – of a group of people produces differences in populations that give rise to ethnicity. It may well be a social construct that is imposed either from within or from outside of the actual ethnic group. In other words, the ethnic label may be the convenience of a social power structure seeking easy exploitation of the labeled group. Biologically, there is only one race – human. All other categories of race are artificial social constructs of classification based on visual differences, cultural expressions, political necessity, and economic priority. What is commonly called race is often really racism. The central defining feature is social power. This is most often expressed through access to wealth and the distribution of civil and human rights.

Racism is when one group in possession of unearned power and privilege to do so labels another group, and disadvantages them socially based on the artificial classifications of race. Individuals become interchangeable objects representing the group. They are named. "They" becomes a category – often a slur or epithet – that means "the same." Each is given identical characteristics which define their place in the social system. It is the system that then does the dirty work. No individual in the power structure need take personal responsibility. "I was just following orders." In times of war, race almost always plays a major part. Heightened by war, racial sensitivity leads to genocide. This is the purposeful war of extermination based on race. A culture of race leads to genocide. Just add power, stir in some fear, and there you have it. It is no wonder that the history of the concept of race parallels the development of the social identity. The hierarchical classification of race and ethnicity in the modern world (Social Darwinism) is a by-product of the same European intellectual influences that generated militant colonialism in general, and the formative philosophies of the United States in particular. Race has regularly been used as a political reason for social conflict and war.

In the case of war, both inside and outside of a society, ethnic diversity becomes a powerful determiner of the direction and intensity of conflict. Either an ethnic group struggles for inclusion into the mainstream society by near-rabid forms of nationalistic patriotism, or the ethnic group becomes a scapegoat for the social system. In the former case, this may mean that the patriotic ethnic group becomes an enthusiastic part of the domestic machinery of war, or that they form the front line in the battlefield. And, of course, ethnic minorities figure high in the casualty lists and body-bags. In the latter case, the ethnic group may well be seen as dissident because of a pro-peace political stance, for instance. This would make the dissident minority the target of government and public attack. In such cases ethnic minorities face the loss of civil and human rights. The extreme expression of the loss of human rights is what we now call "ethnic cleansing." It is just a smooth political term for mass murder. Native Americans, African Americans, Turkish Armenians, Kampucheans Kurds, Tutsi (and Hutu), and European Jews are sadly only a few such groups to face this severe social assault prior to Bosnian "ethnic cleansing." World War One was partly sparked by an assassination carried out by Serbian ethnic nationalists.

The growth of nationalism in social systems is paralleled by an increasing emphasis placed on race and ethnicity. Remembering that they – race and ethnicity – are different, but are often used interchangeably in the political rhetoric of the state, what groups are "in" and what groups are "out" of the national concept of citizenship can mean life or death. But, it is more complex than that. Some ethnic groups are economically and socially marginalized by the ruling and elite power structure. They are not fully excluded from the national enterprise, but are also not fully included. They are what are called minorities, even though collectively all the diverse "minority "groups may even outnumber those in power. This is especially true if the definition of diversity is properly broadened beyond race and ethnicity to include gender, class, religion, etc. The price of greater inclusion into the national inner circle of social benefits, or the freedom from ethnic persecution by the nation is often military service. The career of

Colin Powell (among many others) is an example of military service granting greater access to the "American Dream" than other members of the ethnic minority called Black.

The United States did not invent ethnic nationalism, but it has been particular in its refinement. Race and class have gone hand in hand in the political economy of the U.S. since before it was a Nation. Ethnic groups designated as races have been (and are) legislatively maintained – kept by law – in discreet social classes. This has meant that these groups form a reliable pool of low cost labor, but it also means that these groups form an equally consistent pool of conscripts and "volunteers" for military service. It works like this. If the price for social mobility and opportunity rests on being viewed as the ultimate supporter of the Nation, then no greater public symbol of that support exists that the military uniform showing willingness to die, or kill for that system. Ethnic and immigrant groups are challenged to assimilate and acculturate by showing nationalist patriotism. It should be no wonder that so many members of ethnic groups display extreme examples of patriotism and military volunteerism.

During World War II Executive Order 9066 was issued by President Franklin D. Roosevelt at the request of the Governor of California. The Governor and future Supreme Court Chief Justice, Earl Warren demanded that Japanese American citizens be detained indefinitely. Out of racial fear, Japanese Americans were deprived of property and herded into wasteland internment camps. The camps were called relocation centers or internment camps instead of concentration camps because in the U.S. there was no forced labor or gas chambers. Over half of these

Japanese Americans were born American. Many did not speak Japanese, and none were ever found guilty of any treasonous activity. Nonetheless, they were summarily deprived of rights and due process by the government of the United States because of their race. Many of the Japanese Americans demanded to form their own military units to fight for their country – The U.S.A. They formed the 100th Infantry Battalion and the 442nd Regimental Combat Team, among other units, all from Nisei which is the Japanese word for second born. In other words, they were all born Americans. Many of them volunteered directly from the camps. They became among the most highly decorated soldiers of the history of the United States military. They paid for their martial decorations by having among the highest rate of casualties. Their sacrifices did not free their families, did not regain their lost possessions. It was not until 1988 that the government offered compensation for the formerly interned Japanese Americans.

Although much can be said of patriotism as a force for national unity, there is another domestic problem with race and war. Minority groups that might set aside divisive racial issues in recognition of shared class, and thus form a political front against their oppression become a de-facto threat to the establishment. It is to the advantage then, of the establishment to continue to promote class conflict between ethnic groups and solidarity within ethnic groups. This is what race does when it becomes an institutionally conditioned phenomenon. If the system identifies groups by race and offers differing treatment and opportunities to race groups, then it sets up conditions for resentment of one group for another, and diffuses class awareness. The existing formal social institutions inhibit economic justice and human rights movements that are often characterized as "unpatriotic," or as threats to "national security." The class advantage of the elite is maintained by playing the "race card." Institutionalized racism makes its victims desperate and dangerous. Either through engaging in illegal activity, or by engaging in political struggle against the system, such groups become reactionary targets of the system. A racial minority is "damned if the do, and damned if they don't" conform to institutionalized racism. Ethnic nationalism by minorities becomes by definition a threat to "national security." Interracial and multi-ethnic solidarity movements are likewise a threat to the status quo of entrenched power. The increasing militarization of urban police forces is a sure sign of the establishments' recognition of such threats. War becomes an internal possibility or fact – urban warfare.

There is a darker side of ethnicity and nationalism – war on those who differ. Those who cannot, or do not conform are regularly considered the "other" and often the enemy. In peace or war, members of ethnic populations frequently find themselves in social positions of relative desperation. Ethnic minorities in most nations are not only numerical minorities; they are minorities in political and economic senses, too. Poor people find themselves in jail more frequently than the middle or advantaged classes. Some are politically identified minorities such as members of oppositional parties of those that are in prisons. In most nations, prisoners automatically lose all or part of their civilly protected rights. The imprisoned also often are victims of human rights violations – especially in war. I am reminded of eyewitness revelations of the Soviet treatment of political prisoners during World War II. Soviet leader Josef Stalin used what he called "penal companies" of unarmed prisoners to both empty jails and to win battles. Prisoners were removed from jail and marched to the frontlines of conflict against Nazi troops. The weaponless prisoners were then marched by Soviet troops at gunpoint into the machine guns and artillery of the German forces while Soviet commanders watched to mark the strengths and firing capacities of the Nazi guns. As the unarmed prisoners were mowed down by Nazis, Stalin's Soviet army would attack.

Ethnic groups not supportive of the social power structure are even more expendable than those who conform and end up in front line units and military cemeteries. Such non-supportive ethnic groups are always the targets of the system. This may mean investigation, incarceration, impoverishment (economic genocide), or ethnic cleansing. Ethnic cleansing is a relatively new term for a very old method of dealing with groups that are non-supportive, or challenging to the status quo of the social system. The transfer of wealth out of "their" hands and into the hands of the elite is always an underlying feature of ethnic cleansing. The very old method is genocide – the purposeful policy of a government to exterminate a race – woman, child, and man. American Indians are victims of this type of genocide. Former minister and volunteer Colonel John M. Chivington's order to kill all Cheyenne over the age of twelve just prior to the 1864 Sand Creek Massacre would be initially supported by his superiors. Indian men, women, and children were massacred under a flag of truce. Their bodies were sexually mutilated, with parts displayed as trophies. When the Cheyenne, Arapaho, and Sioux Indians retaliated, William Tecumseh Sherman, the general in charge of the Indian campaigns, wrote: "We must act with vindictive earnestness against the Sioux, exterminating every man, woman, and child."

When a public scapegoat is required to reinforce the power structure, ethnic groups that reside within a nation will often be targeted as the reason for social strife. The ethnic group (and the politics they represent) must be purged. Those in power to actually make a social change create the internal enemy to be cleansed, thus ensuring that the rest of the public view the problem not as one of excessive irresponsible concentration of wealth and power, but as a problem created by the presence of the ethnic "other." A society will then war on itself. Possibilities of peaceful political solutions fade behind the self-serving rhetoric of power blocks primarily interested in diffusing multi-ethnic social justice movements. Their goal is to preserve the human rights of a few over those of many. Social justice becomes a matter of ethnicity. If you are the "right kind" of people, then you can expect justice. The most obvious ethnic cleansing of the twentieth-century was that orchestrated by the Nazi Party against the Gypsies and Jews of Europe. But, even then, Hitler is said to have remarked that no one would care about the Jews, because after all, "who remembers the Armenians?" Aside from Kampuchea, or Bosnia and Serbia, or Rwanda, and all the other ethnic cleansing, it is now the descendant of the European Jew who has the genocidal weapon aimed at the head of the Palestinian.

L. Civil War & Revolution

Civil war entails elements of a social system that is at war with its own people. When the culture, politics, and economics of a large enough social group coalesce in opposition to the ruling power, social justice movements often emerge as counter social systems aimed at change. If these movements are not diffused, or are denied, conflict may result. Because two systems are involved, that conflict usually becomes organized into war. Civil war and revolution only differ in the distance from the power structure and in the rhetoric of politicians. Also, because of the internecine nature of both civil war and revolution, the partisan guerrilla raid produces even more atrocity.

In the American Civil War, both social systems were sizable and arguably viable legitimate structures representing quite similar political and cultural ancestry. The necessity of re-uniting the national unit for the on-going prosperity of the ruling elite meant that the term Civil War was acceptable for a conflict that killed more Americans than all other American wars combined. The war ended Black slavery. But, from the guerrilla activity during the war, postwar organizations such as the Ku Klux Klan emerged. These post war guerrillas survived because despite the moral high ground assumed by the winning side (fairly late in the conflict), the war was about competing economic systems and differing visions of a national future held by the power structures represented by those systems. The system of enslavement of African Americans ended, but it would be another century before American Blacks would win

222

full civil rights. Because of links between ethnicity and nationalism, African Americans still face a host of social and institutional problems in the U.S.

The American Civil War was again a war fought by the poorer members of society, for the advantage of the elite. The moral question of human bondage was a feature of this struggle, not the central most issue.

It is arguable that the war is "civil" if the original power structure prevails, but that it is "revolutionary" if new elite ascends to control. In that sense the American war was indeed "Civil." The French revolution actually changed the system of government as did the American Revolution, although it can easily be argued that those with wealth and power remained (for the most part) wealthy and powerful. The communist revolution in Russia and the communist revolution in China were alike in changing the governing elite of those nations. Even so, the nature of political relationships often remained traditional in both countries. Communist commissars had their dachas on the Black sea just as the Imperial Romanovs had. Mao Zedong exploited the traditional semi-divine status of ancient Chinese rulers in his reign. Neither state, despite revolutionary changes, was communist in much more than name. Both states, regardless of their popular partisan guerrilla origins, continued to support traditional war machines and colonial relationships throughout the Cold war.

Colonial revolution has greater distance politically, economically, and culturally from the central system of power. In either case, war erupts because people in power and in possession of concentrated wealth fail to successfully resort to political process to resolve the inevitable social differences caused by concentrated wealth and power. Indeed, they often cannot resort to peaceful political resolutions, because their prosperity is built on exploitation and manipulation of differences, and on war.

M. International World War

When Nations gang up on nations, we term it World War. It really means that a few nations that have bloodily carved out colonial or neo-colonial territories bully those territories into joining the colonizers into war over the prosperity of a relatively small political and economic elite in the colonizing nations. It is exploitation on top of exploitation. What it became was war for the sake of narrowing the options of the poor majority and in favor of further concentrating wealth and political power in the hands of even fewer. World war allowed the whole of national industrial production to be put into the war effort. It meant the unapologetic suspension of civil liberties and human rights in the name of national security and military victory. Corporations can avoid or set aside labor laws with the support of a government that has been granted extreme centralized authority in the name of victory in war.

It was not the New Deal that got the United States out of the Great Depression. It was the industrial productivity of the war. Of course, the investment by government in the pre-existing war system far outweighed the investment in New Deal reforms. And, there was far less resistance to patriotic war-time economic restructuring than there had been for pre-war programs designed to end the depression. Under the combined influences of the draft and wartime hiring, unemployment plummeted. By the time the United States was engaged in WWII, it would take between 16 and 20 civilians to keep each soldier in the field. Also under the influences of wartime patriotic nationalism, most citizens of the United States willingly set aside civil liberties, among them the democratic right to know and approve of government actions. Those who were dissidents, or whose organizations could form the basis of anti-war activities faced investigation, loss of jobs, and jail for their "un-American activities." The infamous raids of Attorney General A. Mitchell Palmer during WWI, for instance. Nationalism, jingoism, and xenophobia were at an all-time high as well. The internment of Japanese Americans during WWII and the transformation of sauerkraut into "liberty cabbage" are two examples that quickly come to mind (USAFN).

In World War One and World War two, the killing became industrial with efficiency and bottom-line accountant precision that would have made Frederick W. Taylor proud. All forms of human technology and inventiveness were thrown into the effort to efficiently kill more human beings. In World War One, this meant that poison gasses, machine guns, tanks, submarines and airplanes were developed and unashamedly used against combatants. Then there was the fire bombing in the Second World War. The culmination of industrial killing efficiency was, perhaps, the Manhattan Project and the movement into an age of nuclear warfare. Now, tens of thousands could be (and were) incinerated at once, with hundreds of thousands burned and poisoned by radiation. Let us not forget that Hiroshima, and Nagasaki were civilian cities, not military establishments. They were targeted specifically because they were civilian towns. When the world is at war, everyone is a target.

That this new way of war – global conflict – has meant huge numbers of dead among civilian non-combative (innocent) people has been not just expected, but welcomed. That's right, the six million Jews of WWII, and the additional five million plus communists, Gypsies, Poles, disabled, gay and lesbians, were expected to die by Hitler. We all see this as one of the reasons for war. At the time, however, most people did not know that the holocaust was in motion. There is considerable evidence that leaders knew something of the events at places like Dachau or Buchenwald. However, policy concerns dictated that nothing be done. The dead of Dresden, Tokyo, Pearl Harbor, Hiroshima, Nagasaki, Nanking, and Stalingrad – and, countless dead in other cities that all represent the *civilian dead* – became not just possible, but acceptable and *even desirable* in terms of the global political strategy of the elite planners of policy.

By the end of this period two important things were also on the table. At the end of WWI, President Woodrow Wilson proposed a sweeping re-organization of world society called the Fourteen Points. In order to prevent another World War, Wilson sought to reduce militarism and the sources of militarism by general disarmament, by the promotion of self-determination and human rights, and by the formation of an international political body that (he presumed) could be a forum for peaceful conflict resolution. His allies gutted the Fourteen Points with the Treaty of Versailles, and The Congress of the United States refused to endorse or ratify anything that was counter to national sovereignty. The result was, of course, the international retention of the apparatus of war. The product was World War Two. At least 60 million died in this war, with about half of them civilian dead. The overall waste of human life as an indirect result of war may exceed three times that amount – over 180 million dead.

In the face of the obscene death toll of World War II, the newly formed United Nations produced a Universal Declaration of Human Rights in an attempt to reduce the frequency and intensity of war by removing some of the justifications for conflict. By identifying universal rights with all of humanity – irrespective of creed – the U.N. took a major step toward a legal foundation for world peace based on clearly enumerated shared issues. But, armed to the teeth in the wake of World War, the war systems of the victorious nations were far too strong to submit to peace and the universal rights of humanity.

N. Cold War & War by Proxy

At the end of World War Two, there emerged two differing political and economic strategies for global order. Their leadership and respective nationalist identities precluded cooperation. But, their nuclear and conventional militaries were too robust and well balanced for them to fight outright over domination. The result was that they exported violence throughout the globe in a lethal chess game we now call the Cold War. Communist or capitalist, "free" or totalitarian makes no difference here. The product of each was war. It was war by proxy. Each side, the U.S. and the Soviet Union, instigated and bankrolled wars in which they themselves rarely took any overt part. Both sides trained and armed their own special forces, whose mission was often to covertly arm and train soldiers in foreign lands to make war on their neighbors or on their own domestic populations. Assassination and willful disruption of political process became policy. This meant more than half-a-century of war and civil war in as widely separated areas as Greece, and Vietnam, not to mention the continents of Latin America and Africa. Due to the effects of colonialism and world war, the greater concentrations of wealth and power ended up in the hands of the elite class of nations we call "First World." The lesser power, inferior wealth, and lack of self-determination ends up in the nations we term "Third World."

This was a new kind of war, different from the two world wars of the first half of the twentieth century. Instead of getting those militarily and economically under-powered nations to join the nations of wealth and power in war, the powerful nations instead export war and the destruction of people (and valuable property) to the nations least able to bear the destruction. This newer strategy of war preserves profits and power for the elite sponsors to a here-to-fore unprecedented degree. The Cold War was an economic conflict masquerading as a political conflict that caused global warfare to the benefit of the two main sponsors, and to the detriment of nearly everyone else. Millions died, and the political destabilization continues today. The rise in global militarism has spawned the current so-called "War on Terrorism."

The continued military spending of the Cold War benefited American corporations whose productive capability continued to increase. The

Soviet Union had been in poor industrial and economic condition before, during and after World War II. Both governments increased their deficit spending, each to out-do the other in such public competitions as the Space Race, in addition to incessant Cold War military struggles around the world. As U.S. surrogates won in these wars more than the Soviet Union, and because the U.S. economy was better able to withstand the deficits, the United States claimed eventual victory in the Cold War. But it may be termed a victory of capitalism, not a defeat of communism. It was a victory that left many governments around the world destabilized and dramatically reduced in human rights.

Joe McCarthy lent his name to a modern definition of institutionalized oppression. In the United States, McCarthyism perhaps best expresses the assault on human rights and civil liberties during the Cold War. This rabid xenophobe and incompetent congressman led the House Un-American Activities Committee in attack after attack on American citizens. Although we deride his "witch hunt" as extremism, we must not forget that in the paranoid climate of the times he had the utmost support from the bulk of Americans. The ongoing undercurrent of conservative fear of communism allowed others like J. Edgar Hoover to mount a multi-decade campaign of human and civil rights violations against social justice movements such as the Civil Rights movement, the Women's Rights movement, the American Indian Movement, and of course, the Anti-war movement.

O. Terrorism

A particularly modern type of evil, terrorism is an act of war that is illegal. Terrorism is the act of war carried out by those who see no (peaceful) political solution to the problems of self-determination, wealth and power. Terrorism is usually defined as being carried out without the endorsement of legitimate government. It can be called nationalism, but without a nation - or, at least, without the overt support of government. The origins of nearly every group now identified as terrorist can be found in the denial of political and economic self-determination. Almost all were either denied political identity as part of imperial colonial history, or as part of neo-colonial history. The remainders are the by-products of Cold War politics. Add to this the terrorist activities carried out by nation-states as legitimate government policy, and we have another vector of war. Violence in the form of terrorism becomes the tool of state sponsored covert oppression, of it becomes an act of political identity for those who are denied sovereignty and national identity. Terrorists see themselves as warriors in a cause. And, like all warriors they are not born, they are made.

We taught them the lessons of war. It should be no surprise that the weapons and tactics most terrorist employ are those of the larger industrialized and centralized nations. Most use weapons that were manufactured either in the United States, the former Soviet Union, or China. Many of the terrorist leaders were themselves trained in unconventional and guerrilla war by their former colonial masters. Welcome home.

The Cold War was a great breeder of terrorism. In order to spread their ideologies, the nations on any of the sides of the Cold War created organizations to operate militarily outside of the law. The Soviet Union had created Comintern – communism international – as early as 1919. Its job was to spread communist revolution anywhere in the world by any means necessary. Before the Palestinians had Hamass, Israel had the Haganah, the Palmach, and the Mossad. The United States had the Central Intelligence Agency since 1947, and they had Tony Poshepny almost since the beginning.

Tony Poshepny was known as Tony Poe. He was a CIA operative starting in 1951. It was the beginning of the Cold War, and the Communist dominoes seemed to be falling. Poe was among a host of gung-ho agents recruited by former OSS Chief, and now CIA head William "Wild Bill" Donovan. Poe and other agents worked to arm and train anti-communist forces in Southeast Asia. Much of his work was illegal by its very nature. Poe was to do the dirty work of terror that his government could not openly accomplish. Tony Poe attempted to organize a revolution against President Sukarno of Indonesia. He Failed. Later, he trained Tibetan guerrillas. Poe then turned to Laos. There under CIA contract, Tony Poe armed and trained anti-communist Laotian guerrillas in an illegal war. Laos was a country not at war with the U.S. He was known to have decapitated communist heads placed on spikes as warnings. Tony Poe, who gave bounties for human ears, is the model for Colonel Kurtz in "Apocalypse Now."

The origins of terrorism are everywhere. It is an unpleasant fact that the great powers of the modern world have bred terrorism. One side or the other in the Cold War would maintain there own "Tony Poes" all around the world, inciting revolution, arming insurgents, funding violence. Each Superpower creating factions and militarist power bases wherever it seemed to their advantage and regardless of the human rights of the people they were "saving from" whichever "ism." We would like to forget that the United States trained Manuel Noriega and his brutal forces. We would overlook that the U.S. had placed Mohammed Reza Pahlavi on the throne of Iran by using the CIA to overthrow former Iranian leader Mossadeh. That the U.S. had supported Iran until the Ayatollah Khomeini and his religious nationalists took power. And, we would omit that the United States encouraged Saddam Hussein in attacking Iran. But we must all-too-seriously not fail to recall that the United States sponsored and trained arch-terrorist Osama bin Laden.

As part of the anti-communist effort of the CIA, the United States supported the Afghan Mujahadeen against the invading Soviet Union during the 1980s. Mujahadeen means "Holy Warrior." A wealthy Saudi Mujahadeen of the huge bin Laden family was among the U.S. backed Taliban – or students. One reason that Osama bin Laden has not yet been brought to justice – we taught him. He knows all our tricks. The infamous and feared bin Laden terror organization al Qaeda – the base – was structured to defeat the United States. After the Afghan War and into the Iran Iraq War, Osama bin Laden and his followers resented the interference by the West in their affairs. In a fit of fundamentalist religious nationalism bin

232

Laden identified the United States as the most grievous offender. The American government had stationed troops in what was considered holy ground. It was a military insult and a religious threat. Since then, the U.S. presence anywhere in the world has been the target of this formerly U.S.-backed holy warrior.

P. Modified Capitalism – War by the Few Against the Many?

Nationalism and capitalism share a cultural evolution. Although capitalism was first described in detail in the West by Adam Smith in 1776, the concept of abstract wealth that capitalism represents is as old as civilization, which also means it is as old as war. War always profits someone. Capitalism means that – in essence – war is another way to generate capital. One need not be actually fighting the war. Post-industrial war means that an industry or nation can profit quite handsomely from remaining "neutral," and selling to both sides in a conflict. This, of course, sustains and prolongs conflict. United States industry did this prior to its entry into the first two World Wars. It was the production of America's un-bombed factories that brought the U.S. out of the Great Depression. The jump-start to the U.S. economy extended prosperity for decades. Likewise, the industries of many nations prospered from arms and other sales during those and subsequent wars.

Karl Marx saw a different type of war generated by capitalism. His view (equally as antique in some ways as Smith, yet also equally unavoidably applicable to modern economics) was that the productive classes (workers) of society are ever at odds with the owners of the means of production. Workers who make up the bulk of society actually produce wealth, yet they do not benefit from their labor in proportion to that labor. Instead, a historically privileged few who "own" the means of production (factories, businesses, corporations, government, etc.) concentrate the lion's share of wealth and all related social power within the system to themselves. Since Marx this has been called class struggle. He detailed how this could work in the landmark work Das Capital (1867).

To Marx, a class war between workers and owners was a social inevitability, given the state of industrial and early post-industrial civilization of Western Europe at the end of the first colonial period. Marx wrote that capitalism would consume itself in a social war between "haves and have-nots." This war may not be violent, as so many Americans have been taught, but would be all encompassing as far as social organization is concerned (Marx: 1848). The reason that revolutionary social change has not occurred is due to both the myopia of he original Marxist critique (overlooking non-European cultures, race, and gender, for instance), and to continuous modifications of capitalism by capitalists in positions of power since the time of Marx. These modifications have centered on the displacement of social conflict to outside of the nation-state, to the mitigation of social justice movements, to the economic and political distraction of the masses, and to the regular creation of the enemy. In short, modified capitalism counts on war. War has been the most consistent and reliable way to profitably modify capitalism. And, this warfare is not limited to conventional military struggle. Witness the growth and paramilitary development of urban police forces in industrial nations – especially the United States.

The basic critique of capitalism as expressed by Karl Marx has been modified by Marcuse, Keynes, Davis, Cabral, hooks, and others so that the Marxist critique can better apply to real-life issues of race, gender, and political economy. The critique presented in this book describes the cultural evolution of a class of concentrated wealth and political power that was and is based on war. The most important points for us to take from both Marx and Smith in the context of war is that different groups of people promote and profit from war, compared with those who both fight war, and die in war. And, that those who profit manipulate those who fight and die. It is the social system that promotes profit over peace that we must address if war is to actually be put behind humanity.

The 1967 book, <u>Report from Iron Mountain on the Possibility and Desirability of Peace</u>, edited by Leonard C. Lewin (and Victor Navasky) outlines how modern capitalist social systems require regular organization around armed conflict in order to survive and prosper. The <u>Report</u> was the fictional caution of anti-war journalists who wanted to demonstrate how insidious war really is. The once supposedly classified <u>Report</u> allegedly came from a multi-disciplinary team of scientists and thinkers operating in secret during the Vietnam War, at the height of the Cold War. This United States government had purportedly assembled this anonymous group to see what would occur in the unfortunate event that peace actually happened. The <u>Iron Mountain</u> report indicated that war and the threat of war are essential to many aspects of the smooth functioning of the United States. Although the <u>Report</u> was intimately concerned with the U.S., there are clear inferences that all civilization is similarly integrated with war. Over and over, the Report notes that this has been true of all of human history. Scientists described a "war system" that is so indispensable to many other aspects of human society as to be irreplaceable. War, the Report concludes, must continue so that our society will continue. It is striking to the reader of the ultimately fictitious Report how much genuine U.S. Government policy since the 1960's reflects the "war system" strategy. George W. Bush could have been using the Report as a play-book. The "War on Terrorism" that Bush promotes, the posture of global police force that his administration assumes, all predictable social capitalist behaviors if one has read the Iron Mountain data.

Apart from the typical military-industrial complex political economics, the Report also identified other economic, political, sociological, ecological, cultural, and scientific functions of society that war serves. It is sobering reading. And, the Report is a chilling incident of reality in murky blend with fantasy. Understanding war as central to the functioning of the modern capitalist state puts the discussions about peace in a whole new light. The experts, when tested, saw that the "war system [has] demonstrated its effectiveness since the beginning of recorded history; [having] provided the basis for the development of many impressively durable civilizations, including that which is dominant today." If the Report is taken at face value, then governmental posturing toward peace emerges as purposeful hypocrisy and subterfuge by political leaders aimed at placating the masses, and perpetuating war. Peace talks become another strategy in the game of maintaining a threat of war. Wars that will insure the wealth and power of the elite (of any nation) while guaranteeing the body-count of war dead from among poorer, working-class, and ethnic people all over the world.

Even if this damning indictment is only true some of the time for some of the key political and economic leaders, then it is enough. With the weight of tradition and the force of retribution behind it, one contrived conflict can produce plenty of genuine ones. Also, with the bulk of human social organization geared around preserving power relationships and central authority, a few pro-war leaders can produce necessary conflict at will. But, besides the purposeful acts of bellicose political and economic leaders, the structure of society is built so as to allow war, not peace. The investment of society is in war. The Report acknowledges that a peace system can in fact replace the "war system," yet admits that war is the easier and more advisable course for government.

The few (in terms of great power and wealth) must support war in order to remain the few. In capitalism, the natural tension between classes is necessary to the continued disproportionate wealth that class represents. This artificial tension is fueled and maintained by war.

THE FACE OF WAR GALLERY

Images of the Results of Organized Conflict Through Time

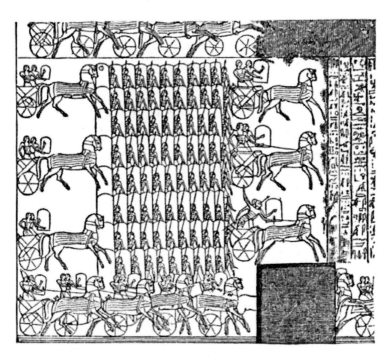

239

War – the original pursuit of kings.

Japanese woodblock print by Chikanobu Toyohara, signed
Yoshu Chikanobu, published by Fukuda Kumajiro, dated Meiji
year 31 (1898 in the Christian calendar). The two samurai are
Sato Tadanobu and Yokogawa Kakuhan, a warrior monk. The
Japanese war system included religious warrior societies that
were staffed by militant priests and monks.

Japanese woodblock print by Chikanobu Toyohara, signed
Yoshu Chikanobu in Meiji year 31 (1898 in the Christian
calendar). The print shows Kusunoki Masatsura engaged in
battle. Kusunoki and his cohorts advanced through a hail of
arrows. Note the lavish highly evoled arms and armor. Consider
the time, energy and resources the social system had invested in
war.

Japanese woodblock print by Chikanobu Toyohara, signed
Yoshu Chikanobu in Meiji year 32 (1899 in the Christian
calendar). Woodblock prints of this type celebrated the act of
killing and dying in service to the lord – or Daimyo. Although the
warrior elite glorified in destroying their foe, the masses of
Japanese farmers who's labor supported the war system lived in
fear and rigid social control.

By the time modern types of photography entered the battlefield, the true, un-glorified horror of war began to leave the battlefield and reveal the disparities between the pro-war propaganda and the dirt and death of real war.

(Photographs in the public domain from the Library of Congress)

George Bellows *The Cigarette* (from the *War* series), 1918
Lithograph. Edition unknown

World War I began a new level in human destruction and war.
The new inventions of machine guns, poison gas, airplanes,
tanks, etc. caused carnage of a level unknown in earlier wars.
WWI also heralded alarming increases in civilian casualties.
These were no accident. Eyewitness accounts of atrocities found
their way into print in many ways. Artist George Bellows created
a series of lithographs specifically to expose atrocity.

George Bellows,
The Bacchanale, 1918, lithograph.

George Bellows,
The Barricade, 1918. Lithograph.

George Bellows,
"Gott Strafh England"

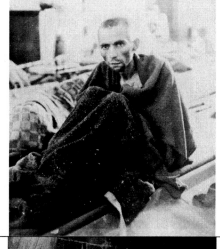

"Starving inmate of Camp Gusen, Austria." T4c. Sam Gilbert, May 12, 1945. 111-SC-264918. NARA

"This victim of Nazi inhumanity still rests in the position in which he died, attempting to rise and escape his horrible death. He was one of 150 prisoners savagely burned to death by Nazi SS troops." Sgt. E. R. Allen, Gardelegen, Germany, April 16, 1945. 111-SC-203572. NARA

And then, there are the atrocities and human rights violations of **World War II** – the "good war." After the death count of this global conflagration, the Nations of the world gathered to prevent future war with the Universal Declaration of Human Rights.

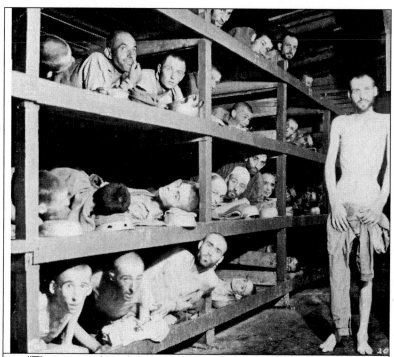

"These are slave laborers in the Buchenwald concentration
camp near Jena; many had died from malnutrition when U.S.
troops of the 80th Division entered the camp." Pvt. H. Miller,
Germany, April 16, 1945. 208-AA-206K-31. NARA

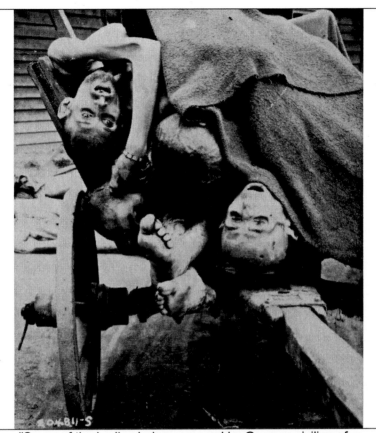

"Some of the bodies being removed by German civilians for decent burial at Gusen Concentration Camp, Muhlhausen, near Linz, Austria. Men were worked in nearby stone quarries until too weak for more, then killed." T4c. Sam Gilbert, May 12, 1945. 111-SC- 204811. NARA

"Bones of anti-Nazi German women still are in the crematoriums in the German concentration camp at Weimar, Germany, taken by the 3rd U.S. Army. Prisoners of all nationalities were tortured and killed." Pfc. W. Chichersky, April 14, 1945. 111-SC- 203461. NARA

"A German girl is overcome as she walks past the exhumed bodies of some of the 800 slave workers murdered by SS guards near Namering, Germany, and laid here so that townspeople may view the work of their Nazi leaders." Cpl. Edward Belfer. May 17, 1945. 111-SC-264895.
NARA

The massacre of South Vietnamese civilians at
My Lai – source unknown

The Vietnam war was driven by the sheer weight of influence of
the war system. It had vague goals, based on abstract notions
compounded by a total lack of cultural understanding. Atrocity
ran amuck, as did civilian victims and refugees.

South Vietnamese police Chief General <u>Nguyen Ngoc Loan</u>
executes Viet Cong Captain
<u>Nguyen Van Lem</u>
Source unknown

4. WHAT IS REALLY GOING ON

Can we explain? What is really going on? Does history repeat itself, or is it a band-aid on cancer? Should we stop war? Can we stop war? How? War was the central problem of the last millennia. What of the next millennium? Will we war?

All social power and concentrated wealth is in some way linked to war, the threat of war, and the war system. Through social organization, war has developed as the ultimate justification for itself and for the current power and wealth structure. A systemic violation of human rights is the result. And, this also promotes war. Upon analysis, then, war is not just the ultimate justification for itself, war is the only justification for itself. The social environment, which was once (and is) the main source of human survival in a natural environment has also become the biggest threat to human survival. This is because cultures center on conflict. Because societies are focused on preserving access to goods and services to a relative few within and between societies, and to excluding the possibilities of sharing through imposing a cult of conflict. War is the "anti-altruism." The global focus on unrestrained capitalism has produced a world in which private property and things are more important than people. It is a world where the basic rights of humanity are for sale. In this climate war thrives. The escalation in the frequency and intensity of war has paralleled the growth of civilization. Civilization as we have practiced it so far.

There rarely is a genuinely implacable enemy poised to threaten social harmony if not the prosperity of the nation. Most often, an enemy is produced by cultural circumstances, or is created and legitimized as a part of the need to reinforce social/economic structure. What is really going on then is that war exists to maintain want and need among many people. War also exists to provide plenty for a few. It is war that prevents peace. History does not repeat itself. There are sets of social and cultural factors that interact to produce conditions. These conditions and the nature of the social and cultural factors represented are the causal options of history. If there is a recurrent set of conditions interrelating with a familiar set of social and cultural factors, then patterns may emerge. War is such a pattern. It relies on sets of conditions that we put into place. War recurs because those conditions we create interrelate to cultures featuring patriarchy and warrior mythos. War also recurs because social conditions favor it. We treat war as a cause, when it is really a result of sets of conditions. We say: "history repeats itself," but history only seems to repeat itself because we overlook the underlying factors and conditions. War is a symptom. You know what a symptom is? It is the result of a set of conditions. A symptom is an indicator, not the thing itself. A symptom may be a cough. The cough may be due to a common cold. Or, the symptom may result from the condition of pneumonia, or lung cancer. War is a symptom. We treat war like a symptom, with superficial topical treatments aimed at temporary relief from that particular symptom, at that particular time. But our efforts have been "over the counter" remedies that cure our pain – only temporarily. Cough syrup will not help cure cancer. It is time to look at causes. To cure cancer, look at the causes of cancer. The cough will take care of itself. The social conditions overlaying the symptom of war need attention. We seek to end *THAT* war or *THIS* war. We need to end war. In that sense, we treat the cancer of war with a band-aid. Then we are surprised at history repeating itself when the cancer of war flares up again. We should stop war. But, if we can, it will be because we approach peace differently.

A. Should We Stop?

What happens if we don't stop? What are the possible consequences? We all know about the most catastrophic. We all fear nuclear holocaust, biological/chemical disaster, the rise of fascism or an unrelenting wave of devastating terrorist attacks. But what if we just don't stop? Some examples can be drawn from history. Take Sparta, for example. A nation founded on militarism, war, and the power of the state, Sparta was also founded upon the systematic denial of human rights. Sparta solved the crises of population pressures common to the Hellenes of the times by the conquest and enslavement of their neighbors, the Messenians in about 725 BCE. To do this, they required all Spartans to commit virtually their entire lives to the Spartan military machine (war system). All Spartan men, women, and children were involved in the training and support of warriors. All Messenians became Helots – permanent serfs. Thus, the Spartan war system claimed two sets of victims who lost their human rights – the slave and the slave master – chattel and citizen soldier. Over the long run, there were many slave uprisings. These were wars of the many who were denied human rights against the few who had them.   Each slave revolt only further entrenched Spartan militarism.

Of course, one also cannot overlook the wars with other Greeks caused by Sparta, or the Spartan military posture.   By the 600s BCE, the reforms of semi-mythic Spartan warrior Lycurgus came into being.   Descendant of Heracles, Lycurgus created a system of pervasive social and cultural militarism in Sparta.   From then on, to be a Spartan meant to be a warrior − birth 'til death.   After the second Messene-Spartan War of 650 BCE resulted in the fixation of the Spartan war system, Spartan cultural development stagnated.   Arts, literature, and architecture that did not contribute to the war system atrophied.   Spartan social and cultural evolution was "side-tracked" into a "blind alley" of post war and pre-war obsessions.

Xenophon noted that Spartan "Peer pressure" and valor at arms were prime motivators for youth.   War became a "categorical imperative" of Spartan social life.   The record (or the huge gap in the record) of Spartan artistic expression is a suggestive glimpse at what militarism and the war system can do to inhibit social and cultural growth.   This bolsters the thesis that the war system has served to impede the evolution of social systems that guarantee increased economic justice and human rights in other cases as well.   Sparta was (we are reminded) the first form of Greek democracy, predating the vaunted Athenian model.   The Athenian form of democracy was itself flawed by being slave based, military, and exclusively upper class male.   And, it was dominated by demagoguery, which often led to war.   As in Sparta, multitudes of slaves, women, the poor, and non-military had no democratic rights whatsoever.   The evolution in Athens of an economy based on concentrated wealth simultaneously checked the expansion of Athenian democracy to other classes and linked class advantage even more to military participation. The result was great elite wealth for Athenian citizens, the hegemony of the Athenian League, great concentration of wealth in Athens, and the Peloponnesian War with Sparta and other fearful envious Greek city-states. This paved the way for the refined militarism of Phillip of Macedon, and the megalomaniac warfare of Alexander the Great.

On a more contemporary front, Matthew White of the Historical Atlas of the Twentieth Century totals the war and war related dead of the 20th Century to be 188,000,000. Zbigniew Brzezinski places the count at 175 million dead in his book: Out of Control: Global Turmoil on the Eve of the Twenty-first Century (1993). This represents an accelerated death toll of the 20th and 21st Centuries. There is a categorically imperative humanity in the combat soldier and in the collateral civilian. Taken to its logical conclusion humanity and human rights dictates an ultimate responsibility of political leadership to cease all war. Peace is a fundamental right of all humans. Government's must be responsible – to make peace as good government – to abolish militarism. If the nation is taken to be the greatest good, then the nation also has the greatest responsibility. Should we stop war? Yes.

B. Can We Stop? – The Case for Change

It may be doubly difficult in light of the clear social and cultural investment that humanity has put into war to see how we can change now. If we accept on top of our militant history that we are biologically determined for war, then stopping may seem impossible. One delusional danger born of the fevered paranoia of Cold Warrior mentality was that the U.S. could force peace on the world through military superiority. Now, with current perceived levels of intense U.S. cultural imperialism and military hegemony, leaders like Bush, Cheney, and Ashcroft who believe they know what's best for all of us continue to do what they have done – make the 21st century even more war-prone than the bloody 20th. More than one-hundred and sixty million died violently in the 20th century. And, if we take into account the peripheral and collateral producers of death such as disease, famine, reduced fertility, increased infant mortality, and other results of war like infrastructural and environmental destruction, then the death toll may well exceed 200 million human lives. Few even seem to tally the children maimed and killed stepping on anti-personnel mines in areas now deemed "peaceful." And yet, with this prophetic history, leaders still support war and the war system as the primary route to peace. But, can war lead to peace?

In the recent award-winning documentary/memoir "The Fog of War," film maker Errol Morris shows through the life of former U.S. Secretary of Defense Robert S. McNamara just how thickly war can fog the peace process. McNamara recounts his insider's role in much of the U.S. involvement in 20th century war. The fog never completely lifts as statements and questions flow. Certain fundamental assumptions remain unchallenged. These include: the role of reason and human nature in war; that one must do evil to do good; that there are just wars; that there are rules in war; that proportional conflict is desirable (or even possible); and, that empathy* (based on race or religion) is valuable, but not for those who are "Evil." It is these very assumptions and others that keep the war system functioning. As experienced and nuanced as McNamara is, he still assumes war to be necessity and not option. This concept of threat and dominance insures war.

With this mentality in place, Should We Stop is moot – How We Stop is an impossibility. It will take a dramatic turn away from assumptions like those of former Secretary McNamara – assumptions that are themselves the *Fog Of War* – before war's reality is itself history.

> "...The paramount aim of any social
> system should be to frame military
> institutions, like all its other institutions,
> with an eye to the circumstances of
> peace-time, when the soldier is off duty.
> And this proposition is borne out by the
> facts of experience. For militarist states
> are apt to survive only so long as they
> remain at war, while they go to ruin as
> soon as they have finished making
> their conquests. Peace causes their metal
> to lose its temper; and the fault lies
> with a social system which does not teach
> its soldiers what to make of their lives
> when they are off duty."
> -Aristotle as quoted in Toynbee (51).

We can be pessimistic. We can accept that as long as peace exists so will war. We only know one in contrast to the other. We can just assume that where there is a chicken, there will be an egg and be done with it.   But, there have been peace and human rights oriented social structures.   There have been and are cultural beliefs centered on peace.   The Jains of India are a sect that is so peaceful as to be vegetarian.   They will go a step further in cultivating non-violence.   The Jain commitment to *ahimsa* – non-injury – conditions every aspect of their lives.   There have been more extroverted activities aimed at human rights and ending the conditions that promote war.   Every religion proselytizes peace.   Some of the religions even practice what they preach.   The "missions" that some groups still send their youth on are particularly noteworthy.   Then, there are the Non-Governmental Organizations (NGOs) such as Human Rights Watch, and institutions like the Peach Corps.   There are the creeds and documents to peace and human rights.   High-minded writings like the Declaration of Independence or the more mechanistic Fourteen Points of Woodrow Wilson stand alongside the post WWII Universal Declaration of Human Rights.   There is even the creed of some of the Asian martial arts aimed at defense and the cultivation of meditative inner peace.   Taken together, these and others offer glimpses at types of social organization that can channel human energy into social and cultural transformation, and the waging of peace.

C. How We Stop - Cultural Evolution

"Neither the genetic evolution of life nor human cultural evolution is deterministic, involving a straightforward unfolding of natural laws.   Both depend on a large degree on all that has gone before (a point made frequently and eloquently by Stephen J.

Gould). All of our natures are a product of our histories, biological and cultural" -Ehrlich: 270.

"The absence of conditions of peace is the cause of war." -Quincy Wright 1935, 1942.

The cost of adequate nutrition for 100% of humanity:
Approximately $19 billion per year
Amount spent on dieting in the United States:
About $35 billion per year

Cost of ending problems in 18 of the world's major trouble spots:
$235 billion per year
World military expenditures:
Over $780 billion per year, and growing.

(Source: Ralph Litwin was certified as a World Game Facilitator in 1996, and presented World Game Workshops in NJ schools from then until 2002 as part-time subcontractor for Education Information & Resource Center (EIRC). http://www.earthcharter.org/)

Why don't we, the human race, do something about it? It's clear we can afford it. Many people and organizations are working to end hunger, yet on a global scale the problem continues. It is hard not to look for a different approach. It will all be in recognizing the systems in which we live, and applying ourselves to peace. The first step must be education. Citizens of every state or nation should be taught not just about their own system, but that of all others. Citizens must broaden, not harrow their world view. People must begin to become what was once called "renaissance" women and men. Objectification must give way to "subjectification" – sympathy is no match for empathy. The "giving mom directions" analogy can be useful, here. Moving a society towards peace has multiple dimensions. Ending war can be seen as giving your mother directions to someplace she has never been. In dealing with others who may not have your points of reference, cultivate a sense of empathy and compassion. Empathy: or feeling like you are experiencing the life of another. Compassion: as in the desire to relieve the suffering of others. You tell mom how to get there by a route that may not be fastest, but that will make sure she gets there safely and soundly. Our route to peace-making institutions may not be fastest, but we need to get there.

Peace must be "managed" like war is. It must become the central intention of our social organization. It means human rights on a grand scale. It means uncompromising economic justice. To disengage humanity from the addiction to mass murder means a fundamental reorganization of our social systems, and that can only happen through culture. People must believe in the reality of peace. Societies must aim to produce conditions where war is not necessary or productive. This means re-examining many aspects of the current political economy, and dramatically shifting existing imbalances and social injustice both real and perceived. This has never historically occurred unless there was a sweeping change in culture. Often as not in history, this has been because of a catastrophe. War is catastrophic. Modern war can become absolutely apocalyptic.

One Strategy for Cultural Evolution

Eliminate standing armed forces and weapons of mass destruction. Political leaders fight it out in person with low technology weapons – like swords – while we watch. Thus, war would occur involving the most people possible with the least actual physical destruction. Leaders should publicly be selected, trained and fight. It would all be televised on cable – pay-per-view, even. The participants in the personal combat would truly represent the interests of his/her nation. Military victory would become political and economic triumph. Whoever won would secure the disputed resource, territory, or authority. You may laugh, but this is not really all a joke. Heads of state would consider casualties and "justifiable collateral damage" much more carefully if they had an intimate stake. Sympathy is no match for empathy.

When war makers had to regularly show personal prowess, wars were limited in scope, in intensity and in duration. I suggest picking up where Ehrlich left off in his book Human Natures, and applying the "conscious evolution" model to the social organization of war and war culture instead of to the environmental dilemma he wrote about (326). Just as no single local bureaucracy is equipped to perceive certain problems with the global environment, we are not fully socially and culturally equipped to see how war has been made essential. We can, however, consciously construct social systems that make war less probable, and far less possible. History does not repeat itself, despite the seeming regularity of war. What has happened is that humankind has been addressing the symptoms, and not the disease. The disease is the lack of uniform human and economic rights.

Our concept of social organization has been limited to reacting to short-term want, and not long term needs. In short, we put a band-aid on cancer.

The symptom is treated using war as the cure. The surface struggle leaves the cancer untouched. The cancer is the lack of human rights as a result of the concentration of wealth and power that gross capitalism and materialism make possible. We have yet to address this question with the intensity we bring to war. What happens is that we fail to solve fundamental problems of social organization. Human rights become secondary. War becomes primary. Profit for a powerful few became the short-term solution to social ills. However, power and wealth for a few has simply maintained the conditions that had brought about war in the first place. By now it should be relatively clear that those conditions still obtain. Human rights are not universal. Vast economic disparity continues. They are the embers ready to spark the next military conflagration – the next fires of war.

Before we can construct institutions of lasting peace, we must demolish the idea that war will somehow end of its own accord. That vague persistent assumption that war will not find a way to make itself necessary keeps us from acting against the war system. Kagan, when he writes of war: "many of them unnecessary" belies the very ubiquity of war he earlier avers (566). There is too much war, too often. To truly resolve war as a temporal and cross-cultural phenomenon, its necessity must be admitted. But, this does not mean that the necessity is not a contrived one. War's necessity may often be a contrived one, but a perceived necessity is no less urgent. This also does not mean that the necessity of war was not itself the product of conditions and forces that can and should be mitigated. We may have decided we need to go to war, but it is a decision.

And, the decision to war is itself the result of earlier decisions. Thus far, social sciences such as anthropology show that much (perhaps all) of the cultural expressions of human behavior emerge as evolutionarily functional or selected for in a Darwinian sense. War cannot be seen as otherwise. It is only the egocentric and species centric social scientist - or the intellectual coward - that fails to see the cloying fecundity of the recurrent theme of human conflict. Promised peace is possible only if we see war's causes and actively seek to preempt them. This is certainly not to presuppose a sublime perfection of either our sciences or of ourselves, nor to mindlessly assume the progressive/positivist paradigm of "new is better" or "perfection is around the corner". But rather, this is to actively assert that change is cause and, that purpose has effect. That action has motivation. The assumption that cause and effect are related in more than proximity, but also in meaning is the apex of science and the not unduly vaunted scientific method.

It misses the point to merely seek a reduction in the frequency of war, or the production of policies promising lasting peace. War is endemically entrenched by nature in human society and culture. War will return – that is the real point. Here is where the past can contribute to the future. This is where history and anthropology can be meaningful in the creation of institutions which can transform or perhaps more importantly reform the manner in which we collectively deal with our own self-annihilation. Following Kagan (569) "in a world of sovereign (ne nationalist economic entities) states, a contest among them...is a normal condition...that will lead to war". We must plan for war, but in a new set of ways. We must plan for war in a way that ends war, not that perpetuates conflict. It is time to be more than simply ready for war. We must be ready for peace. The fatal complexities of the issue demand comprehensive efforts aimed especially at limiting the wholesale demise of countless non-combatants through outright slaughter or through disruption of the infrastructure. This means a greater institutional emphasis on human rights and economic justice. Change being the overriding theme of the human experience dictates that change must be respected in our planning to end war.

There are social and cultural traps here that are both emotional and political.

Emotional trap

Restraint of "wicked, irrational, & unprofitable" impulses ignores the "honorable" calculated economic stimulation of war. Such restraint wastes investigative time and is a waste of educated and educational time. Such denial & suppression of the apparently natural tendencies leading to the collective murder that war represents only produces an increased intensity in the inevitable bloodbath of wars eventual release. Remember what repression did for sex during the Victorian era. The social institutions of the war system count on the emotional, the visceral response. Virtually all war making rhetoric seeks to either create an emotional link between war and the citizen, or to tie in to the existing emotional state of the citizen. To simply seek to repress human natures that give rise to violence plays into the hands of the war system, a system that is both eager, and prepared to tap into the emotional well of conflict that repression fills to overflowing. Also key to the understanding of the emotional trap is the human instinct to imitate, or conform to tradition. It may only be that a few people are really ready to actively engage in organized violence at any given time. But, the imitative and conformist nature of social humanity means that the rest of us tend to follow. Whether the conformist response to leadership advocating war be due to conditioning, or patriotism, or fear of not belonging, the visceral emotional trap of the follower cannot be overlooked.

Political trap

Complex alliance to ensure peace has actually presented - if nothing else - a threat to non-aligned nations, which in reaction again produces war. Some elements of Greek and Roman (classical, or republican, but not imperial) military/political traditions of the past may have signal value in developing movements against institutionalized war of the future. Active participation and understanding of war/military preparation as a precondition of citizenship and social access may help condition populations for peace. However, the trap lies in the assumption that a larger political body will mean peace. The historic reality seems to be that military expansionists and imperialist often promise peace and an end to conflict by force. That is to say, that if an empire is created by force by crushing warring states that peace will be secure. This is the political rhetoric of continued war. Not the end of war, but war on a broader base and for bigger military/police efforts. In this political trap, internal ethnic and class disadvantaged groups get targeted by police, and external states become either subjugated "allies," or enemy threats. Either way war is guaranteed, as is the concentrated wealth and power of the militant elite, and the general lack of human rights and economic justice for the bulk of the population.

As I have shown, war has evolved historically. Humans may be biologically capable of violence, but society has hyper-developed the individual ability (even against the individual will) by distilling violence – conditioning humans to effectively and efficiently kill large numbers of our own kind. Lewin, Grossman, Ehrenreich, and many others reveal in great detail a war system that is integrated into most, if not all aspects of society. The functional approach to explaining organized violence and war goes so far as to suggest that war is essential and irreplaceable to the state. The suggestion is that, in short, human social systems would not exist without war. I differ at this point. War, and the war system may have evolved to fulfill many functions in our social systems – especially supported as war is by a culture of conflict. However, I have also shown that a symbiotic link between hierarchies of social class and war exists. And further, that the wealth, power, and status that class represents means not only the denial of economic rights to most of human society, but that this general deficit in human rights presents the main underlying reason for war. It is not just that those who have wealth want to keep it. Nor is it as simple as the idea that those without wealth and power will go to war to get it. It is that the power group of any society will use war to maintain their position of power and privilege.

Humankind may be biologically capable of aggressive behavior, but we are also biologically capable of cooperative behavior. The data suggests that we are perhaps even more capable of cooperation than of conflict, especially since a precondition to war is social organization. Therefore, social organization need not rely on war and the threat of war, but war relies on social organization. Of the universal needs that human beings face in a natural environment and those in a social environment, war is decidedly absent. Power and privilege are the problem. It is when we turn an eye to the social environment that we see a need to manage conflict. It is when people interfere with the needs of other people that violence becomes organized. It is the disproportionate distribution – the unequal share – of the benefits of society that gives rise to conflicts.

No matter how wealth and power are figured, those who have the most use what they have to keep what they have. In society, that means using people. It means *human lives in exchange for wealth, power, and influence.* Having the means to organize society, those with power and wealth maintain a war system. This system has been made to seem an essential part of human society. But, though it has been made to seem so for all, the war system only serves the interests of a few. War is essential only if human society is structured around the interests of keeping wealth and power in the hands of those few. It is historically the elite class that is obsessed with perpetuating socially sanctioned organized conflict. War is the obsession of the powerful, and the fear of the weak. It has ever been the prerogative of the elite (and of males who hold power due to patriarchic

272

social constructions). Over most of human history, powerful wealthy elite groups have used their authority to convince, coerce or compel the rest of society to join their wars. As technology developed – prodded and lashed by war, funded by, and generator of the wealth of the elite – warfare was made more inclusive. First the longbow, and then the gun, meant that the poorer classes could swell both the battlefield, and the cemetery. "Collateral damages" composed of dead civilians could be accepted. But, elite lives that were by their own assessment too valuable need no longer personally engage the enemy that they themselves had created. Now, standing armies composed of poorer young men socially conditioned to patriotism and violence, eager and not-so-eager for social acceptance and advancement, could be kept in readiness for war. They would always be deployed. But, whether they are deployed immediately or not, the elite class would always be well served by the social economy behind keeping the armies ready.

It is this lopsided equation that war has become. This brings us up-to-date. We war because human societies have evolved toward central authority. We war because we surrender our political autonomy to the authority of a few. Why we war is to maintain the status and wealth of those few in political and economic authority. Modern war is where countless thousands (if not millions) can be made sacrifice to the power and wealth of a few. And all the while that empowered few has less and less responsibility for the well being of the bulk of society. And worse, it becomes so that the concentration of wealth is more important than life itself. War is a created condition that is the product of cultural evolution and social organization. We have looked at why we (make) war, now how to un-make war? Once again, cultural evolution – the long view, and social (re)organization – the short view:

CULTURAL EVOLUTION – How to Cultivate Peace

De-legitimize Killing
Capital Punishment makes collective killing culturally acceptable in defense of society. Self-defense must not mean that another life is expendable. The rape or murder has been committed. Punishment is not simply duplicating the crime. Retribution is rarely justice. Murder does not necessarily deter murder. Seek meaningful alternatives to the death penalty. Blind Justice carries a sword, but she needn't sleep with the Reaper. Justice and death should not go hand in hand.

Teach Peace
Acknowledge that being human means being potentially violent. Reduce this potential in scale to individual non-collective concepts that cultivate self-discipline, self-control and conflict resolution. This will require a shift in patterns of general education. Taoism (Daoism) is an example of a philosophic education towards peace. Despite the current vogue in action movies, some traditional martial arts styles such as Tai Chi Chuan offer methods of re-channeling violent aggression into peaceful paths and humanistic behaviors.

Eliminate Nationalism
Patriotism and nationalism have been two of the central ways that large numbers of people are

assembled for war. Replace nationalism and nationalist expressions for humanism. Use the Universal Declaration of Human Rights as the highest governmental expression of human social political culture, not the nation/state/ethnicity, etc.

Demote Materialist Culture
Reduce and re-evaluate materialism so that people and experiences become more important than things and objects to be acquired at "any expense." Integrate the Universal Declaration of Human Rights with local economies to institutionalize economic justice. The basic quality of life and subsistence aspects of material culture should not be commodities on a competitive market. If basic survival is up to market prices, then many can be convinced to survive at any price – the result, war.

Redefine Masculinity
Masculinity in many cultures has been confused with patriarchy. Humanity is long overdue for a movement that redefines masculinity without patriarchy and dominance. The unfortunate reality of patriarchic male dominance is that men, having the power, have not seen the need to change. To be a male – or a man – does not have to mean being a killer.

Adopt Matriarchy
Reduce male dominance and patriarchy. The Iroquois society featured female property control and confirmation of all male leadership. Earlier in human history and pre-history matriarchies ruled. There is little evidence of widespread war from these times. Matriarchic social organization reduces gender abuses. Also, women become de-commoditized.

SOCIAL ORGANIZATION – Reorganize Society into Institutions of Peace

Remove War Powers
No representative body, or individual should have war powers. If a leader wants a fight, let him fight. If a congress, parliament, or Knesset wants a war, then suit them up and send them. Any declaration of hostilities should be by direct vote. And a pro war vote is enlistment. Those who must fight should be the only ones qualified to vote on a course of war.

De-Militarize the Military
Broaden the scope and obligation of the government military organizations so that their mission is embodied in the Universal Declaration of Human Rights. Democratize the military in a new way, and decentralize authority over them – block the demagogue effect. Partisan politics plays no part in human rights. Rome became an Empire when its armies became professional. It was then that they lost their investment in the common lot of citizens. It was then that demagogues like Julius Caesar could use fear and militarism to seize Imperial authority. If a modern army's mission is embodied in the Universal Declaration of Human Right, for instance, then it keeps them invested in the common lot of citizens. If the modern army is decentralized politically, they form an additional check balanced against imperial demagoguery.

Re-Configure Power and Leadership
Leaders must not be linked to wealth. The wealthy must not become leaders. Anyone seeking political

leadership must give-up all wealth to the state. Campaigns will be federally funded only. Elected leaders will be fed, clothed, and housed by the state. The once-wealthy political leaders can recover their wealth only after their term in office. However, the former wealth of the leader can only be restored after responsible leadership and a direct democratic referendum (vote of confidence). Irresponsible leadership results in the state retaining the wealth of the leader to the degree of the referendum. Irresponsible is defined by a tenure in office that is lacking in human rights and economic justice.

De-Institutionalize Religion
Make a true separation between church and state. The dogmatic blanket of organized religion and the fundamentalist fanaticism it drapes have ever been centers of coercion to war.

Institutionalize Human Rights
Set human rights and economic justice as the fundamental validating principles of government. This must be a foreign as well as a domestic effort. The surrender of individual autonomy to the authority of the state should be based on a social contract consisting of human and economic rights. In order to be legitimate, state authority must rest on a high level of commitment to human rights and economic justice.

De-Capitalize the Basic Quality of Life
Nutrition, housing, fundamental health, education, and general welfare of populations must not be a matter of desperate struggle. Poverty and desperate need makes people open to political manipulation for war. Even when there is an unsupported belief that the

basic quality of life is under threat enemies can be conjured that people respond to viscerally. It must become the primary responsibility of government to de-commoditize the basic quality of life. Without a threat to human rights, a jingoist or demagogue cannot trigger the gut reaction that occurs when the primary elements of one's existence are at risk.

Do Not Socially Reward Violence – Especially Socially Organized Violence
Scale down public presentations of organized violence. Reduce all television coverage contracts of sports such as football, hockey, wrestling, and boxing. People can watch what they want. And, people can do whatever sport they want. But, vast economic empires built on violence should not be socially endorsed.

Will this happen? Sadly, no. Humanity is still a catastrophic species. We act when there is a crisis. Then, we act best. Apparently, we will sometimes create a crisis within which to act. A social system based on concentrated power and wealth favors a war system. The current power and wealth relationships evolved to be accepted as the norm. War is tradition. History has taught us to accept the powerful as the natural way of society. War and the threat of war are particularly necessary in this view. The wealthy are to be emulated. This has, of course, been especially true when the recording and interpretation of history has been supported by the rich and powerful. But human history also supports other views. Social change can happen, and culture can develop along different lines. Something as fundamental and entrenched as concentrated wealth and power – something as compelling as the culture of conflict – will be hard to change. Yet social justice movements have a history of particular success with re-organizing power and re-distributing wealth. The Suffrage movement and the organized labor movement, in the United States, or Gandhi, Mother Theresa, and Polish Solidarity are prime examples of human rights movements that produced radical social change. It will take a new type of struggle to end the war system – a struggle on an evolutionary scale.

It was Frederick Douglass who said that power never concedes anything without a demand – without struggle. Anti-war movements must be aimed at ending all war. This new movement cannot be short sighted. It can not be aimed at ending a war. The movement to end the war system will have to combine aspects of broad social justice, like Gandhi, or Mother Theresa, with the laser beam legal challenge posed by the U.S. Civil Rights movement. It must be an international effort aimed at human rights and economic justice. Expecting assassination and corruption, the anti-war system movement must rely on many leaders. Such a movement must consider longer stretches of time than the administration of any president, prime minister, or monarch. Ending the war system means making peace when war would be easier. After all, the war system is now an embedded aspect of human social organization. It is not just republican or democratic, or parliamentary. War serves power. Until social power is reconsidered and redistributed, centralized authority and wealth will always resort to using that power to organize society for war and the threat of war.

So far, human culture has evolved to the point of representative government. The assumption is that it has been successful and that it is progress. Democracy – true one person one vote government – is still largely a myth. The ancient Athenian Greeks had a democracy in which only wealthy males could participate, and everyone else was a kind of property. The United States is a government with a few limited democratic principles that are allowed under a government that is a Federated Republic.   The nature of capitalism in the U.S. has meant that the government is essentially an oligarchy – a government of the rule by a few.   True direct democracy in a large multi-ethnic nation-state may have only become technologically feasible recently in human history.   So far, true representative government and full democracy, like true communism, do not really exist.

I see the war system as key to why democracy has not evolved and to how government has remained centralized. Centralized government may not be inherently abusive or oppressive, but concentrated wealth and power <u>are</u> inherently oppressive and abusive. This is no arbitrary distinction. Decisions of all types must be made, and centralized government may be expedient and efficient in making them.   However, war powers should not be the purview of a few, or of the one. Certainly war-making powers should not be in the hands of those who can profit from war. The war system facilitates concentrated wealth and power. When the class of wealth is also the class of political power, true representation becomes impossible. By the time they are elected, the so-called representatives are thoroughly and completely insulated by class advantage from the people they pretend to represent. Representative government has proven not to be so. More often the career politicians who make up representative government are really representing the elite class from which their lives flow. This alienation from those "average" citizens that the representative purports to represent means that, instead of peace, the war system is encouraged. Decisions made by such bodies may incidentally reflect some concerns held by the bulk of the population. But, more often public opinion is something to be used, molded and manipulated, or created. I am reminded of the quote on the eve of U.S. imperial colonial expansion at the beginning of the 20th Century. When Frederic Remington was embarking for Cuba, publisher William Randolph Hearst said "you furnish the pictures, and I'll furnish the war."

In the broadcast memorial service for ambushed dead of the U.S. 507th Division in the Second Gulf War, Colonel Robert Woods, Jr. eulogized that "Americans are deployed in front of their television sets." The "Hearsts" of the world – on the "Turners" – are still controlling the pictures, furnishing the wars.

It is not just the democratic, or the republican forms of government. Socialism and communism, likewise, have not yet been tried in the real world. Governments (including the U.S.) have incorporated aspects of socialism to various advantages. Some governments have been communist in name, but have retained the essential nature of their earlier forms. Or, they have blended communism with totalitarian, authoritarian, patriarchic, or Confucian systems. Likewise, as with democracy, I feel that the evolution of government beyond these centralized forms is due to the war system and it's regressive emphasis on concentrated wealth and power. This requires further conflict (or potential conflict) to continue justifying concentration.

This is where anarchists hit the mark. Authority is understood by its very nature to be counter to self-determination (freedom), human potential, and human rights. Ibn Khaldun, Robert Wolff, Rousseau, and others suggest that centralized government only works – can only make war – if people surrender autonomy to authority. Thus far, the idea of popular majority support in the representative systems (above) has given a sturdy illusion. We believe that the surrender of personal autonomy to government (or to the social organization, authority figure, or patriotic movement) is always in the best interest of the majority. Forget for a moment the cogent arguments of minority populations and under-empowered majorities (women and the poor), what is best for the most is what is best – period. Yet, the existence of war and the war system means that the surrender to authority is an end in itself. By conditioning populations to surrender autonomy through patriotic and nationalist appeal, through jingoism and fear, the elite minority maintains economic and political control. Once class advantage is linked to political position, it just isn't possible to keep them from being reinforcing. Those with power use it to seek wealth, and those with wealth use it to consolidate positions of power and authority. The result has been reductions in genuine social and class mobility for the majority, as well as increased centralization of economic and political power in the hands of an elite minority.   The most consistent reason for the majority to surrender autonomy to authority has been the threat of war, or war itself. Thus, war has inhibited the cultural evolution of political process.   Mostly because the evolution of political process may mean peace, and peace would mean no further justifications for disparities in wealth, power, and human rights.

Now, the globe is surrendering autonomy to the hegemony of the United States.

This has a background that goes back to Jimmy Carter, although it is not his fault. Energy in the form of oil became political economy separate from the traditional superpowers in the form of OPEC.   The Organization of Oil Producing Countries helped to shift the global power struggles between the Soviet Union and the United States.   The USSR was in economic decline from which it never recovered. The U.S. began a rise to status as the sole global super power. The foundations were laid for fascism. Then a wall came down. Power became central to one state. Power became again exploitive and manipulative of popular thought by refining elite control of media. Now, economic and media elite like Ted Turner influence popular sentiment in support of politicians who facilitate the accumulation of more wealth by economic elite.   When they retire, these politicians often become CEOs or board members of corporations.

Social organization is in a state of arrested development.   Cultural evolution has been all but defeated. Biologically, humanity is still physically as it was in Neolithic times. Civilization made possible the mitigation of the normal evolutionary principles. Humankind had created a new environment that sheltered and insulated people from natural selection, substituting instead cultural evolution and social selection. Likewise war has made cultural evolution grind to a bone-crunching standstill. The war system inhibits society from an otherwise inevitable progress beyond concentrated power and wealth hierarchies. Be reminded that civilization – society and culture – originally developed to allow a (larger) group of people to meet the needs of survival and prosperity. It has done this and more. On the contrary, war presents the developed and by now dubious qualities of centralized power and condensed capital that limits prosperity and often survival to a few at the direct expense of the group. War does not serve most people and particularly not the poorer majority. War works counter to an increase in survival. War kills not only soldiers and civilians. It also kills chances for social reorganization as well as the development and application of broad-based human rights policies of economic justice.

The next step in cultural evolution should be a concept of world community. Based on human rights and economic justice, this idea offers a global sense of common interest in peace and the general welfare of the people. Based on the common understanding of human rights articulated in the Universal Declaration, and on proactive government, the world community can begin the long task of reforming social and cultural institutions away from large-scale conflict.

But, war wielded as national policy by leaders like George W. Bush, Richard Cheney, John Ashcroft, and Donald Rumsfeld threatens to make the world community a patriarchic fiefdom of U.S. self interest. Of course, the United States will remain the central target, as well.

I started this book by writing about my hypocrisy. My hypocrisy is a beginning. The contradiction to civilization that war represents is its own form of hypocrisy. Maybe it takes someone intimate with violence – a real member of the cult of conflict – to really see it for what it is. Born to peace, socialized into war, yet ultimately willing to change. This book is my beginning – a willingness to make peace.

One day, I took my handguns to the pawnshop. I took the money as a matter of self-respect. I left the guns, and never went back...

Chapter Notes: INTRODUCTION
(All notes are in general order of appearance in the text. All sources are used reference the whole work unless otherwise noted).

McNamara, Robert Strange. "Fog of War." In the 2004 award-winning documentary/memoir "The Fog of War," film maker Errol Morris shows through the life of former U.S. Secretary of Defense Robert McNamara just how thickly war can fog the peace process.

Grossman, Dave, On Killing: The Psychological Cost of Learning to Kill in War and Society. New York: Little, Brown and Co, 1995.

Ehrlich, Paul R. Human Natures: Genes, Cultures, and the Human Prospect. Washington, D.C.: Island Press/Shearwater Books. 2000.

Asimov, Isaac. Foundation. New York: Bantam Books. 1951.

Musashi, Miyamoto. A Book of Five Rings. New York: Overlook Press, 1974.

New World Translation of the Holy Scriptures. New York: Watchtower Bible and Tract Society. 1978.

The Holy Bible New International Version. Grand Rapids Michigan: Zondervan Bible Publishers.1984.

Stone, Merlin. When God Was A Woman. New York: Barnes and Noble. 1976. 116-118, 126-128, 169-172.

Keller, Werner. The Bible as History. William Neil, tr. New York: William Morrow and Company, Inc. 1981.

Zinn, Howard. A People's History of the United States. New York: Harper Perennial. 2001.

Clausewitz, Carl von. On War. Anatol Rapoport, ed. Baltimore: Penguin Books. 1968.

Heidegger, Martin. Basic Writings: Second Edition. Revised and Expanded, ed. David Farrell Krell. New York: Harper Collins, 1993.

Ehrenreich, Barbara. Blood Rites: Origins and History of the Passions of War. New York: Metropolitan Books, Henry Holt and Company. 1997.

Lewin, Leonard C. (& Victor Navasky). Report From Iron Mountain on the Possibility and Desirability of Peace. New York: Delta Books. 1967.

Caesar, Julius. The Conquest of Gaul. Introduction and revisions by Jane F. Gardner. New York: Penguin Putnam. 1982.

Trivers, Robert L. Social Evolution. Benjamin/Cummings, Menlo Park, CA. 1985.

Bodley, John H. Cultural Anthropology: Tribes, States, and the Global System. Mountain View, California: Mayfield Publishing Company. 1997.

Chapter Notes: ANTHROPOLOGY
(All notes are in general order of appearance in the text. All sources are used reference the whole work unless otherwise noted).

Anderson, Benedict. Imagined Communities: Reflections on the Origin and Spread of Nationalism. Revised Edition ed. London and New York: Verso. 1991.

Carr, Edward H. What Is History? The George Macaulay Trevelyan Lectures Delivered at the University of Cambridge, January-March 1961. New York: Vintage Books, A Division of Random House. 1961.

Geertz, Clifford. The Interpretation of Cultures; Selected Essays. New York: Basic Books, 1973.

Kaplan, David and R. A. Manners. Culture Theory. Prospect Heights, Illinois: Waveland Press, 1972.

Feder K.L. and Park M.A. Human Antiquity: An Introduction to Physical Anthropology and Archaeology. Mountain View, California: Mayfield Publishing, 1989. 442-444.

Benedict, Ruth. Patterns of Culture. Boston: Houghton Mifflin, 1961. 12-13.

Peggy McIntosh is associate director of the Wellesley Collage Center for Research on Women. This essay is excerpted from Working Paper 189. "White Privilege and Male Privilege: A Personal Account of Coming To See Correspondences through Work in Women's Studies" (1988), by Peggy McIntosh; available for $4.00 from the Wellesley College Center for Research on Women, Wellesley MA 02181 The working paper contains a longer list of privileges.

Moore, Michael. Dude, Where's My Country? New York: Warner Books. 2003.

Darwin, Charles. The Descent of Man and Selection in Relation to Sex. New York: Appleton and Co. 1883.

Bodley, John H. Cultural Anthropology: Tribes, States, and the Global System. Mountain View, California: Mayfield Publishing Company. 1997. 469.

Ehrlich, Paul R. Human Natures: Genes, Cultures, and the Human Prospect. Washington, D.C.: Island Press/Shearwater Books. 2000.

French, Shannon. The Code of the Warrior: Exploring Warrior Values Past and Present. New York: Rowman & Littlefield Publishers, Inc. 2003.

Kaplan, David and R. A. Manners. Culture Theory. Prospect Heights, Illinois: Waveland Press, 1972. 22-24.

Richards, Howard. Letters from Quebec: a Philosophy for Peace and Justice. San Francisco and London: International Scholars Press, 1994.

Gibson, James William. Warrior Dreams Paramilitary Culture in Post-Vietnam America. New York: Hill and Wang. 1994.

Hedges, Chris. War Is A Force That Gives Us Meaning. New York: Public Affairs, a member of the Perseus Books Group. 2002.

Taylor, Frederick W. The Scientific Principles of Management. New York: Harper and Row. 1911.

Lewin, Leonard C. (& Victor Navasky). Report From Iron Mountain on the Possibility and Desirability of Peace. New York: Delta Books. 1967.

Burke, James. Connections. Boston: Little, Brown & Company. 1978. V. 10.

War in the Age of Technology: The Myriad Faces of Modern Armed Conflict. Geoffrey Jensen and Andrew Wiest, ed. Part of World Of War. Dennis Showalter, General Editor. New York: New York University Press. 2001.

Rieber, Robert W. (ed.), The Psychology of War and Peace; the Image of the Enemy. New York: Plenum Press, 1991.

Davis, Mike. City of Quartz : Excavating the Future in Los Angeles. New York: Knopf. 1992.

Diamond, Jared. Guns, Germs and Steel: The Fates of Human Societies. New York: Norton, 1997.

Clinician's Research Digest. July, 2004, page 5. Author not accompanying article.

Grossman, Dave, On Killing: The Psychological Cost of Learning to Kill in War and Society. New York: Little, Brown and Co, 1995.

Arntz, William, Betsy Chasse, and Mark Vicente writers, producers and directors of What the Bleep Do We Know? Documentary/Drama. A Captive Light Industries, Lord of the Winds Film. 2004.

Capra, Fritjof. The Tao of Physics. Boston: Shambhala. 1991. Introduction.

Kissinger, Henry. A World Restored: Metternich, Castlereagh and the Problems of Peace 1812-22. Boston: Houghton Mifflin, 1957. (Kissinger's doctoral dissertation.)

Zinn, Howard. A People's History of the United States. New York: Harper Perennial. 2001.

Funston, Frederick. Memories of Two Wars: Cuban and Philippine Experiences. New York: Charles Scribners Sons, 1914.

Twain, Mark. Following the Equator and Anti-Imperialist Essays, ed. Shelley
Fisher Fishkin. New York: Oxford Univ. Press, 1996.

Bø, Olav. "Hólmganga and Einvigi: Scandinavian Forms of the Duel." Medieval Scandinavia 2 (1969). 132-148.

Clausewitz, Carl von. On War. Anatol Rapoport, ed. Baltimore: Penguin Books. 1968. 101.
Grossman, Dave, On Killing: The Psychological Cost of Learning to Kill in War and Society. New York: Little, Brown and Co, 1995.

Peters, Ralph. Fighting for the Future: Will America Triumph? Mechanicsburg, Pennsylvania: Stackpole Books. 1999.

Yamamoto, Tsunetomo. Hagakure, The Book of the Samurai, Translated by William Scott Wilson, Kondansha International Ltd., 1979.

Wilson, E.O. Sociobiology: The New Synthesis. Cambridge, Mass.: Harvard University Press. 1975.

Toynbee, Arnold J. War and Civilization. New York: Oxford University Press. 1950. Chap. VIII, paragraph #1.

Gould, Stephen Jay, "Evolution as Fact and Theory," May 1981; from Hen's Teeth and Horse's Toes, New York: W. W. Norton & Company, 1994. 253-262.

Goodall, Jane. Innocent Killers. (with H. van Lawick). Boston: Houghton Mifflin. 1971.

-----------------. Brutal Kinship. (with Michael Nichols). New York: Aperture Foundation. 1999.

Watts, David. "Nature's Deep Jungle: The Beast Within." PBS.org. 2005. In this PBS documentary, David Watts explores and interprets chimpanzee behaviors. The systematic and regular organized murders carried out by chimpanzees appears to have little to do with actual hunting for food, and instead seems focused on social relationships such as dominance, and territorial relationships. Brian Ferguson critiques Watts' interpretations by highlighting the ecological disturbances and imbalances caused by human disruption of the chimpanzee environment. To Ferguson, these imbalances created additional social pressures that prompted organized ritual violence.

Stone, Merlin. When God Was A Woman. New York: Barnes and Noble. 1976.

Ehrenreich, Barbara. Blood Rites: Origins and History of the Passions of War. New York: Metropolitan Books, Henry Holt and Company. 1997.

Trivers, Robert L. Social Evolution. Benjamin/Cummings, Menlo Park, CA. 1985.

Wertham, Frederic, MD. A Sign for Cain: An Exploration of Human Violence. New York: The Macmillan Company. 1966.

Screening Violence. Stephen Prince, ed. New Brunswick, New Jersey: Rutgers University Press. 2000.

Coles, John. Archaeology by Experiment. New York: Charles Scribner's Sons. 1973. 111-134.

Wolpoff, Milford H., et al. 2001. "Modern Human Ancestry at the Peripheries: A Test of the Replacement Theory." Science 291:293-297.

Heidegger, Martin. Basic Writings: Second Edition. Revised and Expanded, ed. David Farrell Krell. New York: Harper Collins, 1993.

Ardrey, Robert. The Social Contract: A Personal Inquiry into the Evolutionary Sources of Order and Disorder. New York: Atheneum, 1970.

Ferguson, R. Brian, "The Birth of War." Natural History. Peter Brown, ed. New York: Natural History Magazine, Inc., July/August, 2003.

Lewin, Roger. Bones of Contention. New York: Touchstone (Simon &Schuster). 1987.

Chapter Notes: PREHISTORY
(All notes are in general order of appearance in the text. All sources are used reference the whole work unless otherwise noted).

Diamond, Jared. Guns, Germs and Steel: The Fates of Human Societies. New York: Norton, 1997.

Ehrlich, Paul R. Human Natures: Genes, Cultures, and the Human Prospect. Washington, D.C.: Island Press/Shearwater Books. 2000.

Toynbee, Arnold J. War and Civilization. New York: Oxford University Press. 1950.

Bodley, John H. Cultural Anthropology: Tribes, States, and the Global System. Mountain View, California: Mayfield Publishing Company. 1997.

Geertz, Clifford. The Interpretation of Cultures; Selected Essays. New York: Basic Books, 1973.

Stone, Merlin. When God Was A Woman. New York: Barnes and Noble. 1976.

Marx, Karl. Capital. Great Books of the Western World edition, Chicago: Encyclopedia Brittanica, 1952, vol. 50.

Giddens, Anthony. Capitalism and Modern Social Theory; an Analysis of the Writings of Marx, Durkheim, and Max Weber. Cambridge UK: Cambridge University Press, 1971.

Ardrey, Robert. The Social Contract: A Personal Inquiry into the Evolutionary Sources of Order and Disorder. New York: Atheneum, 1970.

Ferguson, R. Brian, "The Birth of War." Natural History. Peter Brown, ed. New York: Natural History Magazine, Inc., July/August, 2003.

Feder K.L. and Park M.A. Human Antiquity: An Introduction to Physical Anthropology and Archaeology. Mountain View, California: Mayfield Publishing, 1989.

Brummett, Palmira, et al. Civilization Past and Present. New York: Pearson Longman. 2006.

Upshur, Jiu-Hwa, et al. World History. Belmont, California: Thomson Wadsworth. 2005.

Breisach, Ernst. Historiography: Ancient, Medieval and Modern. 2nd edition. Chicago: University of Chicago Press, 1994.

Campbell. Joseph. The Hero with a Thousand Faces. Princeton, N.J..: Princeton University Press. 1990.

Forty, Jo. Mythology. New York: PRC Publishing, LTD. 1999.

Bonaparte, Napoleon. The Military Maxims of Napoleon. Translated by George C. D'Aguilar with introduction and commentary by David G. Chandler. New York: Macmillan Publishing Company. 1988.

Barraclough, Geoffrey, ed., The Times Concise Atlas of World History. Maplewood, New Jersey: Hammond Inc., 1982.

Plutarch. The Rise and Fall of Athens: Nine Greek Lives. Ian Scott-Kilvert, tr. New York: Penguin Books. 1960.

Barrows, David P. A Decade of American Government in the Philippines. Yonkers, New York: World Book Company, 1914.

Zinn, Howard. A People's History of the United States. New York: Harper Perennial. 2001.

Alfonso, Oscar M. Theodore Roosevelt and the Philippines, 1897 - 1909. Quezon City, Philippine Islands: University of the Philippines Press, 1970.

Blount, James H. The Occupation of the Philippines, 1898 - 1912. New York: Oriole Editions Incorporated, 1973.

Boot, Max. The Savage Wars of Peace: Small Wars and the Rise of American Power. New York: Basic Books, A Member of the Perseus Books Group. 2002.

Pomeroy, William J. American Neo-Colonialism: Its Emergence in the Philippines and Asia. New York: International Publishers, 1970.

Pratt, Julius W. "Ideology of American Expansionism." in Essays in Honor of William E. Dodd, ed. Avery O. Craven, 10-19. Chicago: University of Chicago Press, 1935.

Hofstadter, Richard. "Manifest Destiny and the Philippines." in America in Crisis, ed. Daniel Aaron, 170-81. New York: Alfred A. Knopf, Inc., 1952.

Merk, Frederick. Manifest Destiny and Mission in American History, A Reinterpretation. New York: Alfred A. Knopf, Inc., 1963.

Current, Richard N., et al. American History: A Survey. vol. 2, 1865 to the present. New York: Alfred A. Knopf, Inc., 1987.

Haleem, Harfiyah Abdel et al. The Crescent and the Cross. London: Macmillan, 1998

Keller, Werner. The Bible as History. William Neil, tr. New York: William Morrow and Company, Inc. 1981.

Hourani, Albert. A History of the Arab Peoples. New York: MJF Books. 1991.

Chapter Notes: HISTORY

(All notes are in general order of appearance in the text. All sources are used reference the whole work unless otherwise noted).

Bourne, Randolph. "War is the Health of the State," First draft of an essay, "The State", that was left unfinished by Bourne at the time of his death, 1918. It is now in the Bourne MSS, Columbia University Libraries.

Clausewitz, Carl von. On War. Anatol Rapoport, ed. Baltimore: Penguin Books. 1968.

Geertz, Clifford. The Interpretation of Cultures; Selected Essays. New York: Basic Books, 1973.

Carr, Edward H. What Is History? The George Macaulay Trevelyan Lectures Delivered at the University of Cambridge, January-March 1961. New York: Vintage Books, A Division of Random House. 1961.

Bø, Olav. "Hólmganga and Einvigi: Scandinavian Forms of the Duel." Medieval Scandinavia 2 (1969). 132-148.

Tacitus, P. Cornelius. Germania. In: Medieval Sourcebook: Tacitus's Germania in Latin. Paul Halsall, editor. ORB: The Online Reference Book for Medieval Studies. 1998. (accessed 8/99).

Grant, Michael. Gladiators. New York: Barnes and Noble Books. 1967.

Burton, Richard F. The Book of the Sword. New York: Dover Publications, Inc.1987.

Hedges, Chris. War Is A Force That Gives Us Meaning. New York: Public Affairs, a member of the Perseus Books Group. 2002.

DeLaet, Debra. The Global Struggle for Human Rights: Universal Principles in World Politics. Belmont, California: Thomson Wadsworth. 2006.

Ehrenreich, Barbara. Blood Rites: Origins and History of the Passions of War. New York: Metropolitan Books, Henry Holt and Company. 1997.

Stone, Merlin. When God Was A Woman. New York: Barnes and Noble. 1976.

Keegan, John. A History of Warfare. New York: Vintage Press. 1994.

French, Shannon. The Code of the Warrior: Exploring Warrior Values Past and Present. New York: Rowman & Littlefield Publishers, Inc. 2003.

Toynbee, Arnold J. War and Civilization. New York: Oxford University Press. 1950.

DuBois, W.E.B., The African Roots of War. New York: The Atlantic. 1915.

Bodley, John H. Cultural Anthropology: Tribes, States, and the Global System. Mountain View, California: Mayfield Publishing Company. 1997.

Brummett, Palmira, et al. Civilization Past and Present. New York: Pearson Longman. 2006.

Guevara, Ernesto (Che). Che Guevara on Guerrilla Warfare. New York: Frederick A Praeger, Books that Matter. 1961.

Carson, Clayborne, E. J. Lapsansky-Werner, G. B. Nash. African American Lives: The Struggle for Freedom. New York: Pearson Longman. 2005.

Mackey, Robert R. The UnCivil War: Irregular Warfare in the Upper South, 1861–1865. Norman, Okla.: University of Oklahoma Press. 2004.

Zinn, Howard. A People's History of the United States. New York: Harper Perennial. 2001.

Upshur, Jiu-Hwa, et al. World History. Belmont, California: Thomson Wadsworth. 2005.

Zinn, Howard. Terrorism and War. Canada: Seven Stories. 2002.

Kagan, Donald. On the Origins of War and the Preservation of Peace. New York: Random House. 1996.

Haleem, Harfiyah Abdel et al. The Crescent and the Cross. London: Macmillan, 1998

Keller, Werner. The Bible as History. William Neil, tr. New York: William Morrow and Company, Inc. 1981.

Hourani, Albert. A History of the Arab Peoples. New York: MJF Books. 1991. 22-25, 66, 151.

Twain, Mark. Mark Twain on the Damned Human Race, ed. Janet Smith. New York: Hill and Wang, 1962.

Mayer, H.E. The Crusades. New York: Oxford University Press. 2nd Edition. 1988.

Tuchman, Barbara W. A Distant Mirror: The Calamitous 14th Century. New York: Ballantine Books. 1978. 9, 49-86.

Turnbull, Stephen. The Lone Samurai and the Martial Arts. London, England: Arms and Armour Press. 1990.

Shakespeare, William. Henry V. England. 1599. Film interpretation written by Kenneth Branaugh. 1989.

The Constitution of the United States. Washington: Government Printing Office, 1787.

Reves, Emery. Anatomy of Peace, Random House, Inc. 1945.

Anderson, Benedict. Imagined Communities: Reflections on the Origin and Spread of Nationalism. Revised Edition ed. London

297

and New York: Verso. 1991.

Carneiro: 1981. As discussed in several places in Paul Ehrlich, Human Natures.

Ehrlich: 239-40.

Pomeroy, William J. American Neo-Colonialism: Its Emergence in the Philippines and Asia. New York: International Publishers, 1970.

Pratt, Julius W. "Ideology of American Expansionism." in Essays in Honor of William E. Dodd, ed. Avery O. Craven, 10-19. Chicago: University of Chicago Press, 1935.

Boot, Max. The Savage Wars of Peace: Small Wars and the Rise of American Power. New York: Basic Books, A Member of the Perseus Books Group. 2002.

Twain, Mark. Following the Equator and Anti-Imperialist Essays, ed. Shelley Fisher Fishkin. New York: Oxford Univ. Press, 1996.

Welch, Richard E. Jr. Response to Imperialism: The United States and the Philippine-American War, 1899 - 1902. Chapel Hill, North Carolina: University of North Carolina Press, 1979.

Salamanca, Bonifacio S. The Filipino Reaction to American Rule: 1901 - 1913. np: The Shoe String Press, 1968.

Freire, Paulo. The Pedagogy of the Oppressed . translated by Myra Ramos. New York: Continuum, 1998.

Hofstadter, Richard. "Manifest Destiny and the Philippines." in America in Crisis, ed. Daniel Aaron, 170-81. New York: Alfred A. Knopf, Inc., 1952.

Merk, Frederick. Manifest Destiny and Mission in American History, A Reinterpretation. New York: Alfred A. Knopf, Inc., 1963.

Colley, David P. Blood for Dignity: the Story of the First Integrated Combat Unit in the U.S. Army. New York: St. Martin's

Griffin. 2003.

Cray, Ed. Chief Justice: A Biography of Earl Warren. New York: Simon and Schuster, 1997.

Knoll, Tricia. Becoming Americans: Asian Sojourners, Immigrants, and Refugees in the Western United States. Portland, Oregon: Coast To Coast Books, 1982.

Rieber, Robert W. (ed.), The Psychology of War and Peace; the Image of the Enemy. New York: Plenum Press, 1991.

Cray, Ed. Chief Justice: A Biography of Earl Warren. New York: Simon and Schuster, 1997.

Takaki, Ronald. A Different Mirror: A History of Multicultural America. Boston: Little, Brown and Company, 1993.

McNamara, Robert Strange. "Fog of War." And Errol Morris.

Benedict, Ruth. The Chrysanthemum and the Sword: Patterns of Japanese Culture. New York: Meridian. 1946.

Giddens, Anthony. Capitalism and Modern Social Theory; an Analysis of the Writings of Marx, Durkheim, and Max Weber. Cambridge UK: Cambridge University Press, 1971.

Pyl'cyn, Alexander V. Penalty Strike: The Memoirs of a Red Army Penal Company Commander 1943-45 (Soviet Memories of War vol. 1). [unpublished] Stock Code: HEL0079. July 2006 Series: Soviet Memories of War # 1 1-874622-63-9. Helion & Company, Limited: Solihull, West Midlands, England. 2006.

Turner, Frederick Jackson. The Significance of the Frontier in American History. Ann Arbor: University Microfilms, Incorporated, 1966.

Current, Richard N., et al. American History: A Survey. vol. 2, 1865 to the present. New York: Alfred A. Knopf, Inc., 1987.

Neier, Aryeh. War Crimes: Brutality, Genocide, Terror, and the

Struggle for Justice. New York: Times Books.1998.

Freud, Sigmund "Why War?" in Collected Works of Sigmund Freud, volume XXII. London: The Hogarth Press, 1964.

Bloomfield, Lincoln. International Military Forces: The Question of Peacekeeping in an Armed and Disarmed World. Boston: Little, Brown, 1964.

------------ The Power to Keep Peace: Today in a World Without War. Berkeley, Ca.. World Without War Council Publications, 1971.

Townshend, Charles, ed. The Oxford Illustrated History of Modern War. New York: Oxford University Press. 1997.

White, Matthew. Historical Atlas of the Twentieth Century, 2003. http://users.erols.com/mwhite28/20centry.htm

Hanson, Victor Davis. Carnage and Culture: Landmark Battles in the Rise of Western Power. New York: Anchor, a Division of Random House. 2002.

Zezima, Michael. Saving Private Power: The Hidden History of "The Good War." New York: Soft Skull Press. 2000.

Woodward, Bob. Veil: The Secret Wars of the CIA, 1981-1987. New York: Pocket Books, A Division of Simon & Schuster, Inc. 1987.

Gibson, James William. Warrior Dreams Paramilitary Culture in Post-Vietnam America. New York: Hill and Wang. 1994.

"Tony Poe." http://www.atimes.com/atimes/Southeast_Asia/EG08Ae02.html 2005.

"Osama Bin Ladin." Frontline:2004.

Smith, Adam. An Inquiry into the Nature and Causes of the Wealth of Nations. London: Methuen and Co., Ltd., ed. Edwin Cannan, 1904. Fifth edition. (First published 1776).

Lewin, Leonard C. (& Victor Navasky). Report From Iron Mountain on the Possibility and Desirability of Peace. New York: Delta Books. 1967.

Dunnigan, James F, and Austin Bay. A Quick & Dirty Guide to War: Briefings on Present and Potential Wars. New York: William Morrow and Company, Inc.1991.

Peters, Ralph. Fighting for the Future: Will America Triumph? Mechanicsburg, Pennsylvania: Stackpole Books. 1999.

Moore, Michael. Dude, Where's My Country? New York: Warner Books. 2003.

Chapter Notes: WHAT IS REALLY GOING ON
(All notes are in general order of appearance in the text. All sources are used reference the whole work unless otherwise noted).

Peters, Ralph. Fighting for the Future: Will America Triumph? Mechanicsburg, Pennsylvania: Stackpole Books. 1999.

Brierly, James. The Law of Nations: an Introduction to the International Law of Peace. Oxford: Clarendon Press, 1963.

Thucydides. History of the Peloponnesian War. Betty Radice, ed., New York: Penguin Books, 1972.

Plutarch. The Rise and Fall of Athens: Nine Greek Lives. Ian Scott-Kilvert, tr. New York: Penguin Books. 1960.

Xenophon. Anabasis. Translated by Carleton L. Brownson, Revised by John Dillery. Cambridge, Massachusetts: Harvard University Press. 1998.

Toynbee, Arnold J. War and Civilization. New York: Oxford University Press. 1950.

Brzezinski, Zbigniew. Out of Control: Global Turmoil on the Eve of the Twenty-first Century . New York: Charles Scribner's Sons.

1993.

Anderson, Benedict. Imagined Communities: Reflections on the Origin and Spread of Nationalism. Revised Edition ed. London and New York: Verso. 1991.

Appleby, Joyce, Lynn Hunt, and Margaret Jacob. Telling the Truth About History. New York: W.W. Norton & Company. 1994.

Ardrey, Robert. The Social Contract: A Personal Inquiry into the Evolutionary Sources of Order and Disorder. New York: Atheneum, 1970.

Arntz, William, Betsy Chasse, and Mark Vicente writers, producers and directors of What the Bleep Do We Know? Documentary/Drama. A Captive Light Industries, Lord of the Winds Film. 2004.

Bloomfield, Lincoln. International Military Forces: The Question of Peacekeeping in an Armed and Disarmed World. Boston: Little, Brown, 1964.

------------ The Power to Keep Peace: Today in a World Without War. Berkeley: World Without War Council Publications, 1971.

White, Matthew. Historical Atlas of the Twentieth Century, 2003. http://users.erols.com/mwhite28/20centry.htm

Brzezinski, Zbigniew. Out of Control: Global Turmoil on the Eve of the Twenty-first Century. New York: Charles Scribner's Sons. 1993.

Moore, Michael. Dude, Where's My Country? New York: Warner Books. 2003.

Morris, Errol. "Fog of War: Eleven Lessons from the Life of Robert S. McNamara." Documentary film. Radical.media, The Globe Department Store, SenArt Films. 2003.

War: Opposing Viewpoints. Tamara L. Roleff, ed. San Diego: Greenhaven Press. 1999.

Tsu, Lao. <u>Tao Te Ching</u> Translated by Jane English and Gia Fu-Feng. New York: Vintage Books, a Division of Random House. 1972.

Dalton, Dennis. <u>Indian Ideas of Freedom: the Political Thought of Swami Vivekenanda, Aurobindo Ghose, Mahatma Gandhi, and Rabindranath Tagore</u>. Gurgaon, Haryana: Academic Press, 1982.

Ehrlich, Paul R. <u>Human Natures: Genes, Cultures, and the Human Prospect</u>. Washington, D.C.: Island Press/Shearwater Books. 2000.

Wright, Quincy. <u>The Causes of War and the Conditions of Peace</u>. London: Longmans, Green and Co., 1935.

------------------- <u>A Study of War</u>. Chicago: University of Chicago Press, 1942.

Grossman, Dave, <u>On Killing: The Psychological Cost of Learning to Kill in War and Society.</u> New York: Little, Brown and Co, 1995.

Rieber, Robert W. (ed.), <u>The Psychology of War and Peace; the Image of the Enemy.</u> New York: Plenum Press, 1991.

Wolff, Robert Paul. <u>In Defense of Anarchism</u>. Berkeley: The University of California Press. 1970.

-------------- <u>Understanding Rawls: A Reconstruction and Critique of A Theory of Justice</u>. Princeton, N.J.: Princeton University Press, 1977.

Reardon, Betty. <u>Sexism and the War System</u>. New York: Teachers College Press, 1985.

DeLaet, Debra. <u>The Global Struggle for Human Rights: Universal Principles in World Politics.</u> Belmont, California: Thomson Wadsworth. 2006.

French, Shannon. <u>The Code of the Warrior: Exploring Warrior Values Past and Present</u>. New York: Rowman & Littlefield Publishers, Inc. 2003.

Early, Gerald. The Culture of Bruising: Essays on Prizefighting, Literature, and Modern American Culture. Hopewell New Jersey: The Ecco Press. 1994.

Trivers, Robert L. Social Evolution. Benjamin/Cummings, Menlo Park, CA. 1985.

Burke, James. Connections. Boston: Little, Brown & Company. 1978.

Smoke, Richard, and Willis Harman. Paths to Peace: Exploring the Feasibility of Sustainable Peace. Boulder, Colorado: Westview Press. 1987.

Chadwick, Alger, "Creating Global Visions for Peace Movements," in Elise Boulding, Clovis Brigagao, Kevin Clements (eds.) Peace Culture and Society. Boulder: Westview Press, 1991.

Clark, Ramsey, and others. Challenge to Genocide: Let Iraq Live. New York: International Action Center. 1998.

------------------ et al. NATO in the Balkans. New York: International Action Center.1998.

Cox, Gray. The Ways of Peace: a Philosophy of Peace as Action. New York: Paulist Press, 1986.

Current, Richard N., et al. American History: A Survey. vol. 2, 1865 to the present. New York: Alfred A. Knopf, Inc., 1987.

Dunnigan, James F, and Austin Bay. A Quick & Dirty Guide to War: Briefings on Present and Potential Wars. New York: William Morrow and Company, Inc.1991.

Ehrenreich, Barbara. Blood Rites: Origins and History of the Passions of War. New York: Metropolitan Books, Henry Holt and Company. 1997.

Einstein, Albert. "Why War?" in Collected Works of Sigmund Freud, volume XXII. London: The Hogarth Press, 1964.

Forsberg, Randall and Elise Boulding, <u>Abolishing War</u>. Boston: Boston Research Center for the 21st Century, 1998.

Fuller, R. Buckminster. <u>Operating Manual for Spaceship Earth</u>. New York: Simon and Schuster, 1962.

Geertz, Clifford. <u>The Interpretation of Cultures; Selected Essays</u>. New York: Basic Books, 1973.

Gibson, James William. <u>Warrior Dreams Paramilitary Culture in Post-Vietnam America</u>. New York: Hill and Wang. 1994.

Giddens, Anthony. <u>Capitalism and Modern Social Theory; an Analysis of the Writings of Marx, Durkheim, and Max Weber</u>. Cambridge UK: Cambridge University Press, 1971.

Hart, H. L. A. <u>The Concept of Law</u>. Oxford: Clarendon Press, 1961.

Hedges, Chris. <u>War Is A Force That Gives Us Meaning</u>. New York: Public Affairs, a member of the Perseus Books Group. 2002.

Kant, Immanuel. <u>Perpetual Peace</u>. edited by Lewis White Beck. New York: Liberal Arts Press, 1957.

Lewin, Leonard C. <u>Report From Iron Mountain on the Possibility and Desirability of Peace</u>. New York: Delta Books. 1967.

Neier, Aryeh. <u>War Crimes: Brutality, Genocide, Terror, and the Struggle for Justice</u>. New York: Times Books.1998.

Rawls, John. <u>A Theory of Justice</u>. Cambridge, Massachusetts: Belknap Press of Harvard University Press, 1971.

Reves, Emery. <u>Anatomy of Peace</u>, Random House, Inc. 1945.

Richards, Howard. <u>Letters from Quebec: a Philosophy for Peace and Justice</u>. San Francisco and London: International Scholars Press, 1994.

Townshend, Charles, ed. <u>The Oxford Illustrated History of Modern War</u>. New York:Oxford University Press. 1997.

Zinn, Howard. <u>A People's History of the United States</u>. New York: Harper Perennial. 2001.

------------ <u>Terrorism and War</u>. Canada: Seven Stories. 2002.

Press, Eyal. "Human Rights, The Next Step." <u>The Nation</u>. New York: The Nation Institute. December 25, 2000.

Why We War Supplemental:

Articles, Notes, Documents, Charts, and War Quotes

Articles:

Tony Poe

http://www.atimes.com/atimes/Southeast_Asia/EG08Ae02.html
Death of a dirty fighter
By Richard S Ehrlich

BANGKOK - Anthony A "Tony Poe" Poshepny, a decorated former official of the US Central Intelligence Agency (CIA) who collected enemy ears, dropped decapitated human heads from the air on to communists and stuck heads on spikes, was buried on the weekend in California.

Poshepny, who waged failed secret wars for the United States in Indonesia, Tibet and Laos, was often compared to the Marlon Brando character Kurtz in the movie Apocalypse Now.

"The posting of decapitated heads obviously sent a powerful

message - especially to North Vietnamese troops seeking to invade the homelands of the Hmong and Laotian people," Philip Smith, executive director of the Washington-based Center for Public Policy Analysis, said in an e-mail interview after Poshepny's death on June 27.

"He successfully fought terror with terror. He strove to instill courage and respect in the tribal and indigenous forces that he recruited and trained as well as fear in the enemy. In the post-September 11 security environment, fearless men like Tony Poe are what America needs to combat and counter terrorism and the new unconventional threat that America faces from abroad in exotic and uncharted lands," Smith said.

The heavy-drinking, stocky Poshepny suffered shrapnel and other wounds, diabetes and circulatory problems. He died, aged 78, in the San Francisco Veterans Medical Center after a long illness and his funeral was held in nearby Sonoma, California. He is survived by his Lao-American wife Sheng Ly and their children Usanee, Domrongsin, Maria and Catherine.

He twice won a CIA Star - the agency's highest award - from directors Allen Dulles in 1959 and William Colby in 1975, according to a funeral announcement.

Born on September 18, 1924, in Long Beach, California, much of his legacy remains in unmarked graves half a world away, here in Asia.

In 1942, Poshepny joined the US Marine Corps, was wounded on Iwo Jima and received two Purple Hearts, the decoration awarded Death of a dirty fighter
By Richard S Ehrlich

BANGKOK - Anthony A "Tony Poe" Poshepny, a decorated former official of the US Central Intelligence Agency (CIA) who collected enemy ears, dropped decapitated human heads from the air on to communists and stuck heads on spikes, was buried on the weekend in California.

Poshepny, who waged failed secret wars for the United States in Indonesia, Tibet and Laos, was often compared to the Marlon

Brando character Kurtz in the movie Apocalypse Now.

"The posting of decapitated heads obviously sent a powerful message - especially to North Vietnamese troops seeking to invade the homelands of the Hmong and Laotian people," Philip Smith,
executive director of the Washington-based Center for Public Policy Analysis, said in an e-mail interview after Poshepny's death on June 27.

"He successfully fought terror with terror. He strove to instill courage and respect in the tribal and indigenous forces that he recruited and trained as well as fear in the enemy. In the post-September 11 security environment, fearless men like Tony Poe are what America needs to combat and counter terrorism and the new unconventional threat that America faces from abroad in exotic and uncharted lands," Smith said.

The heavy-drinking, stocky Poshepny suffered shrapnel and other wounds, diabetes and circulatory problems. He died, aged 78, in the San Francisco Veterans Medical Center after a long illness and his funeral was held in nearby Sonoma, California. He is survived by his Lao-American wife Sheng Ly and their children Usanee, Domrongsin, Maria and Catherine.

He twice won a CIA Star - the agency's highest award - from directors Allen Dulles in 1959 and William Colby in 1975, according to a funeral announcement.

Born on September 18, 1924, in Long Beach, California, much of his legacy remains in unmarked graves half a world away, here in Asia.

In 1942, Poshepny joined the US Marine Corps, was wounded on Iwo Jima and received two Purple Hearts, the decoration awarded
by the United States to troops injured in action.
A loud, intense, short-tempered patriot, he joined the CIA as a paramilitary officer in 1951.

"Within weeks, he was running sabotage teams behind enemy lines in Korea. He and former CIA colleagues say Mr Poshepny went on to train anti-communists in Thailand, to foment a failed coup in Indonesia and to help organize the escape of the Dalai Lama from Tibet in 1959," the Wall Street Journal reported in 2000.

During the Korean War, Poshepny went to Korea with the CIA and "worked with the Chondogyo church group, a sort of animist-Christian sect that had fled North Korea and were being trained to be sent back across the 38th parallel", according to William M Leary, a University of Georgia history professor. "At the end of the Korean War, Tony was one of eight [CIA] case officers who were sent to Thailand. He remained there for five years, serving under Walt Kuzmak, who ran the CIA cover company Sea Supply," added Leary in an online condolence website honoring Poshepny's life.

In 1958, Poshepny and fellow CIA operative Pat Landry tried, but failed, to spark an uprising among dissident colonels against Indonesia's then-president Sukarno, father of current President Megawati Sukarnoputri. Outgunned and trapped on the Indonesian island of Sumatra, Poshepny and Landry fled to a fishing trawler that took them to a waiting US submarine, according to the book Feet to the Fire by Kenneth Conboy and James Morrison.

At Camp Hale, Colorado, Poshepny helped train Tibet's tall, fierce Khamba tribesmen to be guerrillas and accompanied them to Dhaka, in what was then East Pakistan, from where Tibetans were flown and parachuted into Tibet in a failed attempt to stop China's People's Liberation Army from occupying their homeland.

Poshepny's CIA work in Laos began in 1961 during America's failed "secret war" against communist North Vietnamese who carved a Ho Chi Minh Trail through Laotian territory to attack US forces in South Vietnam. Pathet Lao communist fighters were also the CIA's foe. The Lao communists achieved victory in 1975 and continue to rule the small nation today.

The loquacious, gravel-voiced Poshepny confirmed to me in 2001 that he rewarded his fighters for bringing in enemy ears. He also confirmed that he let his Lao guerrillas erect a human head on a spike and toss pebbles at it, to boost their anti-communist fervor.

Poshepny said he twice hurled human heads from an aircraft on to his enemies in Laos, to terrify them. "We flew in real low, in front of that bastard's house, and I threw the head so it bounced right on his porch and into his front door," Poshepny, laughing, told me at his San Francisco home in 2001.

Based for several years in the rugged highlands of northern Laos where he was seriously wounded three times, Poshepny also grew angry at Washington's attempts to control his activities. So he sent a bag filled with human ears to the US Embassy in Vientiane to prove his guerrillas were killing communists.

The unopened bag arrived on a Friday and sat in the embassy over the weekend. "Human ears contain a lot of water, and they dried up and shriveled in the heat all weekend, so when the embassy secretary opened the bag on Monday morning it was terrible and she got real sick," Poshepny told me. "I really regret doing that to her, because she wasn't to blame at all."

He unabashedly admitted his horrific acts to other journalists, while insisting his motive was to defeat communism. "I used to collect ears," he was quoted as telling Roger Warner in his book Shooting at the Moon, which won Washington's Overseas Press Club award for the best book on foreign affairs.

"I had a big, green, reinforced cellophane bag as you walked up my steps. I'd tell my people to put them in, and then I'd staple them to this 5,000 kip [Laotian currency] notice that this [ear] was paid for already, and put them in the bag and send them to Vientiane with the report.

"Sent them only once or twice, and then the goddamn office girls [in the US Embassy] were sick for a week. Putrid when they opened up the envelope. Some guy in the office, he told me, 'Jeez, don't ever do that again. These goddamn women don't know anything about this shit, and they throw up all over the place.'

"I still collected them, until one day I went out on an inspection trip ... and I saw this little [Lao] kid out there, he's only about 12, and he had no ears. And I asked, 'What the hell happened to this guy?'

"Somebody said, 'Tony, he heard you were paying for ears. His daddy cut his ears off. For the 5,000 kip,'" Poshepny said.

"Oh, that pissed me off," Poshepny told Warner.

"As for dropping human heads on enemy villages, I only did it twice in my career," Poshepny told the Wall Street Journal - once on a Lao ally who had been flirting with the communists. "I caught hell for that."

Some people considered him mentally unsound, "obnoxious", "a drunk" and an insubordinate "knuckle-dragger" while working for the CIA. But Poshepny inspired strong loyalty and admiration among other Americans and Hmong who knew him.

Said Smith of the Center for Public Policy Analysis: "Tony Poe epitomized what the late Theodore Shackley, former CIA station chief in Laos, called the 'Third Option'. America - to avoid the potential twin options of using nuclear or conventional forces to defend its interests - should instead rely on special, elite clandestine forces to recruit, train and arm indigenous, or tribal forces, to project power, protect its interests and counter guerrilla movements, terrorism or other attacks.

"Clearly, Tony Poe symbolized America's decision to exercise its 'Third Option' in Laos."

After retiring in 1975, Poshepny and his Hmong wife lived in northern Thailand until 1992, when they moved to the United States.

He remained close to the Lao community in the San Francisco Bay Area, advising their sons to join the US Marines, financing Laotians in need and petitioning Washington for aid to Laotian veterans.

The Encyclopeadia of the Orient [sic]
http://i-cias.com/e.o/jihad.htm

Jihad
Arabic: jihād

Islamic term, Arabic for 'battle; struggle; holy war for the religion'.

Jihad has two possible definitions: the greater, which is the spiritual struggle of each man, against vice, passion and ignorance. This understanding of jihad has been presented by apologetics of modern times, but is an understanding of the term rarely used by Muslims themselves.

The lesser jihad is simplified to cover holy war against infidels and infidel countries, aiming at spreading Islam. This kind of jihad is described in both the Koran and in the hadiths.

Koran sura 9: Repentance

41 March ye then, light and heavy, and fight [jāhidū] strenuously with your wealth and persons in God's way; that is better for you if ye did but know! Muslim law has divided the world into two entities, dar al-islam, the abode of Islam, and dar al-harb, the abode of war. Battling against the Abode of war was a duty for a Muslim, as this is the only way for the peace of Islam to take the place of the warlike conditions of the infidels' society. Jihad can be both defence, as well as attacking an enemy.

The enemies of Islam are divided into two groups, the Peoples of the book, ahl al-kitab and the pagans, the kafirun. The first group, defined as Jews, Christians, Zoroastrians, and Mandeans need only to submit to an Islamic ruler, and live in peace with other Muslims to end the situation where jihad is imperative.

For the pagans there is a principle fairly similar, but they get less rights under the Muslim ruler than the Peoples of the book. While this group generally can live safely inside a Muslim society, some Muslims have propagated that these should either convert to Islam or face death penalty. In situations where the Muslim rulers mean that war has to be waged against the infidels, they

312

should be allowed sufficient of time to convert before the Muslim army attacks.

Jihad is a duty for every Muslim community, but not necessarily for every individual: it's sufficient that a certain number of the able men perform jihad. The one who dies in the battle against the infidels, becomes a martyr, a shahid, and is guaranteed a place in Paradise as well as certain privileges there.

While offensive jihad, i.e. attacking, is fully permissible in Sunni Islam, it is prohibited for some of the larger groups of Shi'i Islam, which consider only the Imam, now in occultation, as carrying the right to decide to go to war or not.

The Kharijis regarded jihad as the sixth pillar of Islam, a position that other groups of Islam have adhered to earlier.

The Haganah

http://www.jewishvirtuallibrary.org/jsource/History/haganah.html

The underground military organization of the yishuv in Eretz Yisrael from 1920 to 1948. The Arab riots in 1920 and 1921 (q.v., see also Tel Hai) strengthened the view that it was impossible to depend upon the British authorities and that the yishuv needed to create an independent defense force completely free of foreign authority. In June 1920, the Haganah was founded.

During the first nine years of its existence, the Haganah was a loose organization of local defense groups in the large towns and in several of the settlements. The Arab riots in 1929 (q.v.) brought about a complete change in the Haganah's status.

- It became a large organization encompassing nearly all the youth and adults in the settlements, as well as several thousand members from each of the cities.
- It initiated a comprehensive training program for its members, ran officers' training courses;

- Established central arms depots into which a continuous stream of light arms flowed from Europe.
- Simultaneously, the basis was laid for the underground production of arms.

During1936-1939, the years of the Arab Revolt, were the years in which the Haganah matured and developed from a militia into a military body. Although the British administration did not officially recognize the organization, the British Security Forces cooperated with it by establishing civilian militia (see Jewish Settlement Police—J.S.P., and also, Jewish Auxiliary Police—ghafirs). In the summer of 1938 Sepcial Night Squads—S.N.S. were extablished, under the command of Captain Orde Wingate (see also Plugot Sadeh, Yitzhak Sadeh).

During the years of the riots, the Haganah protected the establishment of over 50 new settlements in new area of the country (see Homa Umigdal—Stockade and Watchtower Settlements). As a result of the British government anti-Zionist policy, expressed in the White Paper of 1939, the Haganah supported illegal immigration and organized demonstrations against the British anti-Zionist policy.

With the outbreak of World War II, the Haganah was faced with new problems. It headed a movement of volunteers, from which Jewish units were formed for service in the British army (see Jewish Brigade Group). It also cooperated with British intelligence units and sent its personnel out on various commando missions in the Middle East. Another example of this cooperation was the dropping of 32 Jewish parachutists in 1943-44 behind enemy lines in the Balkans, Hungary and Slovakia. Europe (see also Hannah Szenesh, Enzo Sereni, Havivah Reik).

At the same time, the Haganah further strengthened its independent basis during the war. A systematic program of training was instituted for the youth of the

314

country. In 1941, the Haganah's first mobilized regiment, the Palmach came into being. At the end of the war, when it became clear that the British government had no intention of altering its anti-Zionist policy, the Haganah began an open, organized struggle against British Mandatory rule in the framework of a unified Jewish Resistance Movement, consisting of Haganah, Irgun Zevai Le'umi - Etzel, and Lohamei Herut Yisrael—Lehi.

Haganah branches were established at Jewish D.P. [displaced person] camps in Europe and Haganah members accompanied the "illegal" immigrant boats. In the spring of 1947, David Ben-Gurion took it upon himself to direct the general policy of the Haganah, especially in preparation for impending Arab attack. On May 26 1948, the Provisional Government of Israel decided to transform the Haganah into the regular army of the State, to be called "Zeva Haganah Le-Yisrael"—The Israel Defense Forces.

Source: The Pedagogic Center, The Department for Jewish Zionist Education, The Jewish Agency for Israel, (c) 1997, 1998, 1999, 2000, Director: Dr. Motti Friedman, Webmaster: Esther Carciente

Ian Black and Benny Morris - Israel's Secret Wars: A History of Israel's Intelligence Service
2). Ze'ev Venia Hadari - Second Exodus: The Full Story of Jewish Illegal Immigration to Palestine, 1945-1948
3). Samuel M. Katz - The Night Raiders: Israel's Naval Commandos at War
4). Dan Raviv and Yossi Melman - Every Spy a Prince: The Complete History of Israel's Intelligence Community
5). Stewart Steven - The Spymasters of Israel

Next week - The Israeli Secret Service's Role in the mass Iraqi Jewish Immigration to Israel in the 1950's.

Evolutionary Psychology

http://en.wikipedia.org/wiki/Evolutionary_psychology

Many traits that are selected for can actually hinder survival of the organism. Consider the classic example of the peacock's tail. It is metabolically costly, cumbersome, and essentially a "predator magnet." What the peacock's tail does do is attract mates. Thus, the type of selective process that is involved here is what Darwin called *sexual selection*. Sexual selection can be divided into two types:

- Intersexual selection, which refers to the traits that one sex generally prefers in the other sex, (e.g. the peacock's tail).
- Intrasexual competition, which refers to the competition among members of the same sex for mating access to the opposite sex, (e.g. two stags locking horns).

Ultimately, no matter how much an organism reproduces, that organism dies, and it is genetic information that gets passed on from one generation to the next. Since it is genetic information that matters, there can also be selection pressures that favor the aid in survival and reproduction of an organism's genetic relatives, since they carry partial copies of varying degrees of an organism's genes. Such pressures are called kin selection.
[edit]

Inclusive fitness

Inclusive fitness theory, which was proposed by William D.Hamilton in 1964 as a revision to evolutionary theory, is basically a combination of natural selection, sexual selection, and kin selection. It refers to the sum of an individual's own reproductive success plus the effects the individual's actions have on the reproductive success of their genetic relatives. General evolutionary theory, in its modern form, **is** essentially inclusive fitness theory.

Inclusive fitness theory resolved the issue of how "altruism" evolved. The dominant, pre-Hamiltonian view was that altruism evolved via group selection: the notion that altruism evolved for the benefit of the group. The problem with this was that if one organism in a group incurred any fitness costs on itself for the benefit of others in the group, (i.e. acted "altruistically"), then that organism would reduce its own ability to survive and/or reproduce, therefore reducing its chances of passing on its altruistic traits. Furthermore, the organism that benefitted from that altruistic act and only acted on behalf of its own fitness would increase its own chance of survival and/or reproduction, thus increasing its chances of passing on its "selfish" traits. Inclusive fitness resolved "the problem of altruism" by demonstrating that altruism can evolve via kin selection as expressed in Hamilton's rule:

$$cost < relatedness \times benefit$$

In other words, altruism can evolve as long as the fitness *cost* of the altruistic act on the part of the actor is less than the *degree of genetic relatedness* of the recipient times the fitness *benefit* to that recipient. This perspective reflects what is referred to as the gene-centered view of evolution and demonstrates that group selection is a very weak selective force. However, in recent years group selection has been making a comeback, (albeit a controversial one), as multilevel selection, which posits that evolution can act on many levels of functional organization, (including the "group" level), and not just the "gene" level.

Middle-level evolutionary theories

Middle-level evolutionary theories are theories that encompass broad domains of functioning. They are compatible with general evolutionary theory but not derived from it. Furthermore, they are applicable across species. During the early 1970's, three very important middle-level evolutionary theories were contributed by then Harvard graduate student, Robert Trivers:

- The theory of reciprocal altruism demonstrates that altruism can arise amongst non-kin, as long as the recipient of the altruistic act reciprocates at a later date.

- Parental investment theory refers to the different levels of investment in offspring on the part of each sex. For example, females in any species are defined as the sex with the larger gamete. In humans, females produce approximately one large, metabolically costly egg per month, as opposed to the millions of relatively tiny and metabolically cheap sperm that are produced each day by males. Females are fertile for only a few days each month, while males are fertile every day of the month. Females also have a nine month gestation period, followed by a few years of lactation. Males' obligatory biological investment can be achieved with one copulatory act. Consequently, females in our species have a significantly higher obligatory investment in offspring than males do, (though in some species, the opposite is true.) Because of this difference in parental investment between males and females, males and females face different adaptive problems in the domains of mating and parenting. Therefore, it is predicted that the higher investing sex will be more selective in mating, and the lesser investing sex will be more competitive for access to mates. Thus, sex differences are predicted to exist not because of maleness or femaleness per se, but because of different levels of parental investment.

- The theory of parent-offspring conflict rests on the fact that even though a parent and his/her offspring are 50% genetically related, they are also 50% genetically different. All things being equal, a parent would want to allocate their resources equally amongst their offspring, while each offspring may want a little more for themselves. Furthermore, an offspring may want a little more resources from the parent than the parent is willing to give. In essence, parent-offspring conflict refers to *a conflict of adaptive interests* between parent and offspring.

However, if all things are not equal, a parent may engage in discriminative investment towards one sex or the other, depending on the *parent's* condition. Recall that females are the heavier parental investors in our species. Because of that, females have a better chance of reproducing at least once in comparison to males. Thus, according to the Trivers-Willard hypothesis, parents in good condition are predicted to favor investment in sons, and parents in poor condition are predicted to favor investment in daughters.

Du Pont: was founded in July 1802 as a gun powder mill by Eleuthère Irénée du Pont on Brandywine Creek, near Wilmington, Delaware, USA. DuPont has evolved into the world's second largest chemical company (first is Dow Chemical Company), and in the 20th century led the polymer revolution by developing many highly successful materials such as Vespel, neoprene, nylon, Corian, Lucite, Teflon, Mylar, Kevlar, M5 fiber, Nomex, and Tyvek.

Human Nature
Isn't Inherently Violent

By Alfie Kohn

Peace activists can tell when it's coming. Tipped off by a helpless shrug or a patronizing smile, they brace themselves to hear the phrase once again. "Sure, I'm in favor of stopping the arms race. But aren't you being idealistic? After all, aggression is just" - here it comes - "part of human nature."

Like the animals, -- "red in tooth and claw," as Tennyson put it - human beings are thought to be unavoidably violent creatures. Surveys of adults, undergraduates, and high school students have found that about 60 percent agree with this statement. "Human nature being what it is, there will always be war." It may be part of our society's folk wisdom, but it sets most of the expert's heads to shaking. Take the belief, popularized by Sigmund Freud and animal researcher Konrad Lorenz, that we have within us, naturally and spontaneously, a reservoir of aggressive energy. This force, which builds by itself, must be periodically drained off - by participating in competitive sports, for instance - lest we explode into violence.

It is an appealing model because it is easy to visualize. It is also false. John Paul Scott, professor emeritus at Bowling Green State University in Bowling Green, Ohio, has written: "All of our present data indicate that fighting behavior among higher mammals, including man, originates in external stimulation and that there is no evidence of spontaneous internal stimulation."

Clearly, many individuals - and whole cultures - manage quite well without behaving aggressively, and there is no evidence of the inexorable buildup of pressure this "hydraulic" model would predict.

The theory also predicts that venting aggressive energy should make us less aggressive - an effect known as "catharsis," which follows Aristotle's idea that we can be purged of unpleasant emotions by watching tragic dramas. But one study after another has shown that we are likely to become more violent after watching or participating in such pastimes.

Although the hydraulic model has been discredited, the more general belief in an innate human propensity for violence has not been so easily shaken. Among the arguments one hears is these: Animals are aggressive and we cannot escape the legacy

320

of our evolutionary ancestors; human history is dominated by takes of war and cruelty, and certain areas of the brain and particular hormones are linked to aggression, proving a biological basis for such behavior.

First, we should be cautious in drawing lessons from other species to explain our own behavior, given the mediating force of culture and our capacity for reflection.

But even animals are not as aggressive as some people think - unless the term "aggression" includes killing to eat. Organized group aggression is rare in other species, and the aggression that does exist is typically a function of the environment in which animals find themselves.

Scientists have discovered that altering animals' environment, or the way they are reared, can have a profound impact on the level of aggression found in virtually all species. Furthermore, animals cooperate both within and among species far more than many of us may assume on the basis of watching nature documentaries.

When we turn to human history, we find an alarming number of aggressive behaviors, but we do not find reason to believe the problem is innate. Here are some of the points made by critics of biological determinism:

- Even if a given behavior is universal, we cannot automatically conclude that it is part of our biological nature. All known cultures may produce pottery, but that does not mean that there is a gene for pottery-making.
- Aggression is no where near universal. Many hunter-gatherer societies in particular are entirely peaceful. And the cultures that are "closer to nature" would be expected to be the most warlike if the proclivity for war were really part of that nature. Just the reverse seems to be true.
- While it is indisputable that wars have been fought, the fact that they seem to dominate our history may say more about how history is presented than about what actually happened.
- Many people have claimed that human nature is aggressive after having lumped together a wide range of emotions and behavior under the label of aggression. While cannibalism, for example, is sometimes perceived as aggression, it might represent a religious ritual rather than an expression of hostility.

It is true that the presence of some hormones or the stimulation of certain sections of the brain has been experimentally linked with aggression. But after describing these mechanisms in some detail, K.E. Moyer, a physiologist at Carnegie-Mellon University in Pittsburgh, emphasizes that "aggressive behavior is stimulus-bound. That is, even though the neural system specific to a particular kind of aggression is well activated, the behavior does not occur unless an appropriate target is available (and even then) it can be inhibited."

Regardless of the evolutionary or neurological factors said to underlie aggression, "biological" simply does not mean "unavoidable." The fact that people voluntarily fast or remain celibate shows that even hunger and sex drives can be overridden.

All this concerns the matter of aggressiveness in general. The idea that war in particular is biologically determined is even more far-fetched.

To begin with, we tend to make generalizations about the whole species on the basis of our own experience. "People in a highly warlike society are likely to overestimate the propensity toward war in human nature," says Donald Greenberg, a sociologist at the University of Missouri.

The historical record, according to the Congressional Research Service, shows the United States is one of the most warlike societies on the planet, having intervened militarily around the world more than 150 times since 1850. Within such a society, not surprisingly, the intellectual traditions supporting the view that aggression is more a function of nature than nurture have found a ready audience. The mass media also play a significant role in perpetuating outdated views on violence, according to Jeffrey Goldstein, a psychologist at Temple University.

Because it is relatively easy to describe and makes for a snappier news story, reporters seem to prefer explanations of aggression that invoke biological necessity, he says. An international conference of experts concluded in 1986 that war is not an inevitable part of human nature. When one member tried to convince reporters that this finding was newsworthy, few news organizations in the United States were interested. One reporter told him, "Call us back when you find a gene for war."

Leonard Eron, a psychologist at the University of Illinois in Chicago, observes, "TV teaches people that aggressive behavior is normative, that the world around you is a jungle when it is

322

actually not so." In fact, research at the University of Pennsylvania's Annenberg School of Communications has shown that the more television an individual watches, the more likely he or she is to believe that "most people would take advantage of you if they got the chance."

The belief that violence in unavoidable, while disturbing at first glance, actually holds a curious attraction for some people. It also allows individuals to excuse their own acts of aggression by suggesting that they have little choice.

"In order to justify, accept, and live with war, we have created a psychology that makes it inevitable," says Dr. Bernard Lown, co-chairman of International Physicians for th4e Prevention of Nuclear War, which received the Nobel peace Prize in 1985. "It is a rationalization for accepting war as a system of resolving human conflict."

To understand these explanations for the war-is-inevitable belief is to realize its consequences. Treating any behavior as inevitable sets up a self-fulfilling prophecy: By assuming we are bound to be aggressive, we are more likely to act that way and provide evidence for the assumption. People who believe that humans are naturally aggressive may also be unlikely to oppose particular wars.

The evidence suggests, then, that humans do have a choice with respect to aggression and war. To an extent, such destructiveness is due to the mistaken assumption that we are helpless to control an essentially violent nature.

"We live in a time," says Lown, "when accepting this as inevitable is no longer possible without courting extinction."

From: Detroit Free Press, August 21, 1988

*This reading is from **The Class of Nonviolence**, prepared by Colman McCarthy of the Center for Teaching Peace, 4501 Van Ness Street, NW, Washington, D.C. 20016 202/537-1372*

INNATE AGGRESSION

This short essay challenges the conventional wisdom that humans are naturally aggressive, violent and war-like. It also makes the point that such beliefs are detrimental to most of us, while benefiting the interests of the ruling elites.

"It is not instinct that drives us to commit atrocities, but our culture."

THE FALLACY

"We are born with aggressive instincts. Human nature is violent. War is inevitable."

Many of our ideas about society and how it should be organized are based on this idea. Much of our political, social, religious and scientific thinking starts with the premise that human beings are born-killers. So much a part of our consciousness has this idea become that we rarely question it. In essence it has become a truth—conventional wisdom that carries with it no requirement to examine the facts with a critical eye.

THE REALITY

One way to determine if aggression is an innate human trait is to examine other cultures. If just one culture can be found that values cooperation and nurturing over violence, then we can conclude that aggression is a learned cultural response, not a human instinct.

And in fact a whole spectrum of aggression levels can be found in pre-literate cultures. Some are extremely violent warrior societies where aggression is highly valued. But other cultures are gentle and peaceful, with few instances of violent crime or war.

We are not "hard-wired" like bugs or ducks, where a given stimulus results in a fixed response. Unlike most animals, we have a large cerebral cortex that allows for reasoning, consideration, creativity and culture. The instinct-controlling part of our brain is relatively insignificant in comparison to the cortex, and can be superseded by will and thought. It is this "flexible response" capability that enabled humans to survive and rise above the rest of the animal kingdom. Many anthropologists feel it was our ability to cooperate, not our ability to fight (compete), that was our evolutionary survival trait.

Because of our ability to reflect and consciously choose the values we instill in our children, as a species we can be whatever we want to be. It can almost be said that there is no such thing as human nature, that almost all our traits and tendencies are culturally defined. This is not as obvious as it should be, because most of us are only exposed to one culture (a culture where everyone pretty much thinks and acts the same) and it's easy to get the impression that the way we are is the only way we can be.

It is not instinct that drives us to commit atrocities, but our culture. Culture is a human creation. Our culture was molded by men who crave power and the domination of others.

Usually fallacies are perpetrated because they serve someone's interests. Not surprisingly, the myth that humans are inherently aggressive benefits the same elites who have had the most influence in shaping our culture: rulers, politicians, militarists, lawyers, clergymen, scientists, the wealthy. If human nature is indeed violent and war is inevitable, then we need large strong states with central governments. We need powerful rulers with mighty armies and brutal security forces. We need repressive laws to protect us from each other. We need guidance from our churches on how to keep our destructive instincts under control.

Of course, when we are constantly told that we are born to be killers, we have an excuse to act like killers. Violence becomes part of our culture, so we act violently. The fallacy perpetrates itself, and the irony comes full circle: our belief in the inevitability of human aggression, sold to us by the ruling elites, creates a world that makes ruling elites necessary. 1997

Can A Video Game Lead To Murder?
March 6, 2005

Imagine if the entertainment industry created a video game in which you could decapitate police officers, kill them with a sniper rifle, massacre them with a chainsaw, and set them on fire.

Think anyone would buy such a violent game?

They would, and they have. The game Grand Theft Auto has sold more than 35 million copies, with worldwide sales approaching $2 billion.

Two weeks ago, a multi-million dollar lawsuit was filed in Alabama against the makers and marketers of Grand Theft Auto, claiming that months of playing the game led a teenager to go on a rampage and kill three men, two of them police officers.

Can a video game train someone to kill? **Correspondent Ed Bradley** reports.

Grand Theft Auto is a world governed by the laws of depravity. See a car you like? Steal it. Someone you don't like? Stomp her. A cop in your way? Blow him away.

There are police at every turn, and endless opportunities to take them down. It is 360 degrees of murder and mayhem: slickly produced, technologically brilliant, and exceedingly violent.

326

And now, the game is at the center of a civil lawsuit involving the murders of three men in the small town of Fayette, Ala. They were gunned down by 18-year-old Devin Moore, who had played Grand Theft Auto day and night for months.

Attorney Jack Thompson, a long-time crusader against video-game violence, is bringing the suit. "What we're saying is that Devin Moore was, in effect, trained to do what he did. He was given a murder simulator," says Thompson.

"He bought it as a minor. He played it hundreds of hours, which is primarily a cop-killing game. It's our theory, which we think we can prove to a jury in Alabama, that, but for the video-game training, he would not have done what he did."

Moore's victims were Ace Mealer, a 911 dispatcher; James Crump, a police officer; and Arnold Strickland, another officer who was on patrol in the early morning hours of June 7, 2003, when he brought in Moore on suspicion of stealing a car.

Moore had no criminal history, and was cooperative as Strickland booked him inside the Fayette police station. Then suddenly, inexplicably, Moore snapped.

According to Moore's own statement, he lunged at Officer Arnold Strickland, grabbing his .40-caliber Glock automatic and shot Strickland twice, once in the head. Officer James Crump heard the shots and came running. Moore met him in the hallway, and fired three shots into Crump, one of them in the head.

Moore kept walking down the hallway towards the door of the emergency dispatcher. There, he turned and fired five shots into Ace Mealer. Again, one of those shots was in the head. Along the way, Moore had grabbed a set of car keys. He went out the door to the parking lot, jumped into a police cruiser, and took off. It all took less than a minute, and three men were dead.

"The video game industry gave him a cranial menu that popped up in the blink of an eye, in that police station," says Thompson. "And that menu offered him the split-second decision to kill the officers, shoot them in the head, flee in a police car, just as the game itself trained them to do."

After his capture, Moore is reported to have told police, "Life is like a video game. Everybody's got to die sometime." Moore is awaiting trial in criminal court. A suit filed by the families of two of his victims claims that Moore acted out a scenario found in Grand Theft Auto: The player is a street thug trying to take over the city. In one scenario, the player can enter a police precinct, steal a uniform, free a convict from jail, escape by shooting police, and flee in a squad car.

"I've now got the entire police force after me. So you have to eliminate all resistance," says Nicholas Hamner, a law student at the University of Alabama, who demonstrated Grand Theft Auto for **60 Minutes**. Like millions of gamers, the overwhelming majority, he says he plays it simply for fun.

David Walsh, a child psychologist who's co-authored a study connecting violent video games to physical aggression, says the link can be explained in part by pioneering brain research recently done at the National Institutes of Health -- which shows that the teenage brain is not fully developed.

Does repeated exposure to violent video games have more of an impact on a teenager than it does on an adult?

"It does. And that's largely because the teenage brain is different from the adult brain. The impulse control center of the brain, the part of the brain that enables us to think ahead, consider consequences, manage urges -- that's the part of the brain right behind our forehead called the prefrontal cortex," says Walsh. "That's under construction during the teenage years. In fact, the wiring of that is not completed until the early 20s."

Walsh says this diminished impulse control becomes heightened in a person who has additional risk factors for criminal behavior. Moore had a profoundly troubled upbringing, bouncing back and forth between a broken home and a handful of foster families.

"And so when a young man with a developing brain, already angry, spends hours and hours and hours rehearsing violent acts, and then, and he's put in this situation of emotional stress, there's a likelihood that he will literally go to that familiar pattern that's been wired repeatedly, perhaps thousands and thousands of times," says Walsh.

"You've got probably millions of kids out there playing violent games like Grand Theft Auto and other violent games, who never hurt a fly," says Bradley. "So what does that do to your theory?"

"You know, not every kid that plays a violent video game is gonna turn to violence. And that's because they don't have all of those other risk factors going on," says Walsh. "It's a combination of risk factors, which come together in a tragic outcome."

Arnold Strickland had been a police officer for 25 years when he was murdered. His brother Steve, a Methodist minister, wants the video game industry to pay.

"Why does it have to come to a point to where somebody's life has to be taken before they realize that these games have repercussions to them? Why does it have to be to where my brother's not here anymore," says Steve Strickland. "There's not a day that goes by that I don't think about him."

Strickland, along with Mealer's parents, are suing Moore, as well as Wal-Mart and GameStop, which sold Moore two versions of Grand Theft Auto. Both companies sent us letters insisting they bear no responsibility for Moore's actions, and that the game is played by millions of law-abiding citizens.

Take-Two Interactive, the creator of Grand Theft Auto, and Sony, which makes the device that runs the game, are also being sued. Both declined to talk to *60 Minutes* on camera. Instead, they referred it to Doug Lowenstein, who represents the video game industry.

Lowenstein is not named in the lawsuit, and says he can't comment on it directly. "It's not my job to defend individual titles," says Lowenstein. "My job is to defend the right of people in this industry to create the products that they want to create. That's free expression."

"A police officer we spoke to said, 'Our job is dangerous enough as it is without having our kids growing up playing those games and having the preconceived notions of "let's kill an officer." It's almost like putting a target on us.' Can you see his point?" asks Bradley.

"Look, I have great respect for the law enforcement officers of this country.... I don't think video games inspire people to commit crimes," says Lowenstein. "If people have a criminal mind, it's not because they're getting their ideas from the video games. There's something much more deeply wrong with the individual. And it's not the game that's the problem."

But shouldn't Moore, alone, face the consequences of his decision to kill three men?

"There's plenty of blame to go around. The fact is we think Devin Moore is responsible for what he did," says Thompson. "But we think that the adults who created these games and in effect programmed Devon Moore and assisted him to kill are responsible at least civilly.

Thompson says video game companies had reason to foresee that some of their products would trigger violence, and bolsters his case with claims that the murders in Fayette were not the first thought to be inspired by Grand Theft Auto.

In Oakland, Calif., detectives said the game provoked a street gang accused of robbing and killing six people. In Newport, Tenn., two teenagers told police the game was an influence when they shot at passing cars with a .22 caliber rifle, killing one person. But to date, not a single court case has acknowledged a link between virtual violence and the real thing.

Paul Smith is a First Amendment lawyer who has represented video game companies. "What you have in almost every generation is the new medium that comes along. And it's subject of almost a hysterical attack," says Smith. "If you went back to the 1950s, it's hard to believe now, but comic books were blamed for juvenile delinquency. And I think what you really have here is very much the same phenomenon playing itself out again with a new medium."

Why does he think the courts have ruled against these kinds of lawsuits?

"If you start saying that we're going to sue people because one individual out there read their book or played their game and decided to become a criminal, there is no stopping point," says Smith. "It's a huge new swath of censorship that will be imposed on the media."

Despite its violence, or because of it, the fact is that millions of people like playing Grand Theft Auto. Steve Strickland can't understand why.

"The question I have to ask the manufacturers of them is, 'Why do you make games that target people that are to protect us, police officers, people that we look up to -- people that I respect -- with high admiration,'" says Strickland.

"'Why do you want to market a game that gives people the thoughts, even the thoughts of thinking it's OK to shoot police officers? Why do you wanna do that?'"

Both Wal-Mart and GameStop, where Moore purchased Grand Theft Auto, say they voluntarily card teenagers in an effort to keep violent games from underage kids. But several states are considering laws that would ban the sale of violent games to those under 17.

Women Today
The Trouble with men?

A Review of: Sacred Cows, by Ros Coward, Harper & Collins, and The Betrayal of Modern Man, by Susan Faludi, Chattow & Windus

"UNLESS MEN CHANGE, the collective evidence seems to suggest that they could become economically, socially and biologically redundant". So wrote the social commentator, Dave Cohen, in The Guardian a few years back. Cohen gave a particularly apocalyptic version of a subject which has preoccupied sociologists, commentators and politicians during the 1990s - the crisis of the male.

NATURE's DEEP JUNGLE: THE BEAST WITHIN. PBS.ORG 2005

David P. Watts (Ph.D., Chicago 1983) is a professor of anthropology at Yale University whose research specialty is the behavior and ecology of nonhuman primates. In Panama, he has done fieldwork on the behavior of white-faced capuchin monkeys; in Rwanda, on the behavioral ecology of mountain gorillas; and in Uganda, on the behavioral ecology of chimpanzees. He was also the Director of the Karisoke Research Centre in Rwanda for two years.

In collaboration with Dr. Jeremiah Lwanga and Dr. John Mitani, David has maintained a research project on chimpanzee behavior at Ngogo, in the Kibale National Park in Uganda, since 1995. With more than 70 adult males and females and approximately 150 individuals in total, this community is the largest that has been reported thus far in the wild. Due to the extremely large number of males in this group, the Ngogo chimpanzees hunt often and with an unusual degree of success. The male chimps also frequently patrol the boundary of their territory. This has led to several documented cases of lethal intergroup aggression. David's work has contributed to our understanding of why chimpanzees hunt and share meat, and has provided insight into the intriguing evolution of sharing.

The Evolution of Violence

It turns out human beings aren't so unique after all. Conventional wisdom once held that humans were the only animals that could make and use tools. Then, researchers discovered that some of our closest relatives, such as chimpanzees and some monkeys, made and used tools too.

http://www.pbs.org/wnet/nature/deepjungle/episode3_watts.html - #Now it turns out that chimps and humans have something else in common: the capacity to kill, and not just for food. In the 1970s, primate researchers shocked many people with the news that chimpanzees hunted and killed colobus monkeys. Then came even more stunning news: Chimps killed, and sometimes ate, their own kind too.

Today, many scientists believe the hunts are a form of organized violence that plays an important role in chimp culture. One of the researchers studying these seemingly ritualized hunts is David Watts, a primatologist and anthropologist at Yale University in New Haven, Connecticut, who is featured in NATURE's DEEP JUNGLE: THE BEAST WITHIN. NATURE recently spoke with Watts about his studies.

How did you get involved in studying chimp violence?

I got into it because I am interested in human evolution and how our behaviors evolved. I first worked with mountain gorillas in Rwanda. Then, [at the suggestion of another scientist,] in the summer of 1993 I went for the first time to study chimps at Ngogo, in Uganda's Kibale National Park. It has one of the biggest known chimp communities in the world, now 140 to 150 animals, and they appear to be in the midst of a baby boom! It's possible we will have 19 births this year, so it turns out to be a fantastic place to observe chimp behavior.

What have you seen?

Well, one of the most fascinating behaviors is chimpanzee hunting. It's incredible to follow a group of chimps and watch them catch colobus monkeys and just go to work on them, sharing the meat. We've also observed groups of male chimps going on patrol and being pretty nasty to their neighbors. Since we've been there, we've documented chimps killing at least seven infant chimps, four adult males, and one juvenile chimp. Other times, they have beaten up females pretty badly.

Why do they do it?

It appears to be a regular part of chimp behavior, although it can vary from population to population and habitat to habitat. And like other forms of aggression, they use it tactically. For instance, we might be following a group of males, and they will switch into what we call patrol mode. They'll go silent, which is unusual for chimps, and just look and listen. When they hear neighboring chimps, they respond in a pretty predictable way. If there are just a few chimps in the group, for instance, they'll quietly move back toward the center of their own territory. If it's a big group, they'll respond vocally and listen to the responses. If they decide they are evenly matched, that can lead to major aggression. They'll chase down, surround, and attack rivals. Sometimes they kill them.

Do they eat the meat?

Chimps that are successful hunters may be eating more meat than some Ugandans. But they don't eat adult chimps, although they will cannibalize the infants. [And even when the prey is a monkey], often chimps don't eat much of the meat. That raises the question of whether the hunts have more important social significance. For instance, we've seen active meat sharing among coalitions of the chimpanzees. If one chimp has a big hunk of meat, and another chimp comes along, [the first chimp] may put a piece of meat into their hand. So it may be a way to build relationships.

So, is this chimp warfare?

I don't personally use the term "warfare" with chimps. It's different. Humans are a lot more complicated, and I have to remind myself regularly that the thoughts I'm putting in [a chimp's] mind aren't the ones it's having. But chimp behavior may give us some insight in[to] the evolution of human behavior.

The Seville Statement on Violence

As republished in the *American Psychologist*, October 1990, 45:10, 1167-1168.

Believing that it is our responsibility to address from our particular disciplines the most dangerous and destructive activities of our species, violence and war; recognizing that science is a human cultural product which cannot be definitive or all-encompassing; and gratefully acknowledging the support of the authorities of Seville and representatives of Spanish UNESCO; we, the undersigned scholars from around the world and from relevant sciences, have met and arrived at the following Statement on Violence. In it, we challenge a number of alleged biological findings that have been used, even by some in our disciplines, to justify violence and war. Because the alleged findings have contributed to an atmosphere of pessimism in our time, we submit that the open, considered rejection of these misstatements can contribute significantly to the International Year of Peace.

Misuse of scientific theories and data to justify violence and war is not new but has been made since the advent of modern science. For example, the theory of evolution has been used to justify not only war, but also genocide, colonialism, and suppression of the weak.

We state our position in the form of five propositions.

334

We are aware that there are many other issues about violence and war that could be fruitfully addressed from the standpoint of our disciplines, but we restrict ourselves here to what we consider a most important first step.

It is scientifically incorrect to say that we have inherited a tendency to make war from our animal ancestors. Although fighting occurs widely throughout animal species, only a few cases of destructive intra-species fighting between organized groups have ever been reported among naturally living species, and none of these involve the use of tools designed to be weapons. Normal predatory feeding upon other species cannot be equated with intra-species violence. Warfare is a peculiarly human phenomenon and does not occur in other animals.

The fact that warfare has changed so radically over time indicates that it is a product of culture. Its biological connection is primarily through language which makes possible the coordination of groups, the transmission of technology, and the use of tools. War is biologically possible, but it is not inevitable, as evidenced by its variation in occurrence and nature over time and space. There are cultures which have not engaged in war for centuries, and there are cultures which have engaged in war frequently at some times and not at others.

It is scientifically incorrect to say that war or any other violent behavior is genetically programmed into our human nature. While genes are involved at all levels of nervous system function, they provide a developmental potential that can be actualized only in conjunction with the ecological and social environment. While individuals vary in their predispositions to be affected by their experience, it is the interaction between their genetic endowment and conditions of nurturance that determines their personalities. Except for rare pathologies, the genes do not produce individuals necessarily predisposed to violence. Neither do they determine the opposite. While genes are co-involved in establishing our behavioral capacities, they do not by themselves specify the outcome.

It is scientifically incorrect to say that in the course of human evolution there has been a selection for aggressive behavior more than for other kinds of behavior. In all well studied species, status within the group is achieved by the ability to cooperate and to fulfill social functions relevant to the structure of that group. "Dominance" involves social bondings and affiliations; it is not simply a matter of the possession and use of superior physical power, although it does involve aggressive behaviors. Where genetic selection for aggressive behavior has been artificially instituted in animals, it has rapidly succeeded in producing hyper-aggressive individuals; this indicates that aggression was not maximally selected under natural conditions. When such experimentally-created hyper-aggressive animals are present in a social group, they either disrupt its social structure or are driven out. Violence is neither in our evolutionary legacy nor in our genes.

It is scientifically incorrect to say that humans have a "violent brain." While we do have the neural apparatus to act violently, it is not automatically activated by internal or external stimuli. Like higher primates and unlike other animals, our higher neural processes filter such stimuli before they can be acted upon. How we act is shaped by how we have been conditioned and socialized. There is nothing in our neurophysiology that compels us to react violently.

It is scientifically incorrect to say that war is caused by "instinct" or any single motivation. The emergence of modern warfare has been a journey from the primacy of emotional and motivational factors, sometimes called "instincts," to the primacy of cognitive factors. Modern war involves institutional use of personal characteristics such as obedience, suggestibility, and idealism; social skills such as language; and rational considerations such as cost-calculation, planning, and information processing. The technology of modem war has exaggerated traits associated with violence both in the training of actual combatants and in the preparation of support for war in the general population. As a result of this exaggeration, such traits are often mistaken to be the causes rather than the consequences of the process.

We conclude that biology does not condemn humanity to war, and that humanity can be freed from the bondage of biological pessimism and empowered with confidence to undertake the transformative tasks needed in this International Year of Peace and in the years to come. Although these tasks are mainly institutional and collective, they also rest upon the consciousness of individual participants for whom pessimism and optimism are crucial factors. Just as "wars begin in the minds of men," peace also begins in our minds. The same species who invented war is capable of inventing peace. The responsibility lies with each of us.

Seville, May 16, 1986

SIGNATORIES:

David Adams, Psychology, Wesleyan University,

Middletown, Connecticut, U.S.A..

S.A. Barnett, Ethology, The Australian National University, Canberra, Australia

N.P. Bechtereva, Neurophysiology, Institute for Experimental Medicine of Academy of Medical Sciences of U.S.S.R., Leningrad, U.S.S.R.

Bonnie Frank Carter, Psychology, Albert Einstein Medical Center, Philadelphia, Pennsylvania, U.S.A.

Jose M. Rodriguez Delgado, Neurophysiology, Centro de Estudios Neurobiologicos, Madrid, Spain

Jose Luis Diaz, Ethology, Instituto Mexicano de Psiquiatria, Mexico D.F., Mexico

Andrej Eliasz, Individual Differences Psychology, Polish Academy of Sciences, Warsaw, Poland

Santiago Genovs, Biological Anthropology, Instituto de Estudios Antropologicos, Mexico D.F., Mexico

Benson E. Ginsburg, Behavior Genetics, University of Connecticut, Storrs, Connecticut, U.S.A.

Jo Groebel, Social Psychology, Erziehungswissenschaftliche Hochschule, Landau, Federal Republic of Germany

Samir-Kumar Ghosh, Sociology, Indian Institute of Human Sciences, Calcutta, India

Robert Hinde, Animal Behavior, Cambridge University, United Kingdom

Richard E. Leakey, Physical Anthropology, National Museums of Kenya, Nairobi, Kenya

Omaha M. Malasi, Psychiatry, Kuwait University, Kuwait

Martin Ramirz, Psychobiology, Universidad de Sevilla, Spain

Federico Mayor Zaragoza, Biochemistry, Universidad Autonoma, Madrid, Spain

Diana L Mendoza, Ethology, Universidad de Sevilla, Spain

Ashis Nandy, Political Psychology, Center for the Study of Developing Societies, Delhi, India
John Paul Scott, Animal Behavior, Bowling Green State University, Bowling Green, Ohio, U.S.A.
Riitta Wahlstrom, Psychology, University of Jyvaskyla, Finland

Teaching Against Stereotypes:
The Seville Statement on Violence
by Christopher Renner (University of Naples, Italy)

The Seville Statement on Violence was drafted by an international committee in 1986. Its purpose is to dispel the widespread belief that human beings are inevitably disposed to war as a result of innate, biologically determined aggressive traits. UNESCO adopted the Statement in 1989 and the findings have been published in journals around the world. Although some view the statement as purely scientific, it also has an important impact on education.

The statement clearly indicates that peace is possible and that wars and violence can be ended. It describes five propositions that underline the incorrectness of commonly held stereotypes that have for centuries doomed the human population to war and aggression.

1. War is not an animal characteristic. Animals do not "make war", and humans are not just like animals. We have reason, and human culture can change as a result. A culture that is war-based in one century can change and live in peace in the following one.

2. It is scientifically incorrect to say that war is part of human nature. Even though the genes transmitted by our parents influence the way we act, arguments stating that war is part of human nature cannot prove anything. This is because human culture gives us the ability to shape and change our natures from one generation to another. It is also true that the social conditioning of the culture in which we grow up influences us and that we can take responsibility

for our own actions.

3. There is no scientific evidence that violent behavior patterns produce a better standard of living, nor do violent people produce more offspring. On the contrary, it can be proved that people who learn to work well with each other produce more and enrich culture more than those who do not. This challenges the notion that might makes right and that only the strong survive.

4. Violence is not a result of our brains. Our brains are part of our bodies, as are hands and legs. All parts can be used for violence or cooperation. It depends on what we want. The brain is the physical basis of our intelligence and enables us to think. The brain has a great capacity for learning and the human race can invent new ways of doing things.

5. Violence is not caused by instinct. Today, the vast majority of behavioral scientists do not use the concept instinct because no part of our behavior is so determined that it cannot be changed through education and learning. Of course, we all have emotions and motivations that can be expressed through violence in terms of war, hate or anger, but we are each responsible for the way we express them. In modern wars, as the Gulf War demonstrated, the decisions of generals are not usually emotional. They are, instead, doing their job as they have been trained. Likewise, soldiers are trained for war and people trained to support war. This training is a teaching process in which people are taught to hate and fear the enemy. The most important question is why they are trained that way in the first place. The Seville Statement emphasizes that we are not condemned to violence by our biology. It is possible to end war and the suffering it causes. We cannot do it alone; we can only change these stereotypes by working together. Most important, we must believe that we can change. "Just as wars begin in the minds of men, peace also begins in our minds." It is up to each of us to do our part.

The Seville Statement provides language teachers with the opportunity to address violence and counter the idea that war is inevitable. It provides us with tools to create value discussions on which peace can be constructed. Most young people believe in the ideals of respect and understanding for all peoples and cultures.

Unfortunately, these ideals are not encouraged and supported by the institutions that most directly affect young people's lives: the schools and the mass media. Young people hunger for a vision of the future that is optimistic and not darkened by war. We can begin to give them this vision. King, Gandhi, Freud, Mead and Einstein are all role models young people should be encouraged to follow. Simply having their photos in a classroom and reading their writings in class gives students insights and hope. The Seville Statement can help people develop a global vision and solidarity with people throughout the world. It shows how enemy images are artificial constructions used to manipulate emotions and not a human trait.

For more information on the Seville Statement, contact a UNESCO office near you or write to David Adams, Director, Culture of Peace Action Program, UNESCO, 1 rue Miollis, 75015 Paris, France.

Notes:

The Birth of War

Ferguson, R. Brian, "The Birth of War" page 28 in Natural History. Peter Brown, ed. New York: Natural History Magazine, Inc., July/August, 2003.

Concluding that warfare has not always been the human condition, Ferguson begins by screening data that may challenge his view. Napoleon A. Chagnon's Yanomamo: The Fierce People had been a staple in the study of organized human conflict. In the 1968 book, Chagnon presented warfare as central to the human condition well prior to what we call civilization. Marvin Harris produced work in 1974 that placed population pressures at the root of Yanomami warfare. But this ecological approach failed to explain war because resources of the natural environment are not scarce or limited. (If we make analogy to other Native Indigenous American groups, such as the Indians of pre-contact California, this environmental balance is wholly plausible. Indians of California found that their food resource base was so plentiful that inter and intra tribal warfare was rare [Kroeber,

Heizer] need to be added to bib.). Ferguson's 1995 book: Yanomami Warfare: A Political History, showed that the Yanomami war was not over natural resources such as food, or human resources like women, but over social resources – outside resources of European manufacture like steel knives, pots, and other goods. In 1996, a new pessimism emerged with works like War Before Civilization, by Lawrence H. Keeley. This archaeological review assembled the most violent evidence from prehistory to support the idea that war is just a natural part of what people do – of who we are. Harvard archaeologist Steven A. LeBlanc asserted that wherever you find people (in the archaeological record) you find warfare. In the book written with Katherine Register, LeBlanc compiled impressive evidence of pre-historic violence. In Constant Battles: The myth of the Peaceful, Noble Savage, signs of war included defensive skeletal fractures, mass burials, missing skulls, trophy skulls, bone-embedded projectile points, paintings, and specialized weapons. Site 117 from the Nile valley is an ancient graveyard of 59 skeletons. Of the 59, twenty-four were found in close association with projectile points. The inference is that these were victims of social patterns of organized violence. Site 117 is 12,000 to 14,000 years old. Rock paintings from Australia dated at 10,000 years ago show duels. Other archaeological signs such as defensive settlement patterns strongly suggest the type of systematic organization around war that also had implications for other aspects of the distribution of wealth and power within early human societies. Though some walled settlements (Jericho) seem to have been walled initially for flood control, the bulk of such architecture dating from 6000+ years ago are structured for military defense. Although Ferguson found no evidence of a direct causal connection between agriculture and war, he does see five preconditions for war. First, he noted the shift from nomadic lifestyle to a sedentary settled lifestyle – protection of local resources that allowed the people to settle down in one location was worth fighting to retain. His second precondition for war was the population growth and the pressure that puts on resource availability. Ferguson's third was the development of hierarchy – elite classes and the internecine rivalries that social class can produce. The fourth precondition was trade and long distance commerce. Trade in especially prestige and luxury items are considered worth organizing to fight for, according to Ferguson. The fifth precondition for war is given as severe ecological disruption. Drought, flood, or any interruption in the natural environment could produce struggle over the resulting shortages and military social organization to control social crises. (permanent settlements, population increase, social class, commerce, ecology).

Kelly, Raymond C. Warless Societies and the Origin of War . War occurs in hunter-gatherer groups when social organization is complex enough to include groups greater in size than the extended family. Clans, bands, and other such groups require retribution and are of a size and structure to allow what we would call war. Of course, social scarcity and war itself may have been reasons for the growth in complexity of social organization. In other words: organized aggression may just as well have required groups to get bigger, and not the other way around. Kelly is silent on this.

Once a group becomes dependant on organized force

to preserve its structural integrity, it also becomes dependant on the industries that supply the materials of war. Once the society is organized around war and the perpetual threat of war, the resources of society are allocated for militarism. The result is that there is less to go around within the society. Because of the mal-distribution of resources allocated to the war system, and the concentrations of wealth and power that are part of any war system, human rights cannot help but be misallocated as well. The nature of wealth is distinction. Wealth manifests distinction through poverty. Power manifests itself through powerlessness. (Toynbee chap. 8 & 9 on tech.-up/HR-down)

While Ferguson does not accept some of the common theories for the origin of war – like cultural ecology – he does accept that social scarcity is usually caused by political and economic conditions within the society. But this artificial "civilized" scarcity itself is a disease of social organization for war. As such, it is itself a cause of conflict. In turn, the desire of the few to hold on to power and wealth requires more force, and further scarcity is the result.

Ferguson's final interpretation is that war is the result (usually) of self-interest on the part of the elite. To use his words: "...leaders often favor war because war favors leaders." It is natural that self-interested act through self-justification.

In the letters to the editor on Ferguson's article nearly all of the anthropologists that he cites disagree with his dismissal of their interpretations. WHY!!! They are perfectly complementary when viewed with less ego...

The Sword and the Chrysanthemum

Benedict, Ruth. The Sword and the Chrysanthemum. New York: Meridian Books. 1946. A World War II approach to anthropology and war in which noted author/anthropologist Benedict studied the Japanese culture and society. [INTRO TO ANTHRO]:

"Religious dogmas, economic practices and politics do not stay dammed up in neat separate little ponds but they overflow their supposed boundaries and their waters mingle inextricably one with the other. Because this is always true, the more a student has seemingly scattered his investigation among facts of economics and sex and religion and the care of the baby, the better he can follow what is happening in the society he studies. He can draw up his hypotheses and get his data in any area of life with profit. He can learn to see the demands any nation makes, whether they are phrased in political, economic, or moral terms, as expressions of habits and ways of thinking which are learned in their social experience." (12-13) and at the bottom: "We do not give ourselves a chance to find out what their habits and values are. If we did, we might discover that a course of action is not necessarily vicious because it is not the one we know."

"The job requires both a certain tough-mindedness and a certain generosity." (14).

"The tough-minded are content that differences should exist. They respect differences. Their goal is a world made safe for differences, where the United States may American to the hilt without threatening the peace of the world,..." (15)

(18-19 cite for definition of culture)

23 – Japanese Imperial investment in militarism grew consistently through the global depression of the 1930's. I might compare the economic recovery

345

strategies of the other pre-WWII future combatants as an introduction to ???? The Japanese were spending roughly half of their GNP to naval/military build up. Only 17% was going to civilian administration. Despite the cultural traditions of deference, this is clearly a disproportionate investment in the Imperial machine to the expense of the human rights of Japanese citizens.

A.J.P. Taylor on War

Historians tend to be reluctant to look for sweeping explanations for all wars. A. J. P. Taylor famously described wars as being like traffic accidents. There are some conditions and situations that make them more likely but there can be no system for predicting where and when each one will occur. Social scientists criticize this approach arguing that at the beginning of every war some leader makes a conscious decision and that they cannot be seen as purely accidental.
wikipedia

The Code Of The Warrior

French, Shannon, The Code Of The Warrior: Exploring Warrior Values Past and Present. New York: Rowman & Littlefield Publishers, Inc. 2003.

At some time in the past, I joined a cult. Not consciously, but thoroughly willing nonetheless, I joined the cult(ure) of the warrior. I became convinced that a warrior is somehow better and more honorable than a murderer or killer. In Code of the Warrior: Exploring Warrior Values Past and Present, author Shannon E. French defined why warriors need a code, and how the code works to form the basis of a kind of masculine culture of conflict. If we are to accept French, this cult operates through a Code. The Code is as timeless as conflict itself, and is both cumulative and cross-cultural. Warrior societies from the Cheyenne Dog Soldiers to Knights Templar – from Samurai to French Foreign Legion maintain a Brotherhood of War. French describes the Code of the Warrior as a necessary civilizing feature to the social organization of war. The Code is an anchor tethered to the warrior's ability to reintegrate into peaceful society. I might agree. The moral and ethical aspects of the Code of the Warrior as outlined by French may well elevate the warrior above some aspects of the habitual atrocity that is war. But, this is where Shannon French and others part company from my view. Anthropologically speaking, the moral and ethical conditions are defined both from within and from outside of the cult of war. Ethical treatment and moral proscription is based on society at large as much as on the "timeless" associations of the warrior hero as documented by French. Rape was honorable for the Viking and the Nazi saw himself as a warrior. This is because things like politics have dipped the warrior into the sewer as thoroughly as Achilles was dipped into the Styx. Nationalism is more recent that the Code, and nationalism has corrupted whatever part of the warrior and his code that does not serve nationalism. The warrior is supposed to serve the greater good – albeit at the point of a sword. The greater good is greater than the state. The soldier serves the state. Patriotism poisons the warrior and reduces his/her Code to a kind of pragmatic utilitarianism. The state gets its soldiers, whose job it is to kill in the service of the goals and objectives of political and economic elite. These leaders "conditionalize" the Code – massaging it to the aims of policy. The warrior in the service of the greatest good becomes the soldier in service to politics. If the warrior seeks to redeem her/himself and the Code, s/he must frequently work against the aim of the state. Sometimes, this means s/he kills for a (supposedly) higher ideal than a flag, and sometimes it means that he does not kill at all. Nonetheless, the state with its political and economic elite manipulates the Code of the Warrior – tailoring it, and Taylorizing* it to fit the maintenance of concentrated wealth and power. The Vietnam War is a fine example. We see a conflict between the soldier and

347

the warrior (as Shannon French defines him) in the James William Gibson book: <u>Warrior Dreams: Paramilitary Culture in Post Vietnam America</u>. It is a struggle between the killer for the state and the killer for higher ethical purposes. One of the reasons for <u>The Code of the Warrior</u> to be written is the post Vietnam War malaise that the American military establishment found itself in. Gibson's dark approach highlights that this dissonance between warrior and soldier all too often occurs in the same individual. Shannon French seeks to resurrect the ancient warrior and his Code to redeem the modern U.S. soldier from the shambles he was left with as a result of Vietnam. At the beginning of Vietnam, American Cold War policy makers joined with corporate elite in promoting the conflict on grounds of public necessity. The people of Vietnam were to be liberated from foreign influence and dominance. Communism must be checked and capitalism freed. To this end, the warrior code was channeled. Films early in the war like the classic John Wayne film: "Green Berets," cloaked the war effort in the noblest of mantles. Valiant U.S. servicemen – soldiers – were warriors in a glorious redemptive struggle. Then, something happened. As time went on, truth came with it. The turning point for civilian America was Tet of 1968. After that massive communist offensive against South Vietnam and their allies, public opinion changed. The war emerged as what it was. Vietnam became an interminable protracted conflict in which the aims and goals shifted with the political necessities of the moment. It was a conflict in which victory was a vague and ill-defined concept not fully understood by most leadership, military personnel, and the American public. The soldier on the ground was caught between warrior ethics and the rather less ethical, often immoral demands of political leaders, of their elite economic backers, and of war itself. In the U.S., the public increasingly turned against the Vietnam War. It was then that the hypocrisy began to show in films like: "The Deer Hunter," and "Apocalypse Now." These films and others since highlighted the ultimate futility of (the) war, as well as the twisted corruption by government of those men who sought to adhere to the Code of the Warrior while serving as a tool of state policy. This does not disparage the warrior or the soldier – or even the Code. Re-read it if you think it does. What this analysis does – as history has – is disparage the political and economic system of leadership that wasted so much human life on all sides. It was a leadership that then turned against the surviving soldiers who questioned the war system. (Here I wrote myself a note to "skip to p 243" I think for a quote, but I can't find it now)

the above has been added to anthro, as intro to culture of conflict.

The search for an "ideal Code for the new millennia" that French advocates (18) should include a commitment to human rights and an end to war.

Chapter 2 (21) begins with the concept of the ideal warrior – based on status and economic benefits in exchange for military prowess – "skill, courage, brute strength." So long as such honorable killing is in keeping with the cultural definition of heroic. She includes "prize woman" as a material reward...

French recounts many myths that built the Code beginning with the Iliad. Noting that alliance (as in WWI) leads to war, and that war leads to gain, she even admits the self-serving nature of the propaganda of this ancient war of aggression. But, her perspective (28+) prevents her from seeing a full modern parallel in the elite warrior propaganda she, herself, preaches earlier and later in the text. Indeed, she is under the spell of the Code – a true member of the Cult – or she would see that (as in the Chris Hedges title) war is the thing that gives her meaning. In the Iliad it was the machinations of the wealthy elite that draws all else into "the brutality of war." She cites Hector's nobility of character as the prime factor in his mythic immortality as a warrior hero. Yet, my perspective cites the war system as the immortalizing agent and laments the unsung nobility of character of the farmer of the Troad, or of the concubine.

The Code may protect the psychology of the warrior, but it does nothing for the intentional and unintentional victims of war (French: 10). And, if Grossman and Ignatieff are correct, any social system as war involved as our own may be headed for a national "Heart of Darkness" (214-215).

On page 16, French notes the quasi-religious ancestor worship nature of the Code connecting identities through time in a kind of bloody amalgamated culture of conflict. I am instantly reminded of the nineties U.S. Marine Corps commercials and their blatant associations between ancient heroic warrior images and the modern Marine.

All the moral pretensions to a Code overlook the fact that soldier's "Warrior Code" is not a guarantee of more than following the moral values of the leaders of society (French: 8). In that sense, the Warrior's Code is socially defined. After all, Nazis had the Code. The Huns of Attila had the Code. In fact, the character issue is moot. And, atrocity may be more consistently flagrant when the Code joins militarily effective behavior with social endorsement – when military morals are consistent with social ones. French makes the assumption that military values imbued in the Code of the Warrior elevate society, when instead, it can very well be said that social institutions have worked against the heroic values of the warrior. In this sense, it is the institutional manipulation of the Code that has made warrior's code moral value relative to the demands of concentrated wealth and power. If the moral behavior of the soldier is relative, not absolute, then there is no Code of the Warrior. Witness Abugraib prison.

Strict adherence to the U.S. Constitution by military personnel does little good for the victims of race-based atrocity, such as Filipinos in the Philippine Insurrection, or Native Americans at Wounded Knee.
And, "inalienable [human] rights" spelled out in the Declaration of Independence, like "life, liberty, and the pursuit of happiness" become political currency.

French 156 – "torturers were mainly the women" – add this to the intro section on gender and reiterate in both the anthro section and the conclusion using the other cites 159 women in warrior societies (kiowa) and 177.

Virtual War

Ignatieff, Michael. Virtual War: Kosovo and Beyond. New York: Henry Holt. 2000.
Despite their patriotic self-sacrifice, the reality is that the military in the abstract and soldiers specifically are instruments of the state – they are means to the ends of the political and economic elite. What cheapens the brotherhood of the warrior band is the expending of their lives for abstract, ill-defined, or non-existent goals. Or, worse, the sacrifice of soldiers lives for goals that result in conditions far worse than prior to military intervention (Gibson) (Hedges).

A Defence of General Funston [sic]

Twain "A Defence of General Funston," "Comments on the Moro Massacre," and "A War Prayer."

"The local population had been ordered to congregate in a few coastal towns. All who did not comply were being shot with "no questions asked." From the Philadelphia Public Ledger, the League quoted this account:

"Our men have been relentless; have killed to exterminate men, women, children, prisoners and captives, active insurgents and suspected people, from lads of ten up, an idea prevailing that the Filipino, as such, was little better than a dog.... Our soldiers have pumped salt water into men to "make them talk," have taken prisoners people who held up their hands and peacefully surrendered, and an hour later, without an atom of evidence to show that they were even insurrectos, stood them on a bridge and shot them down one by one, to drop into the water below and float down, as examples to those who found their bullet-loaded corpses. It is not civilized warfare; but we are not dealing with a civilized people. The only thing they know and fear is force, violence, and brutality, and we give it to them."

WOMEN SLAIN IN MORO SLAUGHTER," he quoted from the headlines, and "With Children They Mixed in Mob in Crater, and All Died Together." Then Twain's interpretation from "Comments":

"They were mere naked savages, and yet there is a soft of pathos about it when that word children falls under your eye, for it always brings before us our perfectest symbol of innocence and helplessness; and by help of its deathless eloquence color, creed and nationality vanish away and we see only that they are children-merely children. And if they are frightened and crying and in trouble, our pity goes out to them by natural impulse. We see a picture. We see small forms. We see the terrified faces. We see the tears. We see the small hands clinging in supplication to the mother, but we do not see those children that we are speaking about. We see in their places the little creatures whom we know and love."

The categorical imperative and humanity of the soldier taken to its logical conclusion dictates an ultimate responsibility of political leadership to cease all war – to make peace – to abolish militarism. If the nation is taken to be the greatest good, then the nation also has the greatest responsibility.

Add an insert from Ordinary Men to round this out.

ADD TO INTRO, THIS STUFF FROM THE OLD PREFACE: As I write, American pacifists are being shouted down by patriotic nationalists bent on revenge for terrorist attacks against the World Trade Center, the Pentagon, and elsewhere. Despite the global popular outcries against the current level of war threat, governments in North Korea and the United States are threatening nuclear conflict. Religious extremists and nationalists who have been twisted by generations of interaction with the greed and violence of the United States government and other colonial powers are suppressing other pacifists in another part of the world. Historically, pacifists have been suppressed by the violent. The sword, the spear, and the gun have silenced the voices of peace. Often the pacifist has been silenced by the state. It is no surprise that civilization has bred far more Colin Powells than Mahatma Gandhis.

On The_Report From Iron Mountain on the Possibility and Desirability of Peace

No by-line found – use for info only- The mystery of who had written the report was revealed in 1972 when Lewin declared in an article in the *New York Times* that he had penned the entire report. In other words, there was no Special Study Group and no government plot to maintain a state of war. The entire report had been a hoax. More details of the creation of the hoax were given in 1996 when Simon & Schuster reprinted the Report with a new introduction.

Apparently, the genesis of the report occurred in 1966 when Victor Navasky, editor of the *Monocle,* a magazine of political satire, noticed a *New York Times* article reporting that the stock market had dipped because of a 'peace scare.' Navasky mentioned this to Lewin who then wrote the report. The two of them presented the report to E.L. Doctorow, editor of the Dial Press. Doctorow agreed to publish the work as nonfiction.

Navasky claimed that the purpose of the hoax had been

"to provoke thinking about the unthinkable—the conversion to a peacetime economy and the absurdity of the arms race."

Even though Lewin and Navasky admitted that the report was a hoax, there still remain some who believe it to be an official government document that was leaked to the public. An ultra-rightwing group known as the Liberty Lobby is one such group. Believing that the report was evidence of a secret government plot, the group printed their own edition of the report. When Lewin found out about this, he sued them for copyright infringement. The case was settled out of court with the Liberty Lobby agreeing to pay Lewin an undisclosed sum.

References:

Leonard C. Lewin, *Report from Iron Mountain On the Possibility and Desirability of Peace,* Free Press, 1996.

Jon Elliston, "Report from Iron Mountain: Highbrow Hoax Mocks National Security Speak," Copyright 1996, Parascope, Inc.

"Hoax or Horror? A Book That Shook White House," *U.S. News & World Report,* November 20, 1967.

". . . so elaborate and ingenious and so substantively original,
acute, interesting and horrifying, that it will receive serious
attention regardless of its origin."
--The New York Times

from 1996 Free Press edition of the Report: It was in that context that *Report From Iron Mountain: On the Possibility and Desirability of Peace* was born. The

354

year was 1966 and one morning the *New York Times* featured a short news item about how the stock market had tumbled because of what the headline called a "Peace Scare."

We had equal luck with our choice of author. We knew that Leonard Lewin, who had edited an anthology of political satire (under the pseudonym of L. L. Case), was a student of the genre. We knew that he cared passionately

about issues of war and peace. And his wicked simultaneous parody of the historian Arthur Schlesinger, Jr., and Eisenhower speechwriter Emmet Hughes's memoir, *The Ordeal of Power*, which *Monocle* magazine had published under Lewin's title "The Ordeal of Rhetoric," showed him to be a sophisticated observer of what Ike had called in his farewell speech (written with the help of Hughes), the military-industrial complex.

There was only one problem. Lewin insisted that he couldn't write the story of the suppression of the so-called report, until there was a report to be suppressed. And so, with the discreet input of his *Monocle* colleagues and folks ranging from Arthur Waskow, then at The Institute for Policy Studies in Washington (who was at work on what he called "A History of the Future"); W. H. Ferry of The Center for the Study of Democratic Institutions in Santa Barbara, California; John Kenneth Galbraith, who was back at Harvard after his stint as JFK's Ambassador to India; and a small cadre of *Monocle* interns to track down original sources, Lewin wrote the report. Titled *Report From Iron Mountain: On the Possibility and Desirability of Peace*, it was a brilliant imitation of think-tankese rendered in impenetrable, bureaucratic prose, replete with obfuscating footnotes, all of them, except for two trick ones, to real if esoteric sources, in a variety of languages.

As it happened, our carefully planned cover story (or "legend" as they say in the C.I.A.) paid off. When John Leo, then a reporter for the *New York Times*, spotted the non-fiction listing of the Report in Dial's catalogue, he made the traditional round of calls to determine whether it was real or a hoax. At Dial he was told if he thought it was a fraud he should check the footnotes, virtually all of which, of course, checked out. No advance reviewer in the trade publications had been willing to label it a hoax, and the State Department's Arms Control and Disarmament Agency carefully said, "To our knowledge no such special study group ever existed." When he called the White House, instead of a denial, Leo got a no-comment—we'll have-to-check-it-out-but-don't-quote-us. (For all the L.B.J. White House knew, the J.F.K. White House *had* commissioned such a study.) The upshot was that the *Times* ran <u>Leo's story</u> saying that the possible hoax was a possibly suppressed report on the front page. The headline, which itself could have been a parody of *Times* style, said "Some see book as hoax/Others take it seriously."

The cold war may be over, but the bloated military budget that undergirds *Iron Mountain's* premise isn't.

But the sad truth may be that the jargonized prose, worst-case scenario thinking, and military value-laden assumptions that Lewin so artfully skewers are still with us. And if that is true, the joke is not on the Michigan and other militias. It is on the rest of us, and it's no longer so funny.

Victor Navasky
November 1995

Fight for the Future

Peters – <u>Fight for the Future</u>: (my evaluation – good for Colonial/Imperial war & maybe part of the conclusion?) Pps. 1-4, Many aspects of thought in this book are either misleading or mistaken when examined in the context of the body of work in this area. Peters does note that the recession of empire has resulted in internal violence within both formerly colonized nations and in the nations were colonizers. But, he blames the "accidental states'" as he calls the post colonial nations, for their own oppression – and not the intrusions of imperial colonizers. His estimation of earlier colonial conditions is that they promoted freedom. To Peters, being (forcibly) colonized meant that those who were occupied were left free to practice their religions and lifestyles. This set of assertions omits or overlooks (neglects?) any of the evidence from colonized sources from the Roman Empire to the modern West Bank. Anything from the writings of Bartolome de las Casas to those of Amilcar Cabral nearly 500 years later show how the "God, Gold, and Glory" justifications for colonial policies of empire left the subject peoples anything but "blissfully unaware" of being colonized. The corrupting disruptive effects of empire changed forever the cultural evolution of states. What cultural failure that has occurred cannot be placed (solely) at the feet of formerly colonized states. This is even more true when one considers the continuous interventions (humanitarian, capitalist, etc.) of the former imperial colonizers.

The class aspect of media and patriotic war propaganda/subliminal violence conditioning: The deep arrogance of Peters, on page 8, gives readers prime example of the depth and tenacity of war system ideal and the effectiveness of conditioning. To Peters, human rights efforts are to blame for the aggressions of the 20th and 21st Centuries. "We" have allowed "Them" to at once see what we have, and what they cannot. "We" have also allowed "Them" to grow so explosively in population as to require more than their resource base can provide. Keep in mind that the same is true for U.S. residents and North Americans in general. But our ability to make war guarantees who gets what. Just as the elite do within the United States, the U.S. as an elite state does to the Third World. The United States consumes up to sixty percent of World resources. In oil alone, the United States consumed 26.1% in 2003 according to BP. This is more than any single nation – and more than the entire oil producing Middle East. It is a figure larger than all of Europe and Eurasia combined (25.9% in 2003).

The Third World (and emergent Fourth World) is not resource poor and overpopulated, it is indeed quite resource rich. The scarcity in resources is created. It is a poverty caused by maldistribution, manipulation, and concentration. It is both the result of war, and the reason for war.

From Howard Richards

(http://www.howardri.org/threetheses.html)
Gray Cox in his book The Ways of Peace proposes to discard the noun "peace," and to replace it with a verb, "peace-ing." "Peace-ing" is the cultivation of agreements. (Cox 1986) It is performing peaceful acts, which when repeated become peaceful practices, and give rise to peaceful traditions. Kenneth Boulding in Stable Peace proposes to learn how to make peace by studying peace that has already been made. He notes, for example, that the border between the United States and Canada is thousands of miles long and completely unfortified, as are the borders that separate Sweden from Finland and Norway. Peace, at some places, at some levels, has become so much a part of networks of trusting relationships that people and nations have

disarmed. Boulding borrows from engineering the idea of strength vs. stress. When the strength of peaceful institutions exceeds any stress that threatens to tear them apart, then peace is stable. (K. Boulding 1978). The other side of the same coin is that there will be sources of recruits for violent adventures as long as there are individuals and classes who find no security or joy in participating in society's peaceful institutions.

It would be misleading, however, to conclude that the world is separated geographically into areas where the peacebuilding process is advanced and areas where it is retarded. It would be more accurate to say that the world as a whole is, in Johan Galtung's terms structurally violent. (Galtung 1980) There are privileged people and poor people. The poor tend to live in geographical areas where overt violence breaks out, but there is no true separation. There are, instead, strong causal relationships which bind privilege and poverty together in a single dance of death.

In large areas of Africa, for example, civil war and other forms of overt violence are now severe, but Africa is not separate from the rest of the world. As Samir Amin has shown in *Maldevelopment*, Africa is a weak and exploited region within the global economic system. (Amin 1990)

Somewhat similarly, on a smaller scale, the inner city and the leafy suburb reflect each other; one exists because the other exists. If the Europeans and the suburb-dwellers are more successful, both in achieving peace among themselves and in other ways, it is success that builds on the failure, or, more precisely, the defeat, of the Africans, and, more generally, of the poor. The South African scholar

Catherine Hoppers writes in *Structural Violence as a Constraint on African Policy Formation*, "Europeans never remember that Africa was incorporated into the world economy by violence. Africans never forget." (Hoppers 1998) The pattern continues today --as the USA, in particular, regularly uses overt military force, when subtler measures are not enough, to keep the world's poor in line. The interdependence of rich and poor neighborhoods is dramatic in Manila, in Sao Paulo, and other third-world cities where the leafy suburbs are protected by armed guards against intruders from neighborhoods that are poorer and more dangerous. Except for occasional visits from the police, armed guards do not patrol the leafy suburbs of London or Los Angeles. Nevertheless, even in the first world, the causes of violence and the fragility of peace exist just as much in places where overt violence is rare as in places where overt violence is common.

The most classic of modern western theories of peace --more classic even than those of Boulding and Galtung cited above-- is that of Immanuel Kant in his *Perpetual Peace*. Like William Penn and others of his fellow forerunners in advancing the idea of world government, Kant envisioned world peace through world law. (Kant 1957, Penn 1912) Kant proposed and predicted the extension of the republican principle of the rule of laws, not of men, to a global scale. In order for this political evolution to come about, he wrote, it is necessary for the spiritual and psychological *(geistliche)* force of law to be as certain and powerful in its operation as a physical force. The rulers of nations are to be counseled by philosophers to follow legal maxims that have moral legitimacy.

Those maxims are, in effect, the basic precepts of respect for persons and property that Kant's philosophy designates as categorical imperatives. Kant had derived the categorical imperative, and the validity of the maxims later proposed as the legitimating framework for international law, from an analysis of what it means to have a good will.

Freud expressed his views on war in a letter to Albert Einstein, who had written to him asking him to state his views on peace. (Freud 1964) But the question Freud answered was different from the question Einstein asked. Freud answered the question, "Is it possible to get rid of men's aggressive inclinations?" Einstein had asked a different question, "Is there any way of delivering mankind from the menace of war ?" (Einstein 1964) To Einstein's question the historian Quincy Wright, the author of a comprehensive study of the history of warfare, had given a good answer, "The absence of conditions of peace is the cause of war." (Wright 1935, 1942) Consequently, mankind can be delivered from the menace of war by establishing the conditions of peace, one of which is "...an organization of the world community adequate to restrain conflicts." Freud gave a good answer too, "No," but it was an answer to his own question. Concerning the question Einstein had asked he admitted that he did not know the answer.

The pessimistic conclusions that some have drawn from the study of violent proclivities of the human body are not valid. The facts on which they draw do, however, imply that the construction of peaceful institutions has real obstacles to overcome. We should resist philosophies of anti-essentialism, deconstruction, anarchism, Rousseauian romanticism, and the notion that discourse constructs its own objects insofar as they tend in practice to bless visions of the world that expect liberation from oppression and all good things to come from dismantling institutions. The existing institutions are bad --we live, as Betty Reardon has put it, not just in a world where wars occur now and then, but rather in a world which is organized and constituted as a war system. (Reardon 1985) But peace can only come from building better institutions. Peace cannot come from an absence of social conventions.

The conclusion I am moving toward is that peacemaking must include the enhancement and extension of existing ethics, in ways that make it possible to establish the rule of law. Following Hart again, Hart defines law as a "union of primary and secondary rules." (Hart 1961) The primary rules govern conduct. The secondary rules (such as the rule that what a court decides is to be accepted) identify which primary rules are valid. Thus law, in principle and in concept, requires the acceptance of rules; and, I am arguing, it requires the acceptance of the core of normative strength (to recur to Kenneth Boulding's notion of the strength of institutions) that rules share with morals, ethics, norms, conventions, customs, and culture.

I have not forgotten Quincy Wright's conclusion that the cause of war is the absence of the organization of peace. Expressing Wright's conclusion juridically, as Emery Reves does in *The Anatomy of Peace*, we can say that we have a war system because we have national sovereignty. (Reves 1945) In the strong sense of "sovereignty" classically articulated by Hugo Grotius in his pioneering work on international law, each nation-state recognizes no authority higher than itself. (Bull 1992) Therefore, each nation-state is legally authorized to make war whenever it wants to. Therefore, the world is governed by a war system in which war is, in principle, in von Clausewitz famous phrase, "the continuation of politics by other means." It should be noted, as Albert Einstein did note, that von Clausewitz's phrase reveals that politics itself, regarded as power politics or *Realpolitik*, assumes that the nation-state recognizes no authority higher than itself, and power politics is therefore, as Einstein also noted, already part of a system based on war, even before any shots are fired.

With my focus on the world as a global economic system, in which rights are an indispensable part of culture, I have not forgotten Wright, Einstein, Reves, von Clausewitz, and others who find war (and, following Hobbes, the same sort of analysis can be extended to violence in general) to be implicit in the logic of independent actors who recognize no authority higher than themselves. What I have done, and what Benito Juarez, Kant, and others did, is to carry the analysis a step farther, by articulating the principle we need to start from to achieve the general recognition of a legitimate authority higher than a nation-state, and (in Huntington's terms) higher than a civilization.

We do not need to go far to find formal legal norms that outlaw violence. War was outlawed by the Kellogg-Briand Treaty of 1924, and then outlawed again in the United Nations Charter of 1948. Other forms of violence were outlawed earlier.

Compare global human rights and peace approaches like this and the UDHR, 14 Points, etc.

Twelve Things We
Can Do Every Day for World Peace and Justice
By Howard Richards
Professor, Earlham College, Peace and Global Justice Studies

1. Use less fossil fuel.

2. Reduce, reuse, and recycle.

3. Support one or more people who cannot (or cannot fully) support themselves.

4. Think of work not as a job but as opportunities for service.

5. Process inner anger by following a spiritual path or getting some form of therapy.

6. Learn and practice conflict resolution techniques.

7. Cultivate an organic garden.

8. Treat property and possessions as held in trust for the benefit of others.

9. Find the good points, not the bad points, in other people's religions, and in their non-religious ethical philosophies.

10. Participate in extended families, family-like communities (e.g. a church), and in multi-generational recreational activities.

11. Buy union-made and environment-friendly goods from cooperative, farmers market, nonprofit, public sector, socially responsible, and locally owned enterprises.

12. Meditate and study about world peace and justice, and then add to, or subtract from, this list.

(These are 3 reasons why Richards says that more than respect for rights is needed) The first was perhaps most famously pointed out by G. W. F. Hegel. (Smith 1989) It is that there are too many rights. Where there is a surplus of rights, Hegel said, force decides. Commonly in a war, or in a barroom brawl, both sides can paint with the language of rights to give their cause the color of moral superiority, and to give themselves the color of knights errant fighting for a righteous cause. To some extent this versatility of the concept of rights can be attributed to the human capacity for deception and self-deception. But it is easy to think of instances that are not mere deception. Often culturally recognized precepts of right really do give both sides good moral arguments, and then it is really true that there is a moral stalemate, where both sides are rhetorically armed with good reasons for declaring the other evil. Then it seems that Hegel may be correct to say that force is necessarily the final arbiter in a culture whose ethics relies solely on concepts of rights.

The second (good for the marx section intro?) was perhaps most famously pointed out by Karl Marx. It is that the stubborn persistence of poverty, the instability of capitalist systems, and the exploitation of labor are all consistent with recognizing the rights of humanity embodied in the laws of commerce. Where everything is sold at its market price, in a free market, with property rights respected, it may well turn out to be the case, and often is the case, that labor is sold for little or nothing. As Marx put it, the deceptive surface of bourgeois society is, "a very Eden of the innate rights of man. There alone rule freedom, equality, property, and Bentham." (Marx)

The third (good for the conclusion social/cultural reorganization) was perhaps most famously pointed out by Alexander Solzhenitsyn and by M. K. Gandhi. (Berman 1980, Dalton 1982) It is that rights without duties are in principle unworkable. Emphasizing rights at the expense of duties is similar to adopting Denis Diderot's 18th century definition of liberty: whatever the law does not forbid is allowed. Like liberty, conceived as being allowed to do anything at all with a few exceptions, rights-talk lends itself to an irresponsible ethic. It authorizes everyone to say what they are supposed to be allowed to do, and are supposed to have and supposed to get. But it does not make anyone responsible for contributing to the welfare of others, or to the common good.

Richards' thesis is then, that we must build on existing cultural and social institutions to create a global civility based on law and that we must promote respect for (human?) rights. However, when the global war system is bigger than any other institution, and itself is the prime denying agent when it comes to rights, and when law is primarily concerned with protection of property, what then can be done? I still maintain that social and cultural reform must undercut the war system before any general condition of human rights can be improved, and that this will lead to peace.

None the less, I can cite Richards on the idea of cultural restructure must parallel economic restructure for peace to be possible

Tournament, joust, holmgang, samurai, and chivalry have the same root. Knights of chivalry were charming killers. Edward, the Black Prince – at Limoges (the slaughter of over 3000 non-combatants) They were a parasitic class. They fed off of all below them in the social structure, even as they, themselves were bled by those few above them. Knights, retainers, and samurai ruled by force of tradition, and by a tradition of force (The Columbia Encyclopedia, Sixth Edition. 2001).

FRONTLINE 11/9/04 "The Persuaders"

Mark Crispin Miller

Cultural and media critic Mark Crispin Miller is a professor of communication and culture at New York University. He explains in this interview the flaw in the claim made by champions of advertising that it is a form of democracy because it is giving people what they want. He also talks about what happens when marketing and advertising techniques spill over into our politics, the great difference between being a citizen and being a consumer and, lastly, the dangers of a culture where marketing is pervasive: "You'll hear [this] from novelists, filmmakers, reporters -- this is not just me. There's a kind of cultural crisis going on now where people are being forced to make the kind of thing that they weren't ever trained to do. ... the kind

367

of thing that's dictated by corporate interests alone, and it tends to make our air thinner. It tends to annihilate all the gorgeousness and novelty and all the challenges posed by really original, passionate works of art and news." This interview was conducted on May 26, 2004.

+ Clotaire Rapaille

Can marketers really get inside a consumer's head to influence the choice they will make? For market researcher Clotaire Rapaille, the answer is yes. He believes all purchasing decisions really lie beyond conscious thinking and emotion and reside at a primal core in human beings. As chairman of Archetype Discoveries Worldwide, he helps Fortune 500 companies discover the unconscious associations for their products - the simple "code" - that will help them sell to consumers: "When you learn a word, whatever it is, "coffee," "love," "mother," there is always a first time. There's a first time to learn everything. The first time you understand, you imprint the meaning of this word; you create a mental connection that you're going to keep using the rest of your life. …So actually every word has a mental highway. I call that a code, an unconscious code in the brain." This interview was conducted on December 15, 2003. Brand loyalty (beyond reason) comes from imprinted associations unconsciously attained early in life. The essential association motivates behavior beyond reason. What do we imprint about war? (Maybe use the hot iron learning model from lecture and link this to the mind stuff from early anthro(?)

+ Frank Luntz

368

A corporate consultant, pollster and political consultant to Republicans, Luntz's specialty is testing language and finding words that will help his clients sell their product or turn public opinion on an issue or a candidate. In this interview, he tells FRONTLINE what it takes to communicate a message effectively, shares some of the advice that he gives clients, and explains why his testing and field research seeks words that move people to act on an emotional level: "It's all emotion. But there's nothing wrong with emotion. When we are in love, we are not rational; we are emotional. When we are on vacation, we are not rational; we are emotional. When we are happy, we are not [rational]. In fact, in more cases than not, when we are rational, we're actually unhappy. Emotion is good; passion is good. Being into what we're into, provided that it's a healthy pursuit, it's a good thing." This interview was conducted on Dec. 15, 2003.

Henry V – Brannagh version. Opening scene: Archbishop of Canterbury is concerned over church power. He urges and legitimizes the claim of England on France. War over land, wealth, and power is given orthodox religious sanction. The famous "Once more unto the breach" appeal to savagery "as a tiger," and to "manhood." Dishonor not your mothers and fathers, he continues, invoking social pride, and national patriotism. "Cry God for Harry, for England, and for Saint George!" After the melee, King Harry threatens the residents with rape and murder, if they do not yield. Later, around the campfire the troubled night before the decisive Battle of Agincourt, King Harry in disguise converses with his soldiers on duty. Finally, after the men at arms chew on duty and death, they agree that "we know enough if the King's cause be right." Then on the day of battle, there is the "upon Saint Crispin's Day" speech, King Harry urges his outnumbered men – common and elite – with the stirring announcement that his company will share the "greater share of honor…" personal fame, and glory. LLewelyn's fanatical grip on the "rules of war," and "laws of arms" leaves him confounded again and again as such rules are violated.

In the end, all of King Harry's poor friends from early life are dead or laid low. But, to Henry V it is "a royal fellowship of death" that attracts his attention. The accounting of the dead was of those of "note," not of those other thousands mired in mud and their own blood.

Conclusion – So what is needed? Certainly we as a race must become more realistically aware of the wages of war. But, martial arts, etc. shows that while this can be done, we still place too much emphasis on war & not enough on peace. It is vital that we engage perpetually both in activity that shows the futility of war, and that we are perennially active structuring social systems of human rights and peace. Each balances the other. Our collective investment in peace must come to outweigh our investment in war. While it seems a "no brainer" that procreation and pleasure have outstripped (surpassed the human tendency toward violence) genocide, it is also indisputable that society has linked sex and violence (Yojimbo). Homo-erotic or hetero-erotic makes no difference. The unifying feature is erotic – the eroticization of violence. Violence, especially group violence, is not a basic instinct like pleasure/sex/procreation. But, socially organized institutions have linked sex and violence as co-equal.

"Temperance!" they shouted, "abstain from sex!" While the same voices shout, "kill for God and country!" Stoicism always had political purpose(s). The result is the unfortunate and revolting fact that well civilized enculturated men get turned on by resistance.

Nation, July 14, 03(?) Assumption that war is part/essential to politics –David Rieff "humanitarian intervention" is always to someone's benefit outside of conflict, or it doesn't happen. Witness the Congo, Rwanda, and the Sudan, where millions died prior to any humanitarian intervention. – Mahmood Mamdani

Killing is made legitimate. It (war) is a reactionary, non-proactive occurrence in this context of "humanitarian intervention." Distinguish this clearly from a proactive HR strategy as outlined in Eyal Press. Aim at "own house in order" posture. Discuss UN/UN security council differences & the idea of legitimate versus legal.

War may be necessary, but call it what it is: a new colonialism – (parallels old colonialism - $, public health, disease/sanitation). Human rights is another ideology, like communism, or Christianity.

No Moral High Ground. – Rieff

I would argue that HR and UDHR has higher legitimacy due to the emphasis on consensus and economic justice.

Global Civil Society: An Answer to War

Kaldor, M., "Global Civil Society: An Answer to War." M. Kaldor, Global Civil Society: An Answer to War, Cambridge: Polity
1) Global Civil Society and New Wars. This work builds on previous research carried out by Mary

Kaldor and others on the nature of new types of war especially in Africa, Eastern Europe and South Asia (Kaldor and Vashee 1998, Kaldor 1999). The aim is to develop arguments about the relationship between processes of globalisation and new wars and the ways in which new wars constitute an obstacle to global civil society; to study, on the one hand, the impact of global economic processes (de industrialisation, the growth of inequality and poverty, corruption, and grey or black economies) and global political and cultural processes (weakening of the state, growing conflict between cosmopolitanism and fundamentalism, emergence of private paramilitary groups) on new forms of violence and threats to the rule of law, and, on the other hand, the ways in which the absence of civil society prevents normal economic development and reconstruction. It is hoped that such research could identify ways in which civil society can be reconstructed through transnational intervention ranging from moral and material support to local groups and independent media to humanitarian intervention.

Mary Kaldor is already engaged in a major research project funded by the British Department of International Development on Strengthening Democratic Governance in War torn societies. The project is investigating the extent to which democracy can offer a mechanism for conflict prevention and management. It will include theoretical enquiry into definitions of democracy and conflict and empirical studies concerning the role of NGOs, in particular women's movements, and of local government in conflict, and the role of security structures, with a focus on Bosnia, Sri Lanka, Uganda and South Africa.

Almost stumped me. But, war, love, and good, and evil all exist. Earlier, I stripped war of it's pathos – I needed us to see the naked vulgarity of war. Then, enter "The Lord of the Rings," the most celebrated series of war movies – a warrior epic of mythic proportion. War. Valor in the service of good. Implacable foes of evil. But, warriors camaraderie and love – in fact all human virtue and more shine in the character of the heroes of legend. Yet, was Tolkien saying that love comes from war, or that love redeems us of the villainy we do in the name of peace? Tolkien was a WWI vet, writing during WWII. In his epic, all enemies are inhuman. Like during any war, the foe was to be dehumanized and distanced. Call them "Orcs," or "Japs," or "Huns," or "Gooks." Well, you get the picture.

Theodore Geisel (Dr. Seuss) wove political and social themes into his work. He worried that there was "too much power in too few hands."

Fahrenheit 911
Bin Ladin Group, John Major, James Baker, George H. W. Bush connections with Carlyle (military contracts) & Halliburton (oil and construction contracts) explored in sections 6,7,8 of the DVD. Bandar Bush is on sections 10 (9-13). Congressman Jim McDermott (D – Wash.) Psychiatrist and member of the House said that "fear does work…yes." "You can make people do anything if they are afraid." The essence is that there was the promotion of a climate of "endless threat." In this, Bush, Rumsfeld, Ashcroft, Cheney, and Wolfowitz are all playing an old tune. They are stoking the war machine. Ultimately, the Bushs – and the Cheneys, the Rumsfelds, and the

Wolfowitzs are the Lords of their tier, but are thralls to the war system. This latest round of organized violence is shocking in immediacy and in its orchestration. But, the war system is as old as civilization itself. Section 28 of the 911 DVD has the Orwell quotes.

Fact is that all exercise of power is unilateral – at least in concept. Generally, power rests in the assumption or belief that one can act unilaterally.

Troy

McCarty, Nick. Troy: <u>The Myth and Reality Behind the Epic Legend</u>. New York: Barnes and Noble Books. 2004. (by arrangement with Carlton Books, LTD.) Schliemann's efforts to find Troy are a tribute to the power and persistence of war myths.
"War itself is never anything but vile and bloody, despite the heroics of some men. It is a story of the darkness of death and of blood seeping into the earth and sand. It tells of men blinded by death…" p. 49.

Vedas 1000 bc – troy 1250.

Joseph Campbell – Joshua taking over from Moses begins a ruthless line of anointed warrior kings – Even Solomon fits into this role.

Alfred P. Sloan of the GM corporation's early history is the individual who decided that you and I would spend more of our money – hard earned money -- on "new and improved" products. Sloan is the originator of "planned obsolescence." This is the idea that manufactured items that did not have to wear out or break down should – instead – be engineered to break down on purpose in order to create even more consumer demand. Consumer demand, of course, relates to profits. Some consumers are military agencies. Such artificially created demand requires a reallocation of social resources that could have been used for human rights, to be instead used for the promotion of the war system. Such seemingly innocuous purchases that you or I may make are always in support of a power structure that promotes war, rape, and the denial of fundamental human rights.

(CONCL?) Often, Pacifists and advocates of peaceful human society simplistically fail to assess the tenacious complexity of the repetitive cycle of human violence. Despite the best of intentions, war will out. However, it is not enough to relegate pacifism to naivete, and thus dismiss deeper study of perhaps the single most potentially transformational element of human culture.

Warrior Dreams

And, in <u>Warrior Dreams: Paramilitary Culture in Post-Vietnam America</u>, James William Gibson traced how a new warrior culture has flourished in the United States since the war in Vietnam. Ethnocentric and fascist, Ralph Peters postmodern approach to war outlined in his book: <u>Fighting for the Future: Will America Triumph?</u> is a look at the mind of an unabashed acolyte of the cult of war.

I may define each aspect of the thesis in the introduction. Example: war is a self-generating system that denies human rights by concentrating wealth and power – I would clarify war, system/systematic, human rights, concentrate, wealth, and power in a sentence or so each.

CULTURAL ANTHROPOLOGY- culture race ethnicity nationality etc. defined

The misuse and misunderstanding of these few key terms can and has distorted human relationships on a historic scale.

All definitions are historically dependent. That is to say that their specifics have all changed over time depending on the factors of their historic context. In anthropological terms, they are products of cultural evolution.

CIVILIZATION
Although definitions of what it means to be civilized differ, a general sense of civilization is that it encompasses the sum total of cooperative human activity. Basically civilization is the socially organized human response to change. Civilization seeks equilibrium, or balance and predictability in an environment that certainly fluctuates, and that may often seem random or chaotic. Being civilized means a division of labor. It means a social system aimed at making that labor count to serve the needs of the whole of society. In the early days of civilization, natural environmental change meant that in order to prosper, people organized. Basic needs were fairly universal and straightforward. People needed food, water, shelter, and the like. These things needed to be predictable and consistently available for people in any numbers to thrive. The basic idea behind civilization was so successful that ultimately

populations could grow beyond the natural capacities of the environment. Specialization of labor forces meant that surpluses of things like food could accumulate to offset times of hardship. This surplus is the basis for the civilized idea of wealth. Around this time came new ideas of private property. Land could be owned. Ownership could be disputed. At this stage, the social environment became as important as the natural one. With wealth came the habit of centralized control. With wealth came the idea of poverty and want. With the concept of wealth came the desire to seize wealth, or a need to defend it. Power and wealth have gone hand in hand ever since. The social power to seize or protect concentrations of wealth meant that new social specializations would develop. A military class came into being whose sole purpose was often the seizure or protection of wealth. War was born. By the time we can read of it, by the advent of literacy, warfare and a lasting concern for the loss of human rights was already synonymous with civilization.

COMMUNITY
Communities are formed from the interactions of culture and society. When individuals are united into groups by complimentary internal (cultural) and external (social) influences, the groups of people can be identified as communities. Such a group of people who share common assumptions about the way the world works, and who are identified within a social context, need not be physically in contact, or segregated in order to feel a sense of community. Always, very few members of such a group share every aspect of cultural belief, or of social role.

Commonalties exist, but members of a community retain individuality. They often share ethnicity, but they are not totally interchangeable. When we speak of a military-industrial complex, or an intelligence community, what is being talked about is groups of people who share both culture and social institutions. They need not even live together in a local sense, but they share beliefs that produce common behavior, and they construct similar institutions accordingly. These institutions in turn produce conditions that are reflected and reinforced in shared beliefs. Like yin and yang, a community uses culture and society in reinforcing ways. Once a productive behavior like war is introduced, there comes with it a culture of conflict that supports institutions of war. It is the community that legitimizes war as a social institution and a cultural norm. When war is believed (culturally) to serve the (social) community, then the community turns to war. The enemy are those who are different – different enough to be considered outside of the community.

War happens because of power. Power is the result of and the motivation for concentrated wealth. Concentrated wealth exists through the denial of human rights. Those with wealth and power deny human rights to others through organized violence and the threat of organized violence – police and soldiers. War occurs because people want to get power, want to keep power, or because they feel powerless.

War and Our World

Keegan, John. <u>War and Our World</u>. New York: Random House.1998.

Celebrated military historian John Keegan explained away social organization and war as a phenomenon in which "civilization, which depends for it's survival on the maintenance of law and order, within and without, is a fragile creation." Presumably, then, he means that civilization depends on organized aggression.

Intro XI
The elite warrior of "character" has been given a bad name by the "hoi polloi."

XII
War is a "predatory affair" showing stages of gradual development from hunter/gatherer, to hunters vs early pastorilists until "slowly" only the farmer-type learn to protect themselves. There is no hint from Keegan, however, as to the raiders' origins. Presumably they are semi nomadic herdspeople, although he makes no case for the development of these aggressors beyond the one dimension of the raid. On the surface, this seems strange. The formation of war would be better understood if both "aggressor" and "defender" were defined. Maybe this is no error of omission, but yet another telling aspect of our interpretation of war. Perhaps Keegan views the raider societies as the dead end systems, not independent of settled society. And, that the true origin of organized systematic warfare should rightfully be credited to settled city-based peoples. These indeed may be valid evaluations of what is inferred in the Keegan interpretation.

In War and Our World, civilization falls when the

military fails as the ultimate "instrument of the state." Predation may be key to the endemic nature of war, but are we not to rise above?

XIII
Keegan errs when he blames Islam for adding religious imperatives to war (9). He not only fails to see this in both Christian and Hebraic history, but also overlooks nationalism. A brief survey of war propaganda – posters, slogans, etc. – and one would find it hard not to recognize the connections between religion, nationalism, and the motivation for universal conscription into the military. It is always "god and country," or in Keegans case, "for Saint Michael and Saint George." Apart from the warrior saints, "God Save the Queen."

There follows a developmental sequence on war through p 10.
Pgs. 9 + 10 list social organization needed for "modern" military.

Human rights issues appear on 11, 12, 13.
Good stuff on the denial of economic justice and various infrastructural hardships for even the winners of war (except the non-bombed U.S.). Also, he concludes that war has become the great enemy of humanity – and the technological irony of Superior force" (15 - compare this with both McNamara and Rumsfeld). He notes on 12 that most bombing casualties in WWII were women and children (but I think he is only counting England).

Chapter II scopes the origins of war from Keegan POV. Nature vs nurture is given as the possibilities, and Keegan is on the nurture side of the argument <Konrad Lorenz> (Keegan cites Ardrey and Freud). Ardrey does the hunting + cooperation = war thing (23).

"Society…is red in tooth and claw" (24).

Pastorialists Nomads and war (26-7) Gist here is that we get better at war as we "advance" in civilization. The war system becomes mre integrated with the rest of society. It became eventually a dominant influence on social organization. Keegan notes that other lifeways are better. He too (see Ferguson) disconnects agriculture from war citing that early agricultural Egypt had no war system while in Mesopotamia war was 1000 years older than Egypt. It is interesting that Keegan nonetheless places the "cradle of civilization" in Mesopotamia – partly just because war is older there. On pages 35-36 Keegan uses Egypt as an example of a state without a war system between 300 and 1700 BC. I do not agree. Narmer/Menes consolidated the Kemet via imperial conquest before 3000 BC. This is clearly a war system in operation. Keegan also envisioned an army without a state in the nomadic warriors of central Asia. I dispute his narrow idea of the state. Again and again Keegan put forth an assumption that the "state" and settled "civilization" to be the same. They are not the same. An important distinction is that a state can organize in a number of ways to satisfy the demands of civilization. But war does not have to be part of that social organization. A state will invariably organize for war as a product of nationalism (cite Howard Richards: "I have not forgotten Quincy

Wright's conclusion that the cause of war is the absence of the organization of peace. Expressing Wright's conclusion juridically, as Emery Reves does in *The Anatomy of Peace*, we can say that we have a war system because we have national sovereignty. (Reves 1945) In the strong sense of "sovereignty" classically articulated by Hugo Grotius in his pioneering work on international law, each nation-state recognizes no authority higher than itself. (Bull 1992) Therefore, each nation-state is legally authorized to make war whenever it wants to. Therefore, the world is governed by a war system in which war is, in principle, in von Clausewitz famous phrase, "the continuation of politics by other means." It should be noted, as Albert Einstein did note, that von Clausewitz's phrase reveals that politics itself, regarded as power politics or *Realpolitik*, assumes that the nation-state recognizes no authority higher than itself, and power politics is therefore, as Einstein also noted, already part of a system based on war, even before any shots are fired.") Keegan: "war evolved with the state" and in chap 3 "war made the state and the state makes war."

Note French and Prussian conscription in "nationalism" and extend it from English archers. Civil virtue and military service as social obligation/education (33-35). Chapter questions the legitimacy of the war/state connection.

28-9 Keegan parallels Gilgamesh as example of early war system – cite in myhology.

page 50. Seems like "human nature" to kill when in power over the weak. K: "…stimulated to kill by the victim's weakness." Speculation runs that remorse is also a product – thus the warrior culture of "fair fight," bringing honor to balance the remorse over atrocity.

K uses a sports analogy. Cite this for "culture of bio-technology" and rename that chapter something sexy.

Social status was also noted by K along the lines already described in my narrative – link to decoration panoply, pomp, & ceremony.

K asserts (52) that the "higher moral code" of Christianity gave warriors "honour," the ethical code of honoring his foe – even in defeat. Well, I guess. If the enemy is Christian – or of high (economic) status. Check the crusader sack of Jerusalem, for instance. The floors of the holy sepulcher were ankle-deep in Christian and non-Christian blood spilled without remorse by the catholic crusaders.

53 – K links nationalism to brutality using the 1930's Japanese invasion of China and Rape of Nanking as examples.

Expand the war system definition after lewin to include broad HR impacts. Link to Toynbee chap VIII & IX.

The Biology of War
In his book, The Biology of War, author G.F. Nicolai supports the view that war is a biologically anachronistic practice – an evolution that has a rise and a fall. We have outlived war, and it has outlived any (biological) usefulness. He may have been premature in the idea that we have outlived war. We

have preserved war through our current forms of social organization, and thus have promoted an unheard of ability to engage in genocide, and species suicide.

War is only an invention – not a biological necessity," Margaret Mead, The Role of Ritualized and Symbolic Conflict (25). – cited from Anthropology Today, June 1989, V5, #3, page 2).

War Crimes
Neier, Aryeh, War Crimes. President of the Open Society Institute and former director of Human Rights Watch as well as the ACLU.

48 – Expectations of rape and looting are the historic expectations "potended" by the approach of any army. Armies made soldiers – soldiers who preyed both on friend and foe.   Woek from 48 to "Colonial Imperialism." Add De Las Casas at this point with links to Hedges and Neier after.
Paintings of Breughel, etc.

Fog of War
McNamara, Robert Strange. "Fog of War" (for Should We Stop, or How We Stop)
One delusional danger born of the fevered paranoia of Cold Warrior mentality is that the U.S. can force peace on the world through military superiority. Now, with current levels of intense cultural imperialism and military hegemony, leaders like Bush, Cheney, and Ashcroft who believe they know what's best for all of us continue to do what they have done – make the 21st century even more war-prone than the bloody

20th. One-hundred and sixty million died violently in the 20th century. And, if we take into account the peripheral and collateral producers of death such as disease, famine, reduced fertility, increased infant mortality, and other results of war like infrastructural and environmental destruction, then the death toll may well exceed 200 million human lives. Few even seem to tally the children maimed and killed stepping on anti-personnel mines in areas now deemed "peaceful." And yet, with this prophetic history, leaders still support war and the war system as the primary route to peace. In the recent award-winning documentary/memoir "The Fog of War," film maker Errol Morris shows through the life of former U.S. Secretary of Defense Robert McNamara just how thickly war can fog the peace process. McNamara recounts his insiders role in much of the U.S. involvement in 20th century war. The fog never completely lifts as statements and questions flow. Certain fundamental assumptions remain unchallenged. These include: the role of reason and human nature in war; that one must do evil to do good; that there are just wars; that there are rules in war; that proportional conflict is desirable (or even possible); and, that empathy* (based on race or religion) is valuable, but not for those who are "Evil." It is these very assumptions and others that keep the war system functioning. As experience and nuanced as McNamara is, he still assumes war to be necessity and not option. This concept of threat and dominance insures war.

With this mentality in place, Should We Stop is moot – How We Stop is an impossibility. It will take a dramatic turn away from assumptions like those of former Secretary McNamara – assumptions that are themselves the Fog Of War – before war's reality is itself history.

*On empathy: McNamara is for empathy when at war, unless they are Nazi or Japanese – but what about empathy as foreign policy before war? What of empathy as a guiding philosophy of culture, and the Universal Declaration of Human Rights as foreign policy?

War and Civilization
Toynbee, Arnold J. War and Civilization. New York: Oxford University Press. 1950.
(Western Civ approach with Christian morality overtones)
On the other hand (other than John Keegan), Toynbee (viii) sees war as a scourge that is key to social breakdown and the decay of civilization. To Toynbee, war is the malignant offspring of all known civilizations because of the wealth and resources demanded. Despite this characterization, Toynbee nonetheless places himself in the camp of those who see war as an unfortunate reality, and perhaps a necessity. In this, he and Keegan agree. Toynbee also links "military virtues with (Judeo) Christian values (compare with Keegan on Honour and French on the Code). But, while discussing the pitfalls of pacifism, Toynbee yet advocates concentrated political action against war.
        This willingness to pay the blood price is the taproot of war – a vein without which war would become anemic and die. But, the selfless ideal of sacrifice to the worthy cause becomes inevitably twisted by those in charge of the war system. In the

moral tug-of-war between the saint (pacifist) and the warrior, the pacifist wins every time. However, the real world has few saints, and many warriors. The average person "flinches from the toil and danger" of war. That the majority of citizens are urged to rise to the level of warrior and not saint is a function of social organization.

Toynbee reasoned that peace could be assured through voluntary international action by a peace-keeping world power. This multi-national power must have sufficient strength to be unassailable militarily, but must also have sagacious enough leadership not to provoke resentful challenges to its authority. I would add that such a world peace-keeping power ought to cultivate the wisdom not to invite militancy by intervening exploitively in the affairs of others, but Toynbee was writing in 1950 – before the height of the Cold War and the emergence of modern post-colonial conflicts.

Toynbee theorized a "ferocious" period of wars of religion from the 16th through the 17th centuries. He then posits an interlude (1648 on the continent and 1660 in the United Kingdom) in which war was again "the sport of kings," followed by another set of ferocious wars of nationality from the 18th into the 20th centuries. I may add two things to this. One, is that these wars spawned both the post-colonial wars of independence (beginning with the United States), and then the current neo-hegemonic wars. And two, that each of the periods of conflict in the western world saw the further concentration of power and wealth into the hands of the elite of the war system. Take, for instance, the wars of (European) nationalism. The quest for a stable national economy with sufficient capital resources forged a bond that is still known as the "military-industrial complex." This is simply the modern expanded industrial version of what has been going on from the beginning of civilization. It is the descendant of the Mesopotamian Lugal who formed bonds of mutual support with Ensi to dominate (and exploit) human and natural resources of the Tigris and Euphrates. The military part of the complex is the power of government, and the industrial part represents concentrated wealth. Together they make a war system. This military industrial complex is descendant of ancient war making machines, but it is also the ancestor of the modern American "international police force" and trans-national corporation. The United States government deploys military force under the doctrine of "enlightened self-interest to protect those same corporations that generate wealth by exploiting the common citizens both within and outside of the U.S.

"The result is that hungry souls which have been given a stone when they have asked for bread cannot be restrained from seeking to satisfy their hunger by devouring the first piece of carrion that comes their way" (Toynbee: 7).

Toynbee supports (my) nationalism-leads-to-war thesis by dividing nationalism into two parts – democracy & industrialism – which he saw as reducing democracy (9).

"is war intrinsically and irredeemably evil in itself?" Toynbee had already likened war to suicide by virtue of the advent of militarism, which he defined as the institutional culture of war (14).

388

Militarism is ingrained enough in myth religion, and history that we value/admire the figure of the "honorable warrior" – transferred via nationalism into the "patriot," or "citizen-soldier" – more than the simply less violent (and less romanticized) figure of the farmer, or teacher. The "military virtues" are distilled from society and the shared values form a foundation for imitation/emulation among the general population. It is through the "code of the warrior" that civil and military authority reinforces each other. This union is essential if the war system is to survive.

14-16 explores the origins of war and assumptions justifying war. Self defense against barbarians and hunting form the sanguine and necessary vectors for socially honorable violence. By extension, Toynbee argued that at an "early and frequently attained" level of social economy hunting becomes superfluous and vestigial as a sport. But war became institutionalized as militarism – and thus war has come to be practiced for the sake of war, and not in defense of unreasonable aggression.

I would add that institutions – the war system included – exist to control group behavior for profit and status. And, that institutions at their best tend to ignore or deny the rights of minorities. Even in a full democracy (which despite U.S. pretensions does not exist) a minority can be as many as 49 percent politically, of 51 percent by gender in the case of women. <refer to both the definitions of social institution, and to the pitfalls of democracy/majority rule in Wolfe>

There is parallel growth in militarism and nationalism

in the 19th century (Toynbee confirms by examination of Prussian source von Moltke), and a split in progressive thought of the era between pacifists and hardened militarists. The militarists sought and found justification more and more to resolve social issues through application of force, and they pushed more and more toward professional soldiery and institutional militarism. It is the movement away from what was earlier christened by Toynbee the "sport of kings" to a business of presidents, premieres, and corporate executive officers.   The product of this course were such extreme forms of nationalism as neo-colonialism, fascism, and nazism.

Nationalism became the filler of the spiritual void created by the failure of Christianity, and the Christian ethic. Modern man [sic] filled this "spiritual vacuum" with a nationalist militarism that was (and is) heavily flavored with an admittedly corrupt spirituality in the form of "military virtues." Nationalist virtues such as – as Mussolini termed them – "obedience, [self] sacrifice, and dedication to country."

Toynbee yearned for a return to Christian values and spiritual sublimation which (he hoped) would replace militarism and war with a unity of spiritual struggle against evil.

While I can see and understand Arnold Toynbee's post-war pining for a lost moral compass – it is in part what produced such documents as the Universal Declaration of Human Rights, and this book – nonetheless, it is also ethnocentric elevation of one doctrine of faith above all others that perpetuates institutionalized violence. See the Crusades, or the concept of Jihad for the practical institutional results of linking a single religious doctrine to an absolute sense of morals, ethics, and values.

<use Sparta and Assyria for examples of social organization committed over time to militarism in "SHOULD WE STOP?">

SPARTA (Ch. 3) A nation founded on militarism, war, and the power of the state was also founded upon the systematic denial of human rights. Sparta solved the crises of population pressures common to the Hellenes of the times by the conquest and enslavement of their neighbors, the Messenians in about 725 BCE. To do this, they required all Spartans to commit virtually their entire lives to the Spartan military machine (war system). All Spartan men, women, and children were involved in the training and support of warriors. All Messenians became Helots – permanent serfs. Thus, the Spartan war system claimed two sets of victims who lost their human rights – the slave and the slave master – chattel and citizen soldier. Of course, one also cannot overlook the wars with other Greeks caused by Sparta, or the Spartan military posture. After the second Meseno-Spartan War of 650 BCE resulted in the fixation of the Spartan war system, Spartan cultural development stagnated. Arts, literature, and architecture that did not contribute to the war system atrophied. Spartan social and cultural evolution was "side-tracked" into a "blind alley" of post war and pre-war obsessions.

Xenophon noted that Spartan "Peer pressure" and valor at arms were prime motivators for youth. War became a "categorical imperative" of Spartan social

life. The record (or the huge gap in the record) of Spartan artistic expression is a suggestive glimpse at what militarism and the war system can do to inhibit social and cultural growth. This bolsters the thesis that the war system has served to impede the evolution of social systems that guarantee increased economic justice and human rights in other cases as well (Toynbee: 40-41). Sparta was (we are reminded) the first form of Greek democracy, predating the vaunted Athenian model. The Athenian form of democracy was itself flawed by being slave based, military, and exclusively upper class male. (& demogoguery) As in Sparta, multitudes of slaves, women, the poor, and non-military had no democratic rights whatsoever (Toynbee: 42-43). The inspiration to a concentrated wealth based economy in Athens simultaneously checked the expansion of Athenian democracy to other classes and linked class advantage even more to military participation.
The result was great elite wealth for Athenian citizens, the hegemony of the Athenian League, great concentration of wealth in Athens, and war with Sparta and other fearful envious Greek city-states.

"...The paramount aim of any social system should be to frame military institutions, like all its other institutions, with an eye to the circumstances of peace-time, when the soldier is off duty. And this proposition is borne out by the facts of experience. For militarist states are apt to survive only so long as they remain at war, while they go to ruin as soon as they have finished making their conquests. Peace causes their metal to lose its temper; and the fault lies with a social system which does not teach its soldiers what to make of their lives when they are off duty."

Aristotle as quoted in Toynbee (51).

I would add that we do not even teach them what they can do non-violently to promote peace when they are on duty....

ASSYRIA (Ch. 4) The case of "there is always a bigger fish" is made using Assyrian history. It is what Toynbee sees as militaristic overconfidence. Assyria met its demise while at the peak of militarism and military capability. All of their armed strength invited (or created) was stronger and more resolved enemies. Incessant warfare and deplorable political and human rights condition promoted coalitions of conflict within and without of Assyria. In the end, escalating militarism engulfed even the formidable and ruthless Assyrian war machine in a storm of swords (Toynbee:71).

98-9. Statistics on the cost of 14th/15th century militarism of Timur Lenk (Tamerlane). 103 quote on overextension of militarism – always a disaster for human rights. "Pax Romana" usually resulted in "frontier forces" turning inward.

On 106-7, Toynbee links the decline of Rome to its victory. Cycle of war: Wealth and human resources enter Rome – provinces stripped of both population and resources to enrich a small group of businessmen and politicos (some, like Caesar ardent militarists). Exploitation and poverty give rise to revolt. More military needed. Militarists become senators and businessmen (the class elevation they sought). New reforms (a'la Marius) allow non-Romans to join the legions. Filling the army with citizens meant filling graves. Newly available lands are gobbled up by senators/businessmen. Labor needs increase. Slavery increases. Wealth and human resources enter Rome. Exploitation and poverty give rise to revolt. More military needed...

Good Gracchus quote – 108 "The wild animals that range over Italy have a hole, and each of them has its lair and nest, but the men who fight and die for Italy have no part or lot in anything but the air and the sunlight...It is for the sake of other men's wealth and luxury that these go to the wars and give their lives. They are called the lords of the World, and they have not a single clod of earth to call their own."

110 – "Intoxification of victory has been the ruin of every militant empire."

And, from chapter 8, "The Price of Progress in Military Technique":

"Militarism has been by far the commonest cause of the breakdowns of civilizations during the four or five millennia which have witnessed the score or so of breakdowns that are on record up to the present date. Militarism breaks a civilization down by causing the local states into which society is articulated to collide with one another in destructive internecine conflicts. In this suicidal process, the entire social fabric becomes fuel to feed the devouring flame in the brazen bosom of Molech. The single art of war makes progress at the expense of all the arts of peace; and, before this deadly ritual has completed the destruction of its votaries, they may have become so expert in the use of their implements of slaughter

394

that, if they happen for a moment to pause in their orgy of mutual destruction and to turn their weapons for a season against the breasts of strangers, they are apt to carry all before them." 130

"...an improvement in military technique is usually, if not invariably, the symptom of a decline in Civilization." 140.

I would refer George W. Bush to chapter 9, "The Failure of the Saviour with the Sword," in which Toynbee outlines how and why a society cannot be saved by the word of war. Although he is making a philosophical point, Toynbee nevertheless develops considerable historical support for the thesis that war and militarism are often (touted erroneously) misleading offered by leaders as solutions to social problems. And, that abuse of force is the only product of militarism.

From an unknown student's paper
"When thinking about the development of social organization, I think it is important to note that so much change has happened because of war. Some of these reason [sic] I found to support this are below: Success in war has, Spencer argued, some ironical consequences: (1) as territories increase in size, logistical problems of control, communication, transportation, and administration escalate; (2) as the span of a territory increases, especially as the result of annexation...of conquered populations, the diversity of the population increases and poses increased internal threat , which in turn, escalates logistical loads; (3) compounding populations, per se, increases population size which, regardless of internal

threats, increases logistical loads; and (4) population growth through compounding trends [sic] to concentrate an increased proportion of population members (due to migration) which then creates a new source of internal threat, and hence, escalated logistical loads. These cycles, as they increase logistical loads, lead to even greater concentrations of power; and, as power is concentrated, it is used in waves of further external conflict, thereby escalating even more than those cycles of increasing logistical loads. At some point, these loads become too great, and the empire implodes back upon itself or dissolve [sic] from (a) internal conflict, (b) overextension beyond the productive, administrative, and distributive capacities, (c) confrontation with a powerful enemy, or (d) some combination of (a), (b), or (c). Indeed, once this process of collapse begins on one front, the other tend to "kick-in" and accelerate dissolution – as can currently be observed in the Russian empire. 256 (Retrieved from the World Wide Web www.unm.edu/~soc101/quoteconstruct.htm)."

Charts:

Inventors and Scientists of wwi	
Hiram Maxim	Alfred Nobel
Gottlieb Daimler	Ernest Swinton
Anton Fokker	Roland Garros
Richard Gatling	Paul Vieille
Peter Paul Mauser	John Moses Browning
Ernst Heinkel	Fritz Haber
Frederick Lindemann	Otto Hahn

Guglielmo Marconi	Hugo Junkers
Benjamin Hotchkis	Robert Whitehead

World War 2 Death Count

Although the precise numbers of deaths is impossible to determine and different sources believe in the accuracy of different numbers, these numbers are one set of figures for the number of deaths that occurred in World War Two. Figures for military and civilian deaths are provided where these were available.

Country	Military	Civilian	Deaths
USSR	13,600,000	7,700,000	21,300,000
China	1,324,000	10,000,000	11,324,000
Germany	3,250,000	3,810,000	7,060,000
Poland	850,000	6,000,000	6,850,000
Japan	-	-	2,000,000
Yugoslavia	300,000	1,400,000	1,706,000
Rumania	520,000	465,000	985,000
France	340,000	470,000	810,000
Hungary	-	-	750,000
Austria	380,000	145,000	525,000
Greece	-	-	520,000
United States	500,000	-	500,000
Italy	330,000	80,000	410,000

Czechoslovakia	-	-	400,000
Great Britain	326,000	62,000	388,000
Netherlands	198,000	12,000	210,000
Belgium	76,000	12,000	88,000
Finland	-	-	84,000
Canada	39,000	-	39,000
India	36,000	-	36,000
Australia	29,000	-	29,000
Albania	-	-	28,000
Spain	12,000	10,000	22,000
Bulgaria	19,000	2,000	21,000
New Zealand	12,000	-	12,000
Norway	-	-	10,262
South Africa	9,000	-	9,000
Luxembourg	-	-	5,000
Denmark	4,000	-	4,000
Total	-	-	56,125,262

Deaths by Mass Unpleasantness:

Estimated Totals for the Entire 20th Century

How many people died in all the wars, massacres, slaughters and oppressions of the Twentieth Century? Here are a few atrocitologists who have made estimates:

- **M. Cherif Bassouni**, from an unspecified "1996" source which I have been unable to track down (Cited in an article in the *Chicago Tribune*, 25 Oct. 1998)
  - ○ 33 million "military casualties" (That's how the article phrased it, but I presume they mean military **deaths**.)
  - ○ 170 million killed in "conflicts of a non-international charater, internal conflicts and tyrannical regime victimization")
    - ▪ 86M since the Second World War
  - ○ TOTAL: 203,000,000
- **Zbigniew Brzezinski**, *Out of Control: Global Turmoil on the Eve of the Twenty-first Century* (1993)
  - ○ "Lives deliberately extinguished by politically motivated carnage":
    - ▪ 167,000,000 to 175,000,000
    - ▪ Including:
      - ▪ War Dead: 87,500,000
        - ▪ Military war dead:
          - ▪ 33,500,000
        - ▪ Civilian war dead:
          - ▪ 54,000,000
      - ▪ Not-war Dead: 80,000,000
        - ▪ Communist oppression:
          - ▪ 60,000,000
- **David Barrett**, *World Christian Encyclopedia* (2001)
  - ○ Christian martyrs only: 45.5M [commentary & context]
- **Stephane Courtois**, *The Black Book of Communism*
  - ○ Victims of Communism only: 85-100M
- **Milton Leitenberg**
  [http://www.pcr.uu.se/Leitenberg_paper.pdf]

- o Politically caused deaths in the 20th C: 214M to 226M, incl...
    - Deaths in wars and conflicts, incl. civilian: 130M-142M
    - Political deaths, 1945-2000: 50M-51M
- **Not The Enemy Media** [http://nottheenemy.com/index_files/Death%20Counts/Death%20Counts.htm]
    - o Killed through U.S. foreign policy since WWII: 10,774,706 to 16,856,361 (1945-May 2003)
- **Rudolph J. Rummel**, *Death By Government*
    - o "Democides" - Government inflicted deaths (1900-87)
        - 169,198,000
        - Including:
            - Communist Oppression: 110,286,000
            - Democratic democides: 2,028,000
    - o Not included among democides:
        - Wars: 34,021,000
        - Non-Democidal Famine (often including famines associated with war and communist mismanagement):
            - China (1900-87): 49,275,000
            - Russia: (1921-47): 5,833,000
    - o Total:
        - 258,327,000 for all the categories listed here.
- Me (**Matthew White**, *Historical Atlas of the Twentieth Century*, 2001):
    - o Deaths by War and Oppression:
        - Genocide and Tyranny:
            - 83,000,000
        - Military Deaths in War:

            42,000,000

        - Civilian Deaths in War:
            - 19,000,000
        - Man-made Famine:
            - 44,000,000
            400

- TOTAL:
  - 188,000,000
- *FAQ: How did you get these totals?*
- *(Note: It's commonly said that more civilians than soldiers die in war, but you may notice that my numbers don't seem to agree with that. Before you jump to any conclusions, however, remember that most civilian deaths in war are intentional, and therefore fall into the "genocide and tyranny" category. Many others are the result of starvation.)*
- My estimate for the Communist share of the century's unpleasantness:
  - Genocide & Tyranny: 44M
    - (incl. intentional famine)
  - Man-made Famine: 37M
    - (excl. intentional famine)
  - Communist-inspired War (for example the Russian Civil War, Vietnam, Korea, etc.)
    - Military: 5M
    - Civilian: 6M
    - NOTE: With these numbers, I'm tallying **every** combat death and accidental civilian death in the war, without differentiating who died, who did it or who started it. According to whichever theory of Just War you are working from, the Communists may be entirely blameless, or entirely to blame, for these 11M dead.
  - TOTAL: 92M deaths by Communism.
  - RESIDUE: 96M deaths by non-Communism.

Costs of Peace

Cost of abundant supplies of food for 100% of humanity: $19 billion per year

Amount spent on dieting in the United States: $35 billion per year

Why don't we, the human race, do something about it? It's clear we can afford it. Many people and organizations are working to end hunger, yet on a global scale, the problem continues.

Cost of solving 18 top global problem areas: $235 billion per year
World military expenditures: $780 billion per year.
Source: Ralph Litwin was certified as a World Game Facilitator in 1996, and presented World Game Workshops in NJ schools from then until 2002 as part-time subcontractor for Education Information & Resource Center (EIRC). Over the years, Ralph & Pete Hecker and other EIRC staff rewrote the script and revised the materials based on their experience. They now present the new and improved experience as Evolution Earth Workshop, focusing on principles expressed in The Earth Charter (www.EarthCharter.org) and giving every participant an opportunity to become a card-carrying Earth Citizen.

For information about The World Game see: www.osearth.com
For a more detailed description of Evolution Earth Workshop ·
(game), see the EIRC website:
www.eirc.org/prodev/Services/EEW.htm
For information on booking Evolution Earth Workshop, contact Melissa Ponce at EIRC:
phone: (856) 582-7000 ext. 127 or email: mponce@eirc.org

Peace Documents:
Keegan (43) mentions the Hague convention(s) 1899, 1903 and 1915 (planned). Arbitration court to avert war – add this and 1928 Kellog-Briand to CAN WE STOP.

The Geneva Conventions – a Summary
From: http://en.wikipedia.org/wiki/Geneva_Conventions
The Geneva Conventions consist of four treaties formulated in Geneva, Switzerland, that set the standards for international law for humanitarian concerns. The conventions were the results of efforts by Henri Dunant, who was motivated by the horrors of war he witnessed at the Battle of Solferino in 1859.
As per article 49, 50, 129 and 146 of the Geneva Conventions I, II, III and IV, respectively, all signatory states are required to enact sufficient national law to make grave violations of the Geneva Conventions a punishable criminal offence. ·

The conventions and their agreements are as follows:
First Geneva Convention "for the Amelioration of the Condition of the Wounded and Sick in Armed Forces in the Field" (first adopted in 1864, last revision in 1949)
Second Geneva Convention "for the Amelioration of the Condition of Wounded, Sick and Shipwrecked Members of Armed Forces at Sea" (first adopted in 1949, successor of the 1907 Hague Convention X)
Third Geneva Convention "relative to the Treatment of Prisoners of War" (first adopted in 1929, last revision in 1949)
Fourth Geneva Convention "relative to the Protection of Civilian Persons in Time of War" (first adopted in 1949, based on parts of the 1907 Hague Convention IV)
In addition, there are three additional protocols to the Geneva Convention:
Protocol I (1977): Protocol Additional to the Geneva Conventions of 12 August 1949, and relating to the Protection of Victims of International Armed Conflicts
Protocol II (1977): Protocol Additional to the Geneva Conventions of 12 August 1949, and relating to the Protection of Victims of Non-International Armed Conflicts
Protocol III (2005): Protocol Additional to the Geneva Conventions of 12 August 1949, and relating to the Adoption of an Additional Distinctive Emblem
The adoption of the First Convention followed the foundation of the International Committee of the Red Cross in 1863. The text is given in the Resolutions of the Geneva International Conference. All four conventions were last revised and ratified in 1949, based on previous revisions and partly on some of the 1907 Hague Conventions; the whole set is referred to as the "Geneva Conventions of 1949" or simply the "Geneva Conventions". Later conferences have added provisions prohibiting certain methods of warfare and addressing issues of civil wars. Nearly all 200 countries of the world are "signatory" nations, in that they have ratified these conventions.
Clara Barton was instrumental in campaigning for the ratification of the First Geneva Convention by the United States; the U.S. signed in 1882. By the Fourth Geneva Convention some 47 nations had ratified the agreements.
[edit]
Other Geneva Conventions
Other conventions of the United Nations taking place in Geneva

and agreements signed there have become part of international and national laws, but are not to be confused with the above-mentioned treaties though they may be referred to as "Geneva Conventions." These include the Convention on the Territorial Sea and the Contiguous Zone, the Convention relating to the Status of Refugees (1951) and Protocol relating to the Status of Refugees (1967), and others.

The Hague Conventions – a Summary

From:
http://en.wikipedia.org/wiki/Hague_Conventions_%281899_and_1907%29
The Hague Conventions were international treaties negotiated at the First and Second Peace Conferences at The Hague, Netherlands in 1899 and 1907, respectively, and were, along with the Geneva Conventions, among the first formal statements of the laws of war and war crimes in the nascent body of international law.

The Hague Convention of 1899:
Signed on July 29, 1899 and entering into force on September 4, 1900, the Hague Convention of 1899 consisted of four main sections and three additional declarations (the final main section is for some reason identical to the first additional declaration):
I - Pacific Settlement of International Disputes
II - Laws and Customs of War on Land
III - Adaptation to Maritime Warfare of Principles of Geneva Convention of 1864
IV - Prohibiting Launching of Projectiles and Explosives from Balloons
Declaration I - On the Launching of Projectiles and Explosives from Balloons
Declaration II - On the Use of Projectiles the Object of Which is the Diffusion of Asphyxiating or Deleterious Gases
Declaration III - On the Use of Bullets Which Expand or Flatten Easily in the Human Body
The main effect of the Convention was to ban the use of certain types of modern technology in war: bombing from the air, chemical warfare, and hollow point bullets. The Convention also set up the Permanent Court of Arbitration.
The conference was summoned by Russia. Its delegates

404

included <u>Fyodor Martens</u> and <u>Ivan Bloch</u>

The Hague Convention of 1907:
The Second Peace Conference was held to expand upon the original Hague Convention, modifying some parts and adding others, with an increased focus on naval warfare. This was signed on <u>October 8</u>, <u>1907</u>, and entered into force on <u>January 26</u>, <u>1910</u>. It consisted of thirteen sections, of which twelve were ratified and entered into force:
I - The Pacific Settlement of International Disputes
II - The Limitation of Employment of Force for Recovery of Contract Debts
<u>III - The Opening of Hostilities</u>
<u>IV - The Laws and Customs of War on Land</u>
<u>V - The Rights and Duties of Neutral Powers and Persons in Case of War on Land</u>
<u>VI - The Status of Enemy Merchant Ships at the Outbreak of Hostilities</u>
<u>VII - The Conversion of Merchant Ships into War-Ships</u>
<u>VIII - The Laying of Automatic Submarine Contact Mines</u>
<u>IX - Bombardment by Naval Forces in Time of War</u>
<u>X - Adaptation to Maritime War of the Principles of the Geneva Convention</u>
<u>XI - Certain Restrictions with Regard to the Exercise of the Right of Capture in Naval War</u>
XII - The Creation of an International Prize Court [Not Ratified]*
<u>XIII - The Rights and Duties of Neutral Powers in Naval War</u>
Two declarations were signed as well:
Declaration I - extending Declaration II from the 1899 Conference to other types of aircraft
Declaration II - on the obligatory arbitration
*The never-ratified Section XII would have established an international court for the resolution of conflicting claims to captured shipping during wartime.
The British delegation included the 11th <u>Lord Reay</u> (Donald James Mackay), Sir <u>Ernest Satow</u> and <u>Eyre Crowe</u>. The Russian delegation was led by <u>Fyodor Martens</u>.

The Geneva Protocol to the Hague Conventions:
Though not negotiated in The Hague, the <u>Geneva Protocol</u> to the Hague Convention is considered an addition to the Convention.

Signed on June 17, 1925 and entering into force on February 8, 1928, it permanently bans the use of all forms of chemical and biological warfare in its single section, entitled Protocol for the Prohibition of the Use in War of Asphyxiating, Poisonous or Other Gases, and of Bacteriological Methods of Warfare. The protocol grew out of the increasing public outcry against chemical warfare following the use of mustard gas and similar agents in World War I, and fears that chemical and biological warfare could lead to horrific consequences in any future war. The protocol has since been augmented by the Biological Weapons Convention (1972) and the Chemical Weapons Convention (1993).

The Kellog-Briand Pact – a Summary

From: http://en.wikipedia.org/wiki/Kellogg-Briand_Pact
The Kellogg-Briand Pact, also known as the Pact of Paris, after the city where it was signed on August 27, 1928, is an international treaty "providing for the renunciation of war as an instrument of national policy." It failed in this purpose, but is significant for later developments in international law. It was named after the American secretary of state, Frank B. Kellogg, and French Foreign minister Aristide Briand, who both drafted the pact.

The Proposal

The pact was proposed 1927 by Aristide Briand, the French foreign minister and a Nobel Peace Prize recipient, as a bilateral treaty between the United States and France outlawing war between the two countries. Briand thought it would both improve the cooled relations between the former allies and, more importantly, ensure that the United States would ally with France in the event of another European war.

Frank B. Kellogg, the US Secretary of State, wanted to avoid any involvement in another European War, and so was indifferent towards the proposal. However, if he opposed the treaty he would be attacked in both Congress and the press by groups which favored such an agreement. Kellogg thus responded with a proposal for a multilateral pact against war open for all nations to become signatories.

Negotiations and Ratifications

After negotiations, it was signed in Paris on August 27, 1928 by eleven states: Australia, Canada, Czechoslovakia, Germany, India, the Irish Free State, Italy, New Zealand, South Africa, the

United Kingdom, and the United States. Four states added their support before it was proclaimed—Poland, Belgium, and France (in March), and Japan (in April). It was proclaimed to go into effect on July 24, 1929. Sixty-two nations ultimately signed the pact.

In the United States, the Senate approved the treaty overwhelmingly, 85-1. However, it did add a reservation that the treaty must not infringe upon America's right of self defense and that the United States was not obliged to enforce the treaty by taking action against those who violated it.

Effect and Legacy

The 1927 Kellogg-Briand Pact was concluded outside the League of Nations, and remains a binding treaty under international law. In the United States it remains in force as part of the supreme positive law, under Article Six of the United States Constitution.

As a practical matter, the Kellogg-Briand Pact did not live up to its aim of ending war, and in this sense it made no immediate contribution to international peace and proved to be ineffective in the years to come; the Japanese invasion of Manchuria in 1931, the Italian invasion of Ethiopia, and the German invasion of Poland, were prime examples of this. However, the pact is an important multilateral treaty because, in addition to binding the particular nations that signed it, it has also served as one of the legal bases establishing the international norm that the use of military force is presumptively unlawful.

Notably, the pact served as the legal basis for the creation of the notion of crime against peace — it was for committing this crime that the Nuremberg Tribunal sentenced a number of persons responsible for starting World War II.

The interdiction of aggressive war was confirmed and broadened by the United Nations Charter, which states in article 2 paragraph 4 that "All Members shall refrain in their international relations from the threat or use of force against the territorial integrity or political independence of any state, or in any other manner inconsistent with the Purposes of the United Nations." The consequence of this is that after World War II, nations have been forced to invoke the right of self-defense or the right of collective defense when using military action and have also been prohibited from annexing territory by force.

President Woodrow Wilson's Fourteen Points

Gentlemen of the Congress:

Once more, as repeatedly before, the spokesmen of the Central Empires have indicated their desire to discuss the objects of the war and the possible basis of a general peace. Parleys have been in progress at Brest-Litovsk between Russsian representatives and representatives of the Central Powers to which the attention of all the belligerents have been invited for the purpose of ascertaining whether it may be possible to extend these parleys into a general conference with regard to terms of peace and settlement.

The Russian representatives presented not only a perfectly definite statement of the principles upon which they would be willing to conclude peace but also an equally definite program of the concrete application of those principles. The representatives of the Central Powers, on their part, presented an outline of settlement which, if runch less definite, seemed susceptible of liberal interpretation until their specific program of practical terms was added. That program proposed no concessions at all either to the sovereignty of Russia or to the preferences of the populations with whose fortunes it dealt, but meant, in a word, that the Central Empires were to keep every foot of territory their armed forces had occupied -- every province, every city, every point of vantage -- as a permanent addition to their territories and their power.

It is a reasonable conjecture that the general principles of settlement which they at first suggested originated with the more liberal statesmen of Germany and Austria, the men who have begun to feel the force of their own people's thought and purpose, while the concrete terms of actual settlement came from the military leaders who have no thought but to keep what they have got. The negotiations have been broken off. The Russian representatives were sincere and in earnest. They cannot entertain such proposals of conquest and domination.

The whole incident is full of signifiances. It is also full of perplexity. With whom are the Russian representatives dealing? For whom are the representatives of the Central Empires speaking? Are they speaking for the majorities of their respective parliaments or for the minority parties, that military and imperialistic minority which has so far dominated their whole policy and controlled the affairs of Turkey and of the Balkan states which have felt obliged to become their associates in this war?

The Russian representatives have insisted, very justly, very wisely, and in the true spirit of modern democracy, that the conferences they have been holding with the Teutonic and Turkish statesmen should be held within open not closed, doors, and all the world has been audience, as was desired. To whom have we been listening, then? To those who speak the spirit and intention of the resolutions of the German Reichstag of the 9th of July last, the spirit and intention of the Liberal leaders and parties of Germany, or to those who resist and defy that spirit and intention and insist upon conquest and subjugation? Or are we listening, in fact, to both, unreconciled and in open and hopeless contradiction? These are very serious and pregnant questions. Upon the answer to them depends the peace of the world.

But, whatever the results of the parleys at Brest-Litovsk, whatever the confusions of counsel and of purpose in the utterances of the spokesmen of the Central Empires, they have again attempted to acquaint the world with their objects in the war and have again challenged their adversaries to say what their objects are and what sort of settlement they would deem just and satisfactory. There is no good reason why that challenge should not be responded to, and responded to with the utmost candor. We did not wait for it. Not once, but again and again, we have laid our whole thought and purpose before the world, not in general terms only, but each time with sufficient definition to make it clear what sort of definite terms of settlement must necessarily spring out of them. Within the last week Mr. Lloyd George has spoken with admirable candor and in admirable spirit for the people and Government of Great Britain.

There is no confusion of counsel among the adversaries of the Central Powers, no uncertainty of principle, no vagueness of detail. The only secrecy of counsel, the only lack of fearless frankness, the only failure to make definite statement of the objects of the war, lies with Germany and her allies. The issues of life and death hang upon these definitions. No statesman who has the least conception of his responsibility ought for a moment to permit himself to continue this tragical and appalling outpouring of blood and treasure unless he is sure beyond a peradventure that the objects of the vital sacrifice are part and parcel of the very life of Society and that the people for whom he speaks think them right and imperative as he does.

There is, moreover, a voice calling for these definitions of principle and of purpose which is, it seems to me, more thrilling and more compelling than any of the many moving voices with which the troubled air of the world is filled. It is the voice of the Russian people. They are prostrate and all but hopeless, it would seem, before the grim power of Germany, which has hitherto known no relenting and no pity. Their power, apparently, is shattered. And yet their soul is not subservient. They will not yield either in principle or in action. Their conception of what is right, of what is humane and honorable for them to accept, has been stated with a frankness, a largeness of view, a generosity of spirit, and a universal human sympathy which must challenge the admiration of every friend of mankind; and they have refused to compound their ideals or desert others that they themselves may be safe.

They call to us to say what it is that we desire, in what, if in anything, our purpose and our spirit differ from theirs; and I believe that the people of the United States would wish me to respond, with utter simplicity and frankness. Whether their present leaders believe it or not, it is our heartfelt desire and hope that some way may be opened whereby we may be privileged to assist the people of Russia to attain their utmost hope of liberty and ordered peace.

It will be our wish and purpose that the processes of peace, when they are begun, shall be absolutely open and that they shall involve and permit henceforth no secret understandings of any kind. The day of conquest and aggrandizement is gone by;

410

so is also the day of secret covenants entered into in the interest of particular governments and likely at some unlooked-for moment to upset the peace of the world. It is this happy fact, now clear to the view of every public man whose thoughts do not still linger in an age that is dead and gone, which makes it possible for every nation whose purposes are consistent with justice and the peace of the world to avow nor or at any other time the objects it has in view.

We entered this war because violations of right had occurred which touched us to the quick and made the life of our own people impossible unless they were corrected and the world secure once for all against their recurrence. What we demand in this war, therefore, is nothing peculiar to ourselves. It is that the world be made fit and safe to live in; and particularly that it be made safe for every peace-loving nation which, like our own, wishes to live its own life, determine its own institutions, be assured of justice and fair dealing by the other peoples of the world as against force and selfish aggression. All the peoples of the world are in effect partners in this interest, and for our own part we see very clearly that unless justice be done to others it will not be done to us. The program of the world's peace, therefore, is our program; and that program, the only possible program, as we see it, is this:

I. Open covenants of peace, openly arrived at, after which there shall be no private international understandings of any kind but diplomacy shall proceed always frankly and in the public view.

II. Absolute freedom of navigation upon the seas, outside territorial waters, alike in peace and in war, except as the seas may be closed in whole or in part by international action for the enforcement of international covenants.

III. The removal, so far as possible, of all economic barriers and the establishment of an equality of trade conditions among all the nations consenting to the peace and associating themselves for its maintenance.

IV. Adequate guarantees given and taken that national armaments will be reduced to the lowest point consistent with domestic safety.

V. A free, open-minded, and absolutely impartial adjustment of all colonial claims, based upon a strict observance of the principle that in determining all such questions of sovereignty the interests of the populations concerned must have equal weight with the equitable claims of the government whose title is to be determined.

VI. The evacuation of all Russian territory and such a settlement of all questions affecting Russia as will secure the best and freest cooperation of the other nations of the world in obtaining for her an unhampered and unembarrassed opportunity for the independent determination of her own political development and national policy and assure her of a sincere welcome into the society of free nations under institutions of her own choosing; and, more than a welcome, assistance also of every kind that she may need and may herself desire. The treatment accorded Russia by her sister nations in the months to come will be the acid test of their good will, of their comprehension of her needs as distinguished from their own interests, and of their intelligent and unselfish sympathy.

VII. Belgium, the whole world will agree, must be evacuated and restored, without any attempt to limit the sovereignty which she enjoys in common with all other free nations. No other single act will serve as this will serve to restore confidence among the nations in the laws which they have themselves set and determined for the government of their relations with one another. Without this healing act the whole structure and validity of international law is forever impaired.

VIII. All French territory should be freed and the invaded portions restored, and the wrong done to France by Prussia in 1871 in the matter of Alsace-Lorraine, which has unsettled the peace of the world for nearly fifty years, should be righted, in order that peace may once more be made secure in the interest of all.

IX. A readjustment of the frontiers of Italy should be effected along clearly recognizable lines of nationality.

X. The peoples of Austria-Hungary, whose place among the nations we wish to see safeguarded and assured, should be accorded the freest opportunity to autonomous development.

XI. Rumania, Serbia, and Montenegro should be evacuated; occupied territories restored; Serbia accorded free and secure access to the sea; and the relations of the several Balkan states to one another determined by friendly counsel along historically established lines of allegiance and nationality; and international guarantees of the political and economic independence and territorial integrity of the several Balkan states should be entered into.

XII. The Turkish portion of the present Ottoman Empire should be assured a secure sovereignty, but the other nationalities which are now under Turkish rule should be assured an undoubted security of life and an absolutely unmolested opportunity of autonomous development, and the Dardanelles should be permanently opened as a free passage to the ships and commerce of all nations under international guarantees.

XIII. An independent Polish state should be erected which should include the territories inhabited by indisputably Polish populations, which should be assured a free and secure access to the sea, and whose political and economic independence and territorial integrity should be guaranteed by international covenant.

XIV. A general association of nations must be formed under specific covenants for the purpose of affording mutual guarantees of political independence and territorial integrity to great and small states alike.

In regard to these essential rectifications of wrong and assertions of right we feel ourselves to be intimate partners of all the governments and peoples associated together against the Imperialists. We cannot be separated in interest or divided in purpose. We stand together until the end. For such arrangements and covenants we are willing to fight and to continue to fight until they are achieved; but only because we wish the right to prevail and desire a just and stable peace such as can be secured only by removing the chief provocations to war, which this program does remove. We have no jealousy of German greatness, and there is nothing in this program that impairs it. We grudge her no achievement or distinction of learning or of pacific enterprise such as have made her record very bright and very enviable. We do not wish to injure her or to block in any way her legitimate influence or power. We do not wish to fight her either with arms or with hostile arrangements of trade if she is willing to associate herself with us and the other peace- loving nations of the world in covenants of justice and law and fair dealing. We wish her only to accept a place of equality among the peoples of the world, -- the new world in which we now live, -- instead of a place of mastery.

Neither do we presume to suggest to her any alteration or modification of her institutions. But it is necessary, we must frankly say, and necessary as a preliminary to any intelligent dealings with her on our part, that we should know whom her spokesmen speak for when they speak to us, whether for the Reichstag majority or for the military party and the men whose creed is imperial domination.

We have spoken now, surely, in terms too concrete to admit of any further doubt or question. An evident principle runs through the whole program I have outlined. It is the principle of justice to all peoples and nationalities, and their right to live on equal terms of liberty and safety with one another, whether they be strong or weak.

Unless this principle be made its foundation no part of the structure of international justice can stand. The people of the United States could act upon no other principle; and to the vindication of this principle they are ready to devote their lives, their honor, and everything they possess. The moral climax of this the culminating and final war for human liberty has come, and they are ready to put their own strength, their own highest purpose, their own integrity and devotion to the test.

(Delivered in Joint Session, January 8, 1918)

Albert Einstein To Sigmund Freud in 1931-32

from <u>Einstein on Peace</u> ed. Otto Nathan and Heinz Norden (New York: Schocken Books, 1960), pp186-203
http://www.cis.vt.edu/modernworld/d/Einstein.html

I greatly admire your passion to ascertain the truth--a passion that has come to dominate all else in your thinking. You have shown with irresistible lucidity how inseparably the aggressive and destructive instincts are bound up in the human psyche with those of love and the lust for life. At the same time, your convincing arguments make manifest your deep devotion to the great goal of the internal and external liberation of man from the evils of war. This was the profound hope of all those who have been revered as moral and spiritual leaders beyond the limits of their own time and country, from Jesus to Goethe and Kant. Is it not significant that such men have been universally recognized as leaders, even though their desire to affect the course of human affairs was quite ineffective?

[2]

I am convinced that almost all great men who, because of their accomplishments, are recognized as leaders even of small groups share the same ideals. But they have little influence on the course of political events. It would almost appear that the very domain of human activity most crucial to the fate of nations is inescapably in the hands of wholly irresponsible political rulers.

[3]

Political leaders or governments owe their power either to the use of force or to their election by the masses. They cannot be regarded as representative of the superior moral or intellectual elements in a nation. In our time, the intellectual elite does not exercise any direct influence on the history of the world; the very fact of its division into many factions makes it impossible for its members to co-operate in the solution of today's problems. Do you not share the feeling that a change could be brought about by a free association of men whose previous work and achievements offer a guarantee of their ability and integrity? Such a group of international scope, whose members would have to keep contact with each other through constant interchange of opinions, might gain a significant and wholesome moral influence on the solution of political problems if its own attitudes, backed by the signatures of its concurring members, were made public through the press. Such an association would, of course, suffer from all the defects that have so often led to degeneration in learned societies; the danger that such a degeneration may develop is, unfortunately, ever present in view of the imperfections of human nature. However, and despite those dangers, should we not make at least an attempt to form such an association in spite of all dangers? It seems to me nothing less than an imperative duty!

[4]

Once such an association of intellectuals--men of real stature--has come into being, it might then make an energetic effort to en-list religious groups in the fight against war. The association would give moral power for action to many personalities whose good intentions are today paralyzed by an attitude of painful resignation. I also believe that such an association of men, who are highly respected for their personal accomplishments, would provide important moral support to those elements in the League of Nations who actively support the great objective for which that institution was created.

[5]

I offer these suggestions to you, rather than to anyone else in the world, because your sense of reality is less clouded by wishful thinking than is the case with other people and since you combine the qualities of critical judgment, earnestness and responsibility.

The high point in the relationship between Einstein and Freud came in the summer of 1932 when, under the auspices of the International Institute of Intellectual Co-operation, Einstein initiated a public debate with Freud about the causes and cure of wars. Einstein's official letter is dated July 30, 1932; it was accompanied by the following private note of the same date:

[6]

I should like to use this opportunity to send you warm personal regards and to thank you for many a pleasant hour which I had in reading your works. It is always amusing for me to observe that even those who do not believe in your theories find it so difficult to resist your ideas that they use your terminology in their thoughts and speech when they are off guard.

This is Einstein's open letter to Freud, which, strangely enough, has never become widely known:

[7]

Dear Mr. Freud:

The proposal of the League of Nations and its International Institute of Intellectual Co-operation at Paris that I should invite a person, to be chosen by myself, to a frank exchange of views on any problem that I might select affords me a very welcome opportunity of conferring with you upon a question which, as things now are, seems the most insistent of all the problems civilization has to face. This is the problem: Is there any way of delivering mankind from the menace of war? It is common knowledge that, with the advance of modern science, this issue has come to mean a matter of life and death for Civilization as we know it; nevertheless, for all the zeal displayed, every attempt at its solution has ended in a lamentable breakdown.

[8]

I believe, moreover, that those whose duty it is to tackle the problem professionally and practically are growing only too aware of their impotence to deal with it, and have now a very lively desire to learn the views of men who, absorbed in the pursuit of science, can see world problems in the perspective distance lends. As for me, the normal objective of my thought affords no insight into the dark places of human will and feeling. Thus, in the inquiry now proposed, I can do little more than to seek to clarify the question at issue and, clearing the ground of the more obvious solutions, enable you to bring the light of your far-reaching knowledge of man's instinctive life to bear upon the problem. There are certain psychological obstacles whose existence a layman in the mental sciences may dimly surmise, but whose interrelations and vagaries he is incompetent to fathom; you, I am convinced, will be able to suggest educative methods, lying more or less outside the scope of politics, which will eliminate these obstacles.

[9]

As one immune from nationalist bias, I personally see a simple way of dealing with the superficial (i.e., administrative) aspect of the problem: the setting up, by international consent, of a legislative and judicial body to settle every conflict arising between nations. Each nation would undertake to abide by the orders issued by this legislative body, to invoke its decision in every dispute, to accept its judgments unreservedly and to carry out every measure the tribunal deems necessary for the execution of its decrees. But here, at the outset, I come up against a difficulty; a tribunal is a human institution which, in proportion as the power at its disposal is inadequate to enforce its verdicts, is all the more prone to suffer these to be deflected by extrajudicial pressure. This is a fact with which we have to reckon; law and might inevitably go hand in hand, and juridical decisions approach more nearly the ideal justice demanded by the community (in whose name and interests these verdicts are pronounced) insofar as the community has effective power to compel respect of its juridical ideal.

But at present we are far from possessing any supranational organization competent to render verdicts of incontestable authority and enforce absolute submission to the execution of its verdicts. Thus I am led to my first axiom: The quest of international security involves the unconditional surrender by every nation, in a certain measure, of its liberty of action--its sovereignty that is to say--and it is clear beyond all doubt that no other road can lead to such security.

[10]

The ill success, despite their obvious sincerity, of all the efforts made during the last decade to reach this goal leaves us no room to doubt that strong psychological factors are at work which paralyze these efforts. Some of these factors are not far to seek. The craving for power which characterizes the governing class in every nation is hostile to any limitation of the national sovereignty. This political power hunger is often supported by the activities of another group, whose aspirations are on purely mercenary, economic lines. I have especially in mind that small but determined group, active in every nation, composed of individuals who, indifferent to social considerations and restraints, regard warfare, the manufacture and sale of arms, simply as an occasion to advance their personal interests and enlarge their personal authority.

[11]

But recognition of this obvious fact is merely the first step toward an appreciation of the actual state of affairs. Another question follows hard upon it: How is it possible for this small clique to bend the will of the majority, who stand to lose and suffer by a state of war, to the service of their ambitions. (*) An obvious answer to this question would seem to be that the minority, the ruling class at present, has the schools and press, usually the Church as well, under its thumb. This enables it to organize and sway the emotions of the masses, and makes its tool of them.

[12]

Yet even this answer does not provide a complete solution. Another question arises from it: How is it that these devices succeed so well in rousing men to such wild enthusiasm, even to sacrifice their lives? Only one answer is possible. Because man has within him a lust for hatred and destruction. In normal times this passion exists in a latent state, it emerges only in unusual circumstances; but it is a comparatively easy task to call it into play and raise it to the power of a collective psychosis. Here lies, perhaps, the crux of all the complex factors we are considering, an enigma that only the expert in the lore of human instincts can resolve.

418

[13]

And so we come to our last question. Is it possible to control man's mental evolution so as to make him proof against the psychosis of hate and destructiveness? Here I am thinking by no means only of the so-called uncultured masses. Experience proves that it is rather the so-called "intelligentsia" that is most apt to yield to these disastrous collective suggestions, since the intellectual has no direct contact with life in the raw but encounters it in its easiest, synthetic form--upon the printed page.

[14]

To conclude: I have so far been speaking only of wars between nations; what are known as international conflicts. But I am well aware that the aggressive instinct operates under other forms and in other circumstances. (I am thinking of civil wars, for instance, due in earlier days to religious zeal, but nowadays to social factors; or, again, the persecution of racial minorities.) But my insistence on what is the most typical, most cruel and extravagant form of conflict between man and man was deliberate, for here we have the best occasion of discovering ways and means to render all armed conflicts impossible.

[15]

I know that in your writings we may find answers, explicit or implied, to all the issues of this urgent and absorbing problem. But it would be of the greatest service to us all were you to present the problem of world peace in the light of your most recent discoveries, for such a presentation well might blaze the trail for new and fruitful modes of action.

Yours very sincerely,

A. Einstein

Leon Steinig, a League of Nations official who did much to inspire this correspondence, wrote Einstein on September 12, 1932:

[16]

. . . When I visited Professor Freud in Vienna, he asked me to thank you for your kind words and to tell you that he would do his best to explore the thorny problem of preventing war. He will have his answer ready by early October and he rather thinks that what he has to say will not be very encouraging. "All my life I have had to tell people truths that were difficult to swallow. Now that I am old, I certainly do not want to fool them." He was even doubtful whether [Henri] Bonnet [Director of the Institute of Intellectual Co-operation in Paris] would want to publish his pessimistic reply. . . .

Einstein replied to Steinig four days later saying that even if Freud's reply would be neither cheerful nor optimistic, it would certainly be interesting and psychologically effective.

Freud's reply, dated Vienna, September 1932, has also never been given the attention it deserved:

[17]

Dear Mr. Einstein:

When I learned of your intention to invite me to a mutual exchange of views upon a subject which not only interested you personally but seemed deserving, too, of public interest, I cordially assented. I expected you to choose a problem lying on the borderland of the knowable, as it stands today, a theme which each of us, physicist and psychologist, might approach from his own angle, to meet at last on common ground, though setting out from different premises. Thus the question which you put me--what is to be done to rid mankind of the war menace?--took me by surprise. And, next, I was dumbfounded by the thought of my (of our, I almost wrote) incompetence; for this struck me as being a matter of practical politics, the statesman's proper study. But then I realized that you did not raise the question in your capacity of scientist or physicist, but as a lover of his fellow men, who responded to the call of the League of Nations much as Fridtjof Nansen, the polar explorer, took on himself the task of succoring homeless and starving victims of the World War. And, next, I reminded myself that I was not being called on to formulate practical proposals but, rather, to explain how this question of preventing wars strikes a psychologist.

[18]

But here, too, you have stated the gist of the matter in your letter--and taken the wind out of my sails! Still, I will gladly follow in your wake and content myself with endorsing your conclusions, which, however, I propose to amplify to the best of my knowledge or surmise.

[19]

You begin with the relations between might and right, and this is assuredly the proper starting point for our inquiry. But, for the term might, I would substitute a tougher and more telling word: violence. In right and violence we have today an obvious antinomy. It is easy to prove that one has evolved from the other and, when we go back to origins and examine primitive conditions, the solution of the problem follows easily enough. I must crave your indulgence if in what follows I speak of well-known, admitted facts as though they were new data; the context necessitates this method.

420

[20]

Conflicts of interest between man and man are resolved, in principle,
by the recourse to violence. It is the same in the animal kingdom, from
which man cannot claim exclusion; nevertheless, men are also prone to
conflicts of opinion, touching, on occasion, the loftiest peaks of abstract
thought, which seem to call for settlement by quite another method.
This refinement is, however, a late development. To start with, group
force was the factor which, in small communities, decided points of
ownership and the question which man's will was to prevail. Very soon
physical force was implemented, then replaced, by the use of various
adjuncts; he proved the victor whose weapon was the better, or handled
the more skillfully. Now, for the first time, with the coming of
weapons, superior brains began to oust brute force, but the object of the
conflict remained the same: one party was to be constrained, by the
injury done him or impairment of his strength, to retract a claim or a
refusal. This end is most effectively gained when the opponent is
definitely put out of action--in other words, is killed. This procedure
has two advantages: the enemy cannot renew hostilities, and, secondly,
his fate deters others from following his example. Moreover, the
slaughter of a foe gratifies an instinctive craving--a point to which we
shall revert hereafter. However, another consideration may be set off
against this will to kill: the possibility of using an enemy for servile
tasks if< his spirit be broken and his life spared. Here violence finds an
outlet not in slaughter but in subjugation. Hence springs the practice of
giving quarter; but the victor, having from now on to reckon with the
craving for revenge that rankles in his victim, forfeits to some extent
his personal security.

[21]

Thus, under primitive conditions, it is superior force--brute violence, or
violence backed by arms-- that lords it everywhere. We know that in
the course of evolution this state of things was modified, a path was
traced that led away from violence to law. But what was this path?
Surely it issued from a single verity: that the superiority of one strong
man can be overborne by an alliance of many weaklings, that l'union
fait la force. Brute force is overcome by union; the allied might of
scattered units makes good its right against the isolated giant. Thus we
may define "right" (i.e., law) as the might of a community. Yet it, too,
is nothing else than violence, quick to attack whatever individual stands
in its path, and it employs the selfsame methods, follows like ends,
with but one difference: it is the communal, not individual, violence
that has its way. But, for the transition from crude violence to the reign
of law, a certain psychological condition must first obtain. The union of

the majority must be stable and enduring. If its sole raison d'etre be the discomfiture of some overweening individual and, after his downfall, it be dissolved, it leads to nothing. Some other man, trusting to his superior power, will seek to reinstate the rule of violence, and the cycle will repeat itself unendingly. Thus the union of the people must be permanent and well organized; it must enact rules to meet the risk of possible revolts; must set up machinery insuring that its rules--the laws--are observed and that such acts of violence as the laws demand are duly carried out. This recognition of a community of interests engenders among the members of the group a sentiment of unity and fraternal solidarity which constitutes its real strength.

[22]

So far I have set out what seems to me the kernel of the matter: the suppression of brute force by the transfer of power to a larger combination, founded on the community of sentiments linking up its members. All the rest is mere tautology and glosses. Now the position is simple enough so long as the community consists of a number of equipollent individuals. The laws of such a group can determine to what extent the individual must forfeit his personal freedom, the right of using personal force as an instrument of violence, to insure the safety of the group. But such a combination is only theoretically possible; in practice the situation is always complicated by the fact that, from the outset, the group includes elements of unequal power, men and women, elders and children, and, very soon, as a result of war and conquest, victors and the vanquished--i.e., masters and slaves--as well. From this time on the common law takes notice of these inequalities of power, laws are made by and for the rulers, giving the servile classes fewer rights. Thenceforward there exist within the state two factors making for legal instability, but legislative evolution, too: first, the attempts by members of the ruling class to set themselves above the law's restrictions and, secondly, the constant struggle of the ruled to extend their rights and see each gain embodied in the code, replacing legal disabilities by equal laws for all. The second of these tendencies will be particularly marked when there takes place a positive mutation of the balance of power within the community, the frequent outcome of certain historical conditions. In such cases the laws may gradually be adjusted to the changed conditions or (as more usually ensues) the ruling class is loath to rush in with the new developments, the result being insurrections and civil wars, a period when law is in abeyance and force once more the arbiter, followed by a new regime of law. There is another factor of constitutional change, which operates in a wholly pacific manner, viz.: the cultural evolution of the mass of the community; this factor, however, is of a different order and an only be dealt with later.

[23]

Thus we see that, even within the group itself, the exercise of violence cannot be avoided when conflicting interests are at stake. But the common needs and habits of men who live in fellowship under the same sky favor a speedy issue of such conflicts and, this being so, the possibilities of peaceful solutions make steady progress. Yet the most casual glance at world history will show an unending series of conflicts between one community and another or a group of others, between large and smaller units, between cities, countries, races, tribes and kingdoms, almost all of which were settled by the ordeal of war. Such war ends either in pillage or in conquest and its fruits, the downfall of the loser. No single all-embracing judgment can be passed on these wars of aggrandizement. Some, like the war between the Mongols and the Turks, have led to unmitigated misery; others, however, have furthered the transition from violence to law, since they brought larger units into being, within whose limits a recourse to violence was banned and a new regime determined all disputes. Thus the Roman conquest brought that boon, the pax Romana, to the Mediterranean lands. The French kings' lust for aggrandizement created a new France, flourishing in peace and unity. Paradoxical as its sounds, we must admit that warfare well might serve to pave the way to that unbroken peace we so desire, for it is war that brings vast empires into being, within whose frontiers all warfare is proscribed by a strong central power. In practice, however, this end is not attained, for as a rule the fruits of victory are but short-lived, the new-created unit falls asunder once again, generally because there can be no true cohesion between the parts that violence has welded. Hitherto, moreover, such conquests have only led to aggregations which, for all their magnitude, had limits, and disputes between these units could be resolved only by recourse to arms. For humanity at large the sole result of all these military enterprises was that, instead of frequent, not to say incessant, little wars, they had now to face great wars which, for all they came less often, were so much the more destructive.

[24]

Regarding the world of today the same conclusion holds good, and you, too, have reached it, though by a shorter path. There is but one sure way of ending war and that is the establishment, by common consent, of a central control which shall have the last word in every conflict of interests. For this, two things are needed: first, the creation of such a supreme court of judicature; secondly, its investment with adequate

executive force. Unless this second requirement be fulfilled, the first is unavailing. Obviously the League of Nations, acting as a Supreme Court, fulfills the first condition; it does not fulfill the second. It has no force at its disposal and can only get it if the members of the new body, its constituent nations, furnish it. And, as things are, this is a forlorn hope. Still we should be taking a very shortsighted view of the League of Nations were we to ignore the fact that here is an experiment the like of which has rarely--never before, perhaps, on such a scale--been attempted in the course of history. It is an attempt to acquire the authority (in other words, coercive influence), which hitherto reposed exclusively in the possession of power, by calling into play certain idealistic attitudes of mind. We have seen that there are two factors of cohesion in a community: violent compulsion and ties of sentiment ("identifications," in technical parlance) between the members of the group. If one of these factors becomes inoperative, the other may still suffice to hold the group together. Obviously such notions as these can only be significant when they are the expression of a deeply rooted sense of unity, shared by all. It is necessary, therefore, to gauge the efficacy of such sentiments. History tells us that, on occasion, they have been effective. For example, the Panhellenic conception, the Greeks' awareness of superiority over their barbarian neighbors, which found expression in the Amphictyonies, the Oracles and Games, was strong enough to humanize the methods of warfare as between Greeks, though inevitably it failed to prevent conflicts between different elements of the Hellenic race or even to deter a city or group of cities from joining forces with their racial foe, the Persians, for the discomfiture of a rival. The solidarity of Christendom in the Renaissance age was no more effective, despite its vast authority, in hindering Christian nations, large and small alike, from calling in the Sultan to their aid. And, in our times, we look in vain for some such unifying notion whose authority would be unquestioned. It is all too clear that the nationalistic ideas, paramount today in every country, operate in quite a contrary direction. Some there are who hold that the Bolshevist conceptions may make an end of war, but, as things are, that goal lies very far away and, perhaps, could only be attained after a spell of brutal internecine warfare. Thus it would seem that any effort to replace brute force by the might of an ideal is, under present conditions, doomed to fail. Our logic is at fault if we ignore the fact that right is founded on brute force and even today needs violence to maintain it.
[25]
I now can comment on another of your statements. You are amazed that it is so easy to infect men with the war fever, and you surmise that man

has in him an active instinct for hatred and destruction, amenable to such stimulations. I entirely agree with you. I believe in the existence of this instinct and have been recently at pains to study its manifestations. In this connection may I set out a fragment of that knowledge of the instincts, which we psychoanalysts, after so many tentative essays and groupings in the dark, have compassed? We assume that human instincts are of two kinds: those that conserve and unify, which we call "erotic" (in the meaning Plato gives to Eros in his Symposium), or else "sexual" (explicitly extending the popular connotation of "sex"); and, secondly, the instincts to destroy and kill, which we assimilate as the aggressive or destructive instincts. These are, as you perceive, the well known opposites, Love and Hate, transformed into theoretical entities; they are, perhaps, another aspect of those eternal polarities, attraction and repulsion, which fall within your province. But we must be chary of passing over hastily to the notions of good and evil. Each of these instincts is every whit as indispensable as its opposite, and all the phenomena of life derive from their activity, whether they work in concert or in opposition. It seems that an instinct of either category can operate but rarely in isolation; it is always blended ("alloyed," as we say) with a certain dosage of its opposite, which modifies its aim or even, in certain circumstances, is a prime condition of its attainment. Thus the instinct of self-preservation is certainly of an erotic nature, but to gain its end this very instinct necessitates aggressive action. In the same way the love instinct, when directed to a specific object, calls for an admixture of the acquisitive instinct if it is to enter into effective possession of that object. It is the difficulty of isolating the two kinds of instinct in their manifestations that has so long prevented us from recognizing them.
[26]
If you will travel with me a little further on this road, you will find that human affairs are complicated in yet another way. Only exceptionally does an action follow on the stimulus of a single instinct, which is per se a blend of Eros and destructiveness. As a rule several motives of similar composition concur to bring about the act. This fact was duly noted by a colleague of yours, Professor G. C. Lichtenberg, sometime Professor of Physics at Gottingen; he was perhaps even more eminent as a psychologist than as a physical scientist. He evolved the notion of a "Compass-card of Motives" and wrote: "The efficient motives impelling man to act can be classified like the thirty-two winds and described in the same manner; e.g., Food-Food-Fame or Fame-Fame-Food." Thus, when a nation is summoned to engage in war, a whole gamut of human motives may respond to this appeal--high and low

motives, some openly avowed, others slurred over. The lust for aggression and destruction is certainly included; the innumerable cruelties of history and man's daily life confirm its prevalence and strength. The stimulation of these destructive impulses by appeals to idealism and the erotic instinct naturally facilitate their release. Musing on the atrocities recorded on history's page, we feel that the ideal motive has often served as a camouflage for the dust of destruction; sometimes, as with the cruelties of the Inquisition, it seems that, while the ideal motives occupied the foreground of consciousness, they drew their strength from the destructive instincts submerged in the unconscious. Both interpretations are feasible.

[26]
You are interested, I know, in the prevention of war, not in our theories, and I keep this fact in mind. Yet I would like to dwell a little longer on this destructive instinct which is seldom given the attention that its importance warrants. With the least of speculative efforts we are led to conclude that this instinct functions in every living being, striving to work its ruin and reduce life to its primal state of inert matter. Indeed, it might well be called the "death instinct"; whereas the erotic instincts vouch for the struggle to live on. The death instinct becomes an impulse to destruction when, with the aid of certain organs, it directs its action outward, against external objects. The living being, that is to say, defends its own existence by destroying foreign bodies. But, in one of its activities, the death instinct is operative within the living being and we have sought to trace back a number of normal and pathological phenomena to this introversion of the destructive instinct. We have even committed the heresy of explaining the origin of human conscience by some such "turning inward" of the aggressive impulse. Obviously when this internal tendency operates on too large a scale, it is no trivial matter; rather, a positively morbid state of things; whereas the diversion of the destructive impulse toward the external world must have beneficial effects. Here is then the biological justification for all those vile, pernicious propensities which we are now combating. We can but own that they are really more akin to nature than this our stand against them, which, in fact, remains to be accounted for.

[27]
All this may give you the impression that our theories amount to species of mythology and a gloomy one at that! But does not every natural science lead ultimately to this--a sort of mythology? Is it otherwise today with your physical sciences?

[28]
The upshot of these observations, as bearing on the subject in hand, is

426

that there is no likelihood of our being able to suppress humanity's aggressive tendencies. In some happy corners of the earth, they say, where nature brings forth abundantly whatever man desires, there flourish races whose lives go gently by; unknowing of aggression or constraint. This I can hardly credit; I would like further details about these happy folk. The Bolshevists, too, aspire to do away with human aggressiveness by insuring the satisfaction of material needs and enforcing equality between man and man. To me this hope seems vain. Meanwhile they busily perfect their armaments, and their hatred of outsiders is not the least of the factors of cohesion among themselves. In any case, as you too have observed, complete suppression of man's aggressive tendencies is not in issue; what we may try is to divert it into a channel other than that of warfare.

[29]

From our "mythology" of the instincts we may easily deduce a formula for an indirect method of eliminating war. If the propensity for war be due to the destructive instinct, we have always its counter-agent, Eros, to our hand. All that produces ties of sentiment between man and man must serve us as war's antidote. These ties are of two kinds. First, such relations as those toward a beloved object, void though they be of sexual intent. The psychoanalyst need feel no compunction in mentioning "love" in this connection; religion uses the same language: Love thy neighbor as thyself. A pious injunction, easy to enounce, but hard to carry out! The other bond of sentiment is by way of identification. All that brings out the significant resemblances between men calls into play this feeling of community, identification, whereon is founded, in large measure, the whole edifice of human society.

[30]

In your strictures on the abuse of authority I find another suggestion for an indirect attack on the war impulse. That men are divided into the leaders and the led is but another manifestation of their inborn and irremediable inequality. The second class constitutes the vast majority; they need a high command to make decisions for them, to which decisions they usually bow without demur. In this context we would point out that men should be at greater pains than heretofore to form a superior class of independent thinkers, unamenable to intimidation and fervent in the quest of truth, whose function it would be to guide the masses dependent on their lead. There is no need to point out how little the rule of politicians and the Church's ban on liberty of thought encourage such a new creation. The ideal conditions would obviously be found in a community where every man subordinated his instinctive life to the dictates of reason. Nothing less than this could bring about so thorough and so durable a union between men, even if this involved the severance of mutual ties of sentiment. But surely such a hope is utterly utopian, as things are. The other indirect methods of preventing war are certainly more feasible, but entail no quick results. They conjure up an ugly picture of mills that grind so slowly that, before the flour is ready, men are dead of hunger.

[31]

As you see, little good comes of consulting a theoretician, aloof from worldly contact, on practical and urgent problems! Better it were to tackle each successive crisis with means that we have ready to our hands. However, I would like to deal with a question which, though it is not mooted in your letter, interests me greatly. Why do we, you and I and many another, protest so vehemently against war, instead of just accepting it as another of life's odious importunities? For it seems a natural thing enough, biologically sound and practically unavoidable. I trust you will not be shocked by my raising such a question. For the better conduct of an inquiry it may be well to don a mask of feigned aloofness. The answer to my query may run as follows: Because every man has a right over his own life and war destroys lives that were full of promise; it forces the individual into situations that shame his manhood, obliging him to murder fellow men, against his will; it ravages material amenities, the fruits of human toil, and much besides. Moreover, wars, as now conducted, afford no scope for acts of heroism according to the old ideals and, given the high perfection of modern arms, war today would mean the sheer extermination of one of the combatants, if not of both. This is so true, so obvious, that we can but wonder why the conduct of war is not banned by general consent. Doubtless either of the points I have just made is open to debate. It may be asked if the community, in its turn, cannot claim a right over the individual lives of its members. Moreover, all forms of war cannot be indiscriminately condemned; so long as there are nations and empires, each prepared callously to exterminate its rival, all alike must be equipped for war. But we will not dwell on any of these problems; they lie outside the debate to which you have invited me. I pass on to another point, the basis, as it strikes me, of our common hatred of war. It is this: We cannot do otherwise than hate it. Pacifists we are, since our organic nature wills us thus to be. Hence it comes easy to us to find arguments that justify our standpoint.

[32]

This point, however, calls for elucidation. Here is the way in which I see it. The cultural development of mankind (some, I know, prefer to call it civilization) has been in progress since immemorial antiquity. To

this process we owe all that is best in our composition, but also much that makes for human suffering. Its origins and causes are obscure, its issue is uncertain, but some of its characteristics are easy to perceive. It well may lead to the extinction of mankind, for it impairs the sexual function in more than one respect, and even today the uncivilized races and the backward classes of all nations are multiplying more rapidly than the cultured elements. This process may, perhaps, be likened to the effects of domestication on certain animals--it clearly involves physical changes of structure--but the view that cultural development is an organic process of this order has not yet become generally familiar. The psychic changes which accompany this process of cultural change are striking, and not to be gainsaid. They consist in the progressive rejection of instinctive ends and a scaling down of instinctive reactions. Sensations which delighted our forefathers have become neutral or unbearable to us; and, if our ethical and aesthetic ideals have undergone a change, the causes of this are ultimately organic. On the psychological side two of the most important phenomena of culture are, firstly, a strengthening of the intellect, which tends to master our instinctive life, and, secondly, an introversion of the aggressive impulse, with all its consequent benefits and perils. Now war runs most emphatically counter to the psychic disposition imposed on us by the growth of culture; we are therefore bound to resent war, to find it utterly intolerable. With pacifists like us it is not merely an intellectual and affective repulsion, but a constitutional intolerance, an idiosyncrasy in its most drastic form. And it would seem that the aesthetic ignominies of warfare play almost as large a part in this repugnance as war's atrocities.
[33]
How long have we to wait before the rest of men turn pacifist? Impossible to say, and yet perhaps our hope that these two factors-- man's cultural disposition and a well-founded dread of the form that future wars will take--may serve to put an end to war in the near future, is not chimerical. But by what ways or byways this will come about, we cannot guess. Meanwhile we may rest on the assurance that whatever makes for cultural development is working also against war.
[34]
With kindest regards and, should this expose prove a disappointment to you, my sincere regrets,

Yours,

SIGMUND FREUD

Einstein was apparently not disappointed when Freud's reply was received. He addressed the following letter to Freud on December 3, 1932:

[35]

You have made a most gratifying gift to the League of Nations and myself with your truly classic reply. When I wrote you I was thoroughly convinced of the insignificance of my role, which was only meant to document my good will, with me as the bait on the hoof; to tempt the marvelous fish into nibbling. You have given in return something altogether magnificent. We cannot know what may grow from such seed, as the effect upon man of any action or event is always incalculable. This is not within our power and we do not need to worry aboutit.

[36]

You have earned my gratitude and the gratitude of all men for having devoted all your strength to the search for truth and for having shown the rarest courage in professing your convictions all your life. . . . By the time the exchange between Einstein and Freud was published in 1933, under the title Why War?, Hitler, who was to drive both men into exile, was already in power, and the letters never achieved the wide circulation intended for them. Indeed, the first German edition of the pamphlet is reported to have been limited to only 2,000 copies, as was also the original English edition.

Besides the four major projects in 1932 that were just recorded, some of the messages, replies to inquiries, and similar statements which Einstein prepared during that same period give evidence of the increasing political tensions of those days. On April 20, 1932, he submitted to the Russian-language journal Nord-Ost, published in Riga, Latvia (then still an independent country), a contribution to a symposium on "Europe and the Coming War":

[37]

As long as all international conflicts are not subject to arbitration and the enforcement of decisions arrived at by arbitration is not guaranteed, and as long as war production is not prohibited we may be sure that war will follow upon war. Unless our civilization achieves the moral strength to overcome this evil, it is bound to share the fate of former civilizations: decline and decay.

To Arnold Kalisch, editor of the magazine Die Friedensfront, who asked him to sponsor a book against war by a Czechoslovakian physician, Einstein wrote on April 26, 1932:

[38]

No doubt you know how anxious I am to support anything that could effectively help combat the militaristic orientation of the public. But I have reservations . . . about this book. If war psychosis could be regarded as anillness like, say, paranoia, then any panic in a meeting would likewise have to be considered a sickness. It appears to be quite normal for people to raise little resistance to the emotional attitude of their fellow human beings. . . . In the case of war, to describe the psychosis that may then exist as an illness does not bring us one single step closer to solving the problem of wars. . . .

* (In speaking of the majority I do not exclude soldiers of every rank who have chosen war as their profession, in the belief that they are serving to defend the highest interests of their race, and that attack is often the best method of defense.)

Universal Declaration of Human Rights

PREAMBLE

Whereas recognition of the inherent dignity and of the equal and inalienable rights of all members of the human family is the foundation of freedom, justice and peace in the world,

Whereas disregard and contempt for human rights have resulted in barbarous acts which have outraged the conscience of mankind, and the advent of a world in which human beings shall enjoy freedom of speech and belief and freedom from fear and want has been proclaimed as the highest aspiration of the common people,

Whereas it is essential, if man is not to be compelled to have recourse, as a last resort, to rebellion against tyranny and oppression, that human rights should be protected by the rule of law,

Whereas it is essential to promote the development of friendly relations between nations,

Whereas the peoples of the United Nations have in the Charter reaffirmed their faith in fundamental human rights, in the dignity and worth of the human person and in the equal rights of men and women and have determined to promote social progress and better standards of life in larger freedom,

Whereas Member States have pledged themselves to achieve, in co-operation with the United Nations, the promotion of universal respect for and observance of human rights and fundamental freedoms,

Whereas a common understanding of these rights and freedoms is of the greatest importance for the full realization of this pledge,

Now, Therefore,

THE GENERAL ASSEMBLY

proclaims

THIS UNIVERSAL DECLARATION OF HUMAN RIGHTS as a common standard of achievement for all peoples and all nations, to the end that every individual and every organ of society, keeping this Declaration constantly in mind, shall strive by teaching and education to promote respect for these rights and freedoms and by progressive measures, national and international, to secure their universal and effective recognition and observance, both among the peoples of Member States themselves and among the peoples of territories under their jurisdiction.

Article 1. All human beings are born free and equal in dignity and rights. They are endowed with reason and conscience and should act towards one another in a spirit of brotherhood.

Article 2. Everyone is entitled to all the rights and freedoms set forth in this Declaration, without distinction of any kind, such as race, colour, sex, language, religion, political or other opinion, national or social origin, property, birth or other status.

Furthermore, no distinction shall be made on the basis of the political, jurisdictional or international status of the country or territory to which a person belongs, whether it be independent, trust, non-self-governing or under any other limitation of sovereignty.

Article 3. Everyone has the right to life, liberty and security of person.

Article 4. No one shall be held in slavery or servitude; slavery and the slave trade shall be prohibited in all their forms.

Article 5. No one shall be subjected to torture or to cruel, inhuman or degrading treatment or punishment.

Article 6. Everyone has the right to recognition everywhere as a person before the law.

Article 7. All are equal before the law and are entitled without any discrimination to equal protection of the law. All are entitled to equal protection against any discrimination in violation of this Declaration and against any incitement to such discrimination.

Article 8. Everyone has the right to an effective remedy by the competent national tribunals for acts violating the fundamental rights granted him by the constitution or by law.

Article 9. No one shall be subjected to arbitrary arrest, detention or exile.

Article 10. Everyone is entitled in full equality to a fair and public hearing by an independent and impartial tribunal, in the determination of his rights and obligations and of any criminal charge against him.

Article 11. (1) Everyone charged with a penal offence has the right to be presumed innocent until proved guilty according to law in a public trial at which he has had all the guarantees necessary for his defence.

(2) No one shall be held guilty of any penal offence on account of any act or omission which did not constitute a penal offence, under national or international law, at the time when it was committed.

Nor shall a heavier penalty be imposed than the one that was applicable at the time the penal offence was committed.

Article 12. No one shall be subjected to arbitrary interference with his privacy, family, home or correspondence, nor to attacks upon his honour and reputation. Everyone has the right to the protection of the law against such interference or attacks.

Article 13. (1) Everyone has the right to freedom of movement and residence within the borders of each state.

(2) Everyone has the right to leave any country, including his own, and to return to his country.

Article 14. (1) Everyone has the right to seek and to enjoy in other countries asylum from persecution.

(2) This right may not be invoked in the case of prosecutions genuinely arising from non-political crimes or from acts contrary to the purposes and principles of the United Nations.

Article 15. (1) Everyone has the right to a nationality.

(2) No one shall be arbitrarily deprived of his nationality nor denied the right to change his nationality.

Article 16. (1) Men and women of full age, without any limitation due to race, nationality or religion, have the right to marry and to found a family. They are entitled to equal rights as to marriage, during marriage and at its dissolution.

(2) Marriage shall be entered into only with the free and full consent of the intending spouses.

(3) The family is the natural and fundamental group unit of society and is entitled to protection by society and the State.

Article 17. (1) Everyone has the right to own property alone as well as in association with others.

(2) No one shall be arbitrarily deprived of his property.

Article 18. Everyone has the right to freedom of thought, conscience and religion; this right includes freedom to change his religion or belief, and freedom, either alone or in community with others and in public or private, to manifest his religion or belief in teaching, practice, worship and observance.

Article 19. Everyone has the right to freedom of opinion and expression; this right includes freedom to hold opinions without interference and to seek, receive and impart information and ideas through any media and regardless of frontiers.

Article 20. (1) Everyone has the right to freedom of peaceful assembly and association.

(2) No one may be compelled to belong to an association.

Article 21. (1) Everyone has the right to take part in the government of his country, directly or through freely chosen representatives.

(2) Everyone has the right of equal access to public service in his country.

(3) The will of the people shall be the basis of the authority of government; this will shall be expressed in periodic and genuine elections which shall be by universal and equal suffrage and shall be held by secret vote or by equivalent free voting procedures.

Article 22. Everyone, as a member of society, has the right to social security and is entitled to realization, through national effort and international co-operation and in accordance with the organization and resources of each State, of the economic, social and cultural rights indispensable for his dignity and the free development of his personality.

Article 23. (1) Everyone has the right to work, to free choice of employment, to just and favourable conditions of work and to protection against unemployment.

(2) Everyone, without any discrimination, has the right to equal pay for equal work.

(3) Everyone who works has the right to just and favourable remuneration ensuring for himself and his family an existence worthy of human dignity, and supplemented, if necessary, by other means of social protection.

(4) Everyone has the right to form and to join trade unions for the protection of his interests.

Article 24. Everyone has the right to rest and leisure, including reasonable limitation of working hours and periodic holidays with pay.

Article 25. (1) Everyone has the right to a standard of living adequate for the health and well-being of himself and of his family, including food, clothing, housing and medical care and necessary social services, and the right to security in the event of unemployment, sickness, disability, widowhood, old age or other lack of livelihood in circumstances beyond his control.

(2) Motherhood and childhood are entitled to special care and assistance. All children, whether born in or out of wedlock, shall enjoy the same social protection.

Article 26. (1) Everyone has the right to education. Education shall be free, at least in the elementary and fundamental stages. Elementary education shall be compulsory. Technical and professional education shall be made generally available and higher education shall be equally accessible to all on the basis of merit.

(2) Education shall be directed to the full development of the human personality and to the strengthening of respect for human rights and fundamental freedoms.

It shall promote understanding, tolerance and friendship among all nations, racial or religious groups, and shall further the activities of the United Nations for the maintenance of peace.

(3) Parents have a prior right to choose the kind of education that shall be given to their children.

Article 27. (1) Everyone has the right freely to participate in the cultural life of the community, to enjoy the arts and to share in scientific advancement and its benefits.

(2) Everyone has the right to the protection of the moral and material interests resulting from any scientific, literary or artistic production of which he is the author.

Article 28. Everyone is entitled to a social and international order in which the rights and freedoms set forth in this Declaration can be fully realized.

Article 29. (1) Everyone has duties to the community in which alone the free and full development of his personality is possible.

(2) In the exercise of his rights and freedoms, everyone shall be subject only to such limitations as are determined by law solely for the purpose of securing due recognition and respect for the rights and freedoms of others and of meeting the just requirements of morality, public order and the general welfare in a democratic society.

(3) These rights and freedoms may in no case he exercised contrary to the purposes and principles of the United Nations.

Article 30. Nothing in this Declaration may be interpreted as implying for any State, group or person any right to engage in any activity or to perform any act aimed at the destruction of any of the rights and freedoms set forth herein.

The Russell-Einstein Manifesto

From http://www.pugwash.org/about/manifesto.htm

Issued in London, 9 July 1955

By Bertrand Russell and Albert Einstein

IN the tragic situation which confronts humanity, we feel that scientists should assemble in conference to appraise the perils that have arisen as a result of the development of weapons of mass destruction, and to discuss a resolution in the spirit of the appended draft.

We are speaking on this occasion, not as members of this or that nation, continent, or creed, but as human beings, members of the species Man, whose continued existence is in doubt. The world is full of conflicts; and, overshadowing all minor conflicts, the titanic struggle between Communism and anti-Communism.

Almost everybody who is politically conscious has strong feelings about one or more of these issues; but we want you, if you can, to set aside such feelings and consider yourselves only as members of a biological species which has had a remarkable history, and whose disappearance none of us can desire.

We shall try to say no single word which should appeal to one group rather than to another. All, equally, are in peril, and, if the peril is understood, there is hope that they may collectively avert it.

We have to learn to think in a new way. We have to learn to ask ourselves, not what steps can be taken to give military victory to whatever group we prefer, for there no longer are such steps; the question we have to ask ourselves is: what steps can be taken to prevent a military contest of which the issue must be disastrous to all parties?

The general public, and even many men in positions of authority, have not realized what would be involved in a war with nuclear bombs. The general public still thinks in terms of the obliteration of cities. It is

438

understood that the new bombs are more powerful than the old, and that, while one A-bomb could obliterate Hiroshima, one H-bomb could obliterate the largest cities, such as London, New York, and Moscow.

No doubt in an H-bomb war great cities would be obliterated. But this is one of the minor disasters that would have to be faced. If everybody in London, New York, and Moscow were exterminated, the world might, in the course of a few centuries, recover from the blow. But we now know, especially since the Bikini test, that nuclear bombs can gradually spread destruction over a very much wider area than had been supposed.

It is stated on very good authority that a bomb can now be manufactured which will be 2,500 times as powerful as that which destroyed Hiroshima. Such a bomb, if exploded near the ground or under water, sends radio-active particles into the upper air. They sink gradually and reach the surface of the earth in the form of a deadly dust or rain. It was this dust which infected the Japanese fishermen and their catch of fish. No one knows how widely such lethal radio-active particles might be diffused, but the best authorities are unanimous in saying that a war with H-bombs might possibly put an end to the human race. It is feared that if many H-bombs are used there will be universal death, sudden only for a minority, but for the majority a slow torture of disease and disintegration.

Many warnings have been uttered by eminent men of science and by authorities in military strategy. None of them will say that the worst results are certain. What they do say is that these results are possible, and no one can be sure that they will not be realized. We have not yet found that the views of experts on this question depend in any degree upon their politics or prejudices. They depend only, so far as our researches have revealed, upon the extent of the particular expert's knowledge. We have found that the men who know most are the most gloomy.

Here, then, is the problem which we present to you, stark and dreadful and inescapable: Shall we put an end to the human race; or shall mankind renounce war? People will not face this alternative because it is so difficult to abolish war.

The abolition of war will demand distasteful limitations of national

439

sovereignty. But what perhaps impedes understanding of the situation more than anything else is that the term "mankind" feels vague and abstract. People scarcely realize in imagination that the danger is to themselves and their children and their grandchildren, and not only to a dimly apprehended humanity. They can scarcely bring themselves to grasp that they, individually, and those whom they love are in imminent danger of perishing agonizingly. And so they hope that perhaps war may be allowed to continue provided modern weapons are prohibited.

This hope is illusory. Whatever agreements not to use H-bombs had been reached in time of peace, they would no longer be considered binding in time of war, and both sides would set to work to manufacture H-bombs as soon as war broke out, for, if one side manufactured the bombs and the other did not, the side that manufactured them would inevitably be victorious.

Although an agreement to renounce nuclear weapons as part of a general reduction of armaments would not afford an ultimate solution, it would serve certain important purposes. First, any agreement between East and West is to the good in so far as it tends to diminish tension. Second, the abolition of thermo-nuclear weapons, if each side believed that the other had carried it out sincerely, would lessen the fear of a sudden attack in the style of Pearl Harbour, which at present keeps both sides in a state of nervous apprehension. We should, therefore, welcome such an agreement though only as a first step.

Most of us are not neutral in feeling, but, as human beings, we have to remember that, if the issues between East and West are to be decided in any manner that can give any possible satisfaction to anybody, whether Communist or anti-Communist, whether Asian or European or American, whether White or Black, then these issues must not be decided by war. We should wish this to be understood, both in the East and in the West.

There lies before us, if we choose, continual progress in happiness, knowledge, and wisdom. Shall we, instead, choose death, because we cannot forget our quarrels? We appeal as human beings to human beings: Remember your humanity, and forget the rest. If you can do so, the way lies open to a new Paradise; if you cannot, there lies before you the risk of universal death.

Resolution:

WE invite this Congress, and through it the scientists of the world and the general public, to subscribe to the following resolution:

"In view of the fact that in any future world war nuclear weapons will certainly be employed, and that such weapons threaten the continued existence of mankind, we urge the governments of the world to realize, and to acknowledge publicly, that their purpose cannot be furthered by a world war, and we urge them, consequently, to find peaceful means for the settlement of all matters of dispute between them."

Signatories:
Max Born
Percy W. Bridgman
Albert Einstein
Leopold Infeld
Frederic Joliot-Curie
Herman J. Muller
Linus Pauling
Cecil F. Powell
Joseph Rotblat
Bertrand Russell
Hideki Yukawa

War Quotes:

Author	Quote
Richard M. Nixon	A riot is a spontaneous outburst. A war is subject to advance planning.
Napoleon Bonaparte	A soldier will fight long and hard for a bit of colored ribbon.
Herbert V. Prochnow	A visitor from Mars could easily pick out the civilized nations. They have the best implements of war.

Sun Tzu	All war is deception.
Francois Fenelon	All wars are civil wars, because all men are brothers.
Marcus Tullius Cicero	An unjust peace is better than a just war.
Gregory Clark	Are bombs the only way of setting fire to the spirit of a people? Is the human will as inert as the past two world-wide wars would indicate?
John Stuart Mill	Can treaties be more faithfully enforced between aliens than laws can among friends? Suppose you go to war, you cannot fight always; and when, after much loss on both sides, and no gain on either, you cease fighting, the identical old questions as to term
Karl Kraus	Confidence in the principles of an enemy must remain even during war, otherwise a peace could never be concluded; and hostilities would degenerate into a war of extermination since war in fact is but the sad resource employed in a state of nature in defen
David G. Farragut	Damn the torpedoes! Full speed ahead!
David G. Farragut	Every gun that is made, every warship launched, every rocket fired signifies, in the final sense, a theft from those who hunger and are not fed, those who are cold and are not clothed. This world in arms is not spending money alone. It is spending the sw
Colman McCarthy	Everyone's a pacifist between wars. It's like being a vegetarian between meals.
D. W. Brogan	For Americans war is almost all of the time a nuisance, and military skill is a luxury like Mah-Jongg. But when the issue is brought home to them, war becomes as important, for the necessary period, as business or sport. And it is hard to decide which is
Charles Sumner	Give me the money that has been spent in war and I will clothe every man, woman, and child in an attire of which kings and queens will be proud. I will build a schoolhouse in every valley over the whole earth. I will crown every hillside with a place of w
Charles Sumner	Give me the money that has been spent in war and I will clothe every man, woman, and child in an attire of

	which kings and queens will be proud. I will build a schoolhouse in every valley over the whole earth. I will crown every hillside with a place of worship consecrated to peace.
Albert Einstein	He who joyfully marches to music in rank and file has already earned my contempt. He has been given a large brain by mistake, since for him the spinal cord would suffice.
Gen. H. Norman Schwarzkopf	History teaches that wars begin when governments believe the price of aggression is cheap. To keep the peace, we and our allies must be strong enough to convince any potential aggressor that war could bring no benefit, only disaster.
Agatha Christie	http://unpress.bandersnatch.org/suntzu/artofwar.html#n0.58
Kahlil Gibran	http://www.eisenhower.archives.gov/chance.htm
Franklin D. Roosevelt	http://www.pitt.edu/~pugachev/greatwar/owen.html
General John Stark	http://www.reagan.utexas.edu/archives/speeches/1984/11684a.htm
Ronald Reagan	I couldn't help but say to Mr. Gorbachev just think how easy his task and mine might be in these meetings that we held if suddenly there was a threat to this world from another planet. We'd find out once and for all that we really are all human beings here on this earth together.
Ulysses S. Grant	I have never advocated war except as a means of peace.
John Paul Jones	I have not yet begun to fight!
Sun-Tzu	I have seen war. I have seen war on land and sea. I have seen blood running from the wounded. I have seen men coughing out their gassed lungs. I have seen the dead in the mud. I have seen cities destroyed. I have seen 200 limping, exhausted men come out o
John Adams	I must study politics and war that my sons may have liberty to study mathematics and philosophy.

Joan Baez	If it's natural to kill, how come men have to go into training to learn how?
H. G. Wells	If we don't end war, war will end us.
Ernest Hemingway	In modern war... you will die like a dog for no good reason.
?Immanuel Kant	In peace, as a wise man, he should make suitable preparation for war.
Jose Narosky	In war, there are no unwounded soldiers.
Fred Woodworth	It seems like such a terrible shame that innocent civilians have to get hurt in wars, otherwise combat would be such a wonderfully healthy way to rid the human race of unneeded trash.
Isaac Asimov	John Dalton's records, carefully preserved for a century, were destroyed during the World War II bombing of Manchester. It is not only the living who are killed in war.
Percy Bysshe Shelley	Man has no right to kill his brother. It is no excuse that he does so in uniform: he only adds the infamy of servitude to the crime of murder.
John F. Kennedy	Mankind must put an end to war before war puts an end to mankind.
Ssu-ma Ch`ien	Military weapons are the means used by the Sage to punish violence and cruelty, to give peace to troublous times, to remove difficulties and dangers, and to succor those who are in peril. Every animal with blood in its veins and horns on its head will fig
Ernest Hemingway	Never think that war, no matter how necessary, nor how justified, is not a crime.
Henry A. Kissinger	No country can act wisely simultaneously in every part of the globe at every moment of time.
Herbert Hoover	Older men declare war. But it is the youth that must fight and die.
Martin Luther King, Jr.	One of the greatest casualties of the war in Vietnam is the Great Society... shot down on the battlefield of Vietnam.
Plato	Only the dead have seen the end of the war.

Omar N. Bradley	Ours is a world of nuclear giants and ethical infants. We know more about war that we know about peace, more about killing that we know about living.
Euripides	Ten soldiers wisely led will beat a hundred without a head.
Sir Winston Churchill	That was what, ultimately, war did to you. It was not the physical dangers--the mines at sea, the bombs from the air, the crisp ping of a rifle bullet as you drove over a desert track. No, it was the spiritual danger of learning how much easier life was i
Louis Simpson	The aim of military training is not just to prepare men for battle, but to make them long for it.
John F. Kennedy	The basic problems facing the world today are not susceptible to a military solution.
Joseph Stalin	The death of one man is a tragedy. The death of millions is a statistic.
George McGovern	The Establishment center... has led us into the stupidest and cruelest war in all history. That war is a moral and political disaster - a terrible cancer eating away at the soul of our nation.
John Paul Jones	The general who is able to persuade his forces that there is victory, even where there seems to be defeat, is one who will inspire them to fight against apparently impossible odds. They will, indeed, never suffer defeat, but will fight on until annihilate
Albert Einstein	The release of atom power has changed everything except our way of thinking... the solution to this problem lies in the heart of mankind. If only I had known, I should have become a watchmaker.
Richard Jordan Gatling	It occurred to me that if I could invent a machine - a gun - which could by its rapidity of fire, enable one man to do as much battle duty as a hundred, that it would, to a large extent supersede the necessity of large armies, and consequently, exposure to battle and disease [would] be greatly diminished.
Robert Oppenheimer	We knew the world would not be the same. A few people laughed, a few people cried, most people were silent. I remembered the line from

	the Hindu scripture, the *Bhagavad-Gita*. Vishnu is trying to persuade the Prince that he should do his duty and to impress him takes on his multi-armed form and says, 'I am become Death, the destroyer of worlds.' I suppose we all thought that one way or another.
Randolph Bourne,	from War and the Intellectuals, 1964. "War is the health of the State. It automatically sets in motion throughout society these irresistible forces for uniformity, for passionate cooperation with the government in coercing into obedience the minority groups and individuals which lack the larger herd sense."

BIBLIOGRAPHY

Abanes, Richard. American Militias. Downers Grove, Illinois: InterVarsity Press. 1996.

Alfonso, Oscar M. Theodore Roosevelt and the Philippines, 1897 - 1909. Quezon City, Philippine Islands: University of the Philippines Press, 1970.

Anderson, Benedict. Imagined Communities: Reflections on the Origin and Spread of Nationalism. Revised Edition ed. London and New York: Verso. 1991.

Appleby, Joyce, Lynn Hunt, and Margaret Jacob. Telling the Truth About History. New York: W.W. Norton & Company. 1994.

Ardrey, Robert. The Social Contract: A Personal Inquiry into the Evolutionary Sources of Order and Disorder. New York: Atheneum, 1970.

Arntz, William, Betsy Chasse, and Mark Vicente writers, producers and directors of What the Bleep Do We Know? Documentary/Drama. A Captive Light Industries, Lord of the Winds Film. 2004.

Asimov, Isaac. Foundation. New York: Bantam Books. 1951.

Barraclough, Geoffrey, ed., The Times Concise Atlas

of World History. Maplewood, New Jersey: Hammond Inc., 1982.

Barrows, David P. A Decade of American Government in the Philippines. Yonkers, New York: World Book Company, 1914.

Benedict, Ruth. Patterns of Culture. Boston: Houghton Mifflin, 1961.

------------- The Chrysanthemum and the Sword: Patterns of Japanese Culture. New York: Meridian. 1946.

Beowulf and the Fight at Finnsburgh. ed. Frederick Klaeber, 3d ed., Lexington MA: DC Heath & Co. 1950.

Bloomfield, Lincoln. International Military Forces: The Question of Peacekeeping in an Armed and Disarmed World. Boston: Little, Brown, 1964.

------------- The Power to Keep Peace: Today in a World Without War. Berkeley, Ca.. World Without War Council Publications, 1971.

Blount, James H. The Occupation of the Philippines, 1898 - 1912. New York: Oriole Editions Incorporated, 1973.

Bø, Olav. "Hólmganga and Einvigi: Scandinavian Forms of the Duel." Medieval Scandinavia 2 (1969). 132-148.

Bodley, John H. Cultural Anthropology: Tribes, States, and the Global System. Mountain View, California:

Mayfield Publishing Company. 1997.

Bohannan, Paul, and Mark Glazer. Highpoints in Anthropology. New York: Alfred A. Knopf, Inc., 1988.

Bonaparte, Napoleon. The Military Maxims of Napoleon. Translated by George C. D'Aguilar with introduction and commentary by David G. Chandler. New York: Macmillan Publishing Company. 1988.

Boot, Max. The Savage Wars of Peace: Small Wars and the Rise of American Power. New York: Basic Books, A Member of the Perseus Books Group. 2002.

Boulding, Kenneth. Stable Peace. Austin: University of Texas Press, 1978.

Bourne, Randolph. "War is the Health of the State," First draft of an essay, "The State", that was left unfinished by Bourne at the time of his death, 1918. It is now in the Bourne MSS, Columbia University Libraries.

Breisach, Ernst. Historiography: Ancient, Medieval and Modern. 2nd edition. Chicago: University of Chicago Press, 1994.

Brierly, James. The Law of Nations: an Introduction to the International Law of Peace. Oxford: Clarendon Press, 1963.

Brummett, Palmira, et al. Civilization Past and Present. New York: Pearson Longman. 2006.

Brzezinski, Zbigniew. Out of Control: Global Turmoil on the Eve of the Twenty-first Century . New York: Charles Scribner's Sons. 1993.

Burke, James. Connections. Boston: Little, Brown & Company. 1978.

Burton, Richard F. The Book of the Sword. New York: Dover Publications, Inc. 1987.

Caesar, Julius. The Conquest of Gaul. Introduction and revisions by Jane F. Gardner. New York: Penguin Putnam. 1982.

Campbell. Joseph. The Hero with a Thousand Faces. Princeton, N.J..: Princeton University Press. 1990.

Capra, Fritjof. The Tao of Physics. Boston: Shambhala. 1991.

Carr, Edward H. What Is History? The George Macaulay Trevelyan Lectures Delivered at the University of Cambridge, January-March 1961. New York: Vintage Books, A Division of Random House. 1961.

Carson, Clayborne, E. J. Lapsansky-Werner, G. B. Nash. African American Lives: The Struggle for Freedom. New York: Pearson Longman. 2005.

Chadwick, Alger, "Creating Global Visions for Peace Movements," in Elise Boulding, Clovis Brigagao, Kevin Clements (eds.) Peace Culture and Society. Boulder: Westview Press, 1991.

Che Man, W. K. Muslim Separatism: The Moros of the Southern Philippines and the Malays of Southern Thailand. Singapore: Oxford University Press, 1990.

Clark, Ramsey, and others. Challenge to Genocide: Let Iraq Live. New York: International Action Center. 1998.

------------------ et al. NATO in the Balkans. New York: International Action Center. 1998.

Clausewitz, Carl von. On War. Anatol Rapoport, ed. Baltimore: Penguin Books. 1968.

Coles, John. Archaeology by Experiment. New York: Charles Scribner's Sons. 1973.

Colley, David P. Blood for Dignity: the Story of the First Integrated Combat Unit in the U.S. Army. New York: St. Martin's Griffin. 2003.

Cox, Gray. The Ways of Peace: a Philosophy of Peace as Action. New York: Paulist Press, 1986.

Cray, Ed. Chief Justice: A Biography of Earl Warren. New York: Simon and Schuster, 1997.

Current, Richard N., et al. American History: A Survey. vol. 2, 1865 to the present. New York: Alfred A. Knopf, Inc., 1987.

Dalton, Dennis. Indian Ideas of Freedom: the Political Thought of Swami Vivekenanda, Aurobindo Ghose, Mahatma Gandhi, and Rabindranath Tagore.

Gurgaon, Haryana: Academic Press, 1982.

Darwin, Charles. The Descent of Man and Selection in Relation to Sex. New York: Appleton and Co. 1883.

Davis, Mike. City of Quartz : Excavating the Future in Los Angeles. New York: Knopf. 1992.

Dees, Morris with James Corcoran. Gathering Storm: America's Militia Threat. New York: HarperCollins Publishers, Inc. 1996.

DeLaet, Debra. The Global Struggle for Human Rights: Universal Principles in World Politics. Belmont, California: Thomson Wadsworth. 2006.

Diamond, Jared. Guns, Germs and Steel: The Fates of Human Societies. New York: Norton, 1997.

DuBois, W.E.B., The African Roots of War. New York: The Atlantic. 1915.

Dunnigan, James F, and Austin Bay. A Quick & Dirty Guide to War: Briefings on Present and Potential Wars. New York: William Morrow and Company, Inc. 1991.

Early, Gerald. The Culture of Bruising: Essays on Prizefighting, Literature, and Modern American Culture. Hopewell New Jersey: The Ecco Press. 1994.

Ehrenreich, Barbara. Blood Rites: Origins and History of the Passions of War. New York: Metropolitan Books, Henry Holt and Company. 1997.

Ehrlich, Paul R. Human Natures: Genes, Cultures, and the Human Prospect. Washington, D.C.: Island Press/Shearwater Books. 2000.

Einstein, Albert. "Why War?" in Collected Works of Sigmund Freud, volume XXII. London: The Hogarth Press, 1964.

Feder K.L. and Park M.A. Human Antiquity: An Introduction to Physical Anthropology and Archaeology. Mountain View, California: Mayfield Publishing, 1989.

Ferguson, R. Brian, "The Birth of War." Natural History. Peter Brown, ed. New York: Natural History Magazine, Inc., July/August, 2003.

Forsberg, Randall and Elise Boulding, Abolishing War. Boston: Boston Research Center for the 21st Century, 1998.

Forty, Jo. Mythology. New York: PRC Publishing, LTD. 1999.

Freire, Paulo. The Pedagogy of the Oppressed . translated by Myra Ramos. New York: Continuum, 1998.

French, Shannon. The Code of the Warrior: Exploring Warrior Values Past and Present. New York: Rowman & Littlefield Publishers, Inc. 2003.

Freud, Sigmund "Why War?" in Collected Works of Sigmund Freud, volume XXII. London: The Hogarth

Press, 1964.

Fuller, R. Buckminster. Operating Manual for
Spaceship Earth. New York: Simon and Schuster,
1962.

Funston, Frederick. Memories of Two Wars: Cuban
and Philippine Experiences. New York: Charles
Scribners Sons, 1914.

Gates, John Morgan. Schoolbooks and Krags: The
United States Army in the Philippines 1898 -1902.
Westport, Connecticut: Greenwood Press, Inc., 1973.

Geertz, Clifford. The Interpretation of Cultures;
Selected Essays. New York: Basic Books, 1973.

Gibson, James William. Warrior Dreams Paramilitary
Culture in Post-Vietnam America. New York: Hill and
Wang. 1994.

Giddens, Anthony. Capitalism and Modern Social
Theory; an Analysis of the Writings of Marx,
Durkheim, and Max Weber. Cambridge UK:
Cambridge University Press, 1971.

Goodall, Jane. Innocent Killers. (with H. van Lawick).
Boston: Houghton Mifflin. 1971.

------------------. Brutal Kinship. (with Michael Nichols).
New York: Aperture Foundation. 1999.

Gould, Stephen Jay, "Evolution as Fact and Theory,"
May 1981; from Hen's Teeth and Horse's Toes, New
York: W. W. Norton & Company, 1994.

Grant, Michael. Gladiators. New York: Barnes and Noble Books. 1967.

Grossman, Dave, On Killing: The Psychological Cost of Learning to Kill in War and Society. New York: Little, Brown and Co, 1995.

Guevara, Ernesto (Che). Che Guevara on Guerrilla Warfare. New York: Frederick A Praeger, Books that Matter. 1961.

Haleem, Harfiyah Abdel et al. The Crescent and the Cross. London: Macmillan, 1998.

Hanson, Victor Davis. Carnage and Culture: Landmark Battles in the Rise of Western Power. New York: Anchor, a Division of Random House. 2002.

Harris, Marvin. Cows, Pigs, Wars and Witches: the Riddles of Culture. New York: Random House, 1974.

------------- Cannibals and Kings: the Origins of Cultures. New York: Vintage Books. 1977.

Hart, H. L. A. The Concept of Law. Oxford: Clarendon Press, 1961.

Hedges, Chris. War Is A Force That Gives Us Meaning. New York: Public Affairs, a member of the Perseus Books Group. 2002.

Heidegger, Martin. Basic Writings: Second Edition. Revised and Expanded, ed. David Farrell Krell. New York: Harper Collins, 1993.

Heizer, Robert F., ed. The Destruction of California Indians. Salt Lake City: Peregrine Press. 1974.

Hofstadter, Richard. "Manifest Destiny and the Philippines." in America in Crisis, ed. Daniel Aaron, 170-81. New York: Alfred A. Knopf, Inc., 1952.

Hourani, Albert. A History of the Arab Peoples. New York: MJF Books. 1991.

Kagan, Donald. On the Origins of War and the Preservation of Peace. New York: Random House. 1996.

Kanigel, Robert. The One Best Way: Frederick Winslow Taylor and the Enigma of Efficiency. New York: Penguin Penguin, 1997.

Kant, Immanuel. Perpetual Peace. edited by Lewis White Beck. New York: Liberal Arts Press, 1957.

Kaplan, David and R. A. Manners. Culture Theory. Prospect Heights, Illinois: Waveland Press, 1972.

Keegan, John. A History of Warfare. New York: Vintage Press. 1994.

Kegley, Jr., Charles W. and Gregory A. Raymond, How Nations Make Peace. New York: St. Martins Press, Inc. 1999.

Keller, Werner. The Bible as History. William Neil, tr. New York: William Morrow and Company, Inc. 1981.

Kiefer, Thomas M. The Tausug: Violence and Law in Philippine Moslem Society. New York: Holt, Rinehart and Winston, Inc., 1972.

Kissinger, Henry. A World Restored: Metternich, Castlereagh and the Problems of Peace 1812-22. Boston: Houghton Mifflin, 1957.

Knoll, Tricia. Becoming Americans: Asian Sojourners, Immigrants, and Refugees in the Western United States. Portland, Oregon: Coast To Coast Books, 1982.

Kormáks saga. Lee M. Hollander, trans. In: The Sagas of Kormák and the Sworn Brothers. Princeton: Princeton University Press. 1949.

Kormáks saga. W. Collinew, trans. In: The Life and Death of Cormac the Skald. AMS Press. 1940.

Lee, Bruce. Tao of Jeet Kune Do. Burbank, California: Ohara Publications. 1975.

Lewin, Leonard C. Report From Iron Mountain on the Possibility and Desirability of Peace. New York: Delta Books. 1967.

Lewin, Roger. Bones of Contention. New York: Touchstone (Simon &Schuster). 1987.

Mackey, Robert R. The UnCivil War: Irregular Warfare in the Upper South, 1861–1865. Norman, Okla.: University of Oklahoma Press. 2004.

Marx, Karl. Capital. Great Books of the Western World edition, Chicago: Encyclopedia Brittanica, 1952, vol. 50.

Mayer, H.E. The Crusades. New York: Oxford University Press. 2nd Edition. 1988.

McClintock, Anne. Imperial Leather: Race, Gender, and Sexuality in the Colonial Contest. New York: Routledge. 1995.

Merk, Frederick. Manifest Destiny and Mission in American History, A Reinterpretation. New York: Alfred A. Knopf, Inc., 1963.

-------------- The Monroe Doctrine and American Expansionism, 1843 - 1849. New York: Alfred A. Knopf, Inc., 1966.

Moore, Michael. Dude, Where's My Country? New York: Warner Books. 2003.

Morris, Errol. "Fog of War: Eleven Lessons from the Life of Robert S. McNamara." Documentary film. Radical.media, The Globe Department Store, SenArt Films. 2003.

Morton, W. Scott. China: Its History and Culture. New York: McGraw-Hill Book Co., 1984.

--------------- Japan: Its History and Culture. New York: McGraw-Hill Book Co., 1984.

Musashi, Miyamoto. A Book of Five Rings. New York: Overlook Press, 1974.

"Nature's Deep Jungle: The Beast Within." Pbs.org. 2005.

Neier, Aryeh. War Crimes: Brutality, Genocide, Terror, and the Struggle for Justice. New York: Times Books.1998.

New World Translation of the Holy Scriptures. New York: Watchtower Bible and Tract Society. 1978.

Oman, C.W.C. The Art of War in the Middle Ages: A.D. 378-1515. John H. Beeler, ed. Ithaca, New York: Great Seal Books, A Division of Cornell University Press. 1953.

Past Imperfect: History According to the Movies. Mark C. Carnes, General Ed. New York: An Owl Book of Henry Holt And Company. 1996.

Peters, Ralph. Fighting for the Future: Will America Triumph? Mechanicsburg, Pennsylvania: Stackpole Books. 1999.

Plutarch. The Rise and Fall of Athens: Nine Greek Lives. Ian Scott-Kilvert, tr. New York: Penguin Books. 1960.

Pomeroy, William J. American Neo-Colonialism: Its Emergence in the Philippines and Asia. New York: International Publishers, 1970.

Pratt, Julius W. "Ideology of American Expansionism." in Essays in Honor of William E. Dodd, ed. Avery O. Craven, 10-19. Chicago: University of Chicago Press,

1935.

Press, Eyal. "Human Rights, The Next Step." The Nation. New York: The Nation Institute. December 25, 2000.

Pyl'cyn, Alexander V. Penalty Strike: The Memoirs of a Red Army Penal Company Commander 1943-45 (Soviet Memories of War vol. 1). [unpublished] Stock Code: HEL0079. July 2006 Series: Soviet Memories of War # 1 1-874622-63-9. Helion & Company, Limited: Solihull, West Midlands, England. 2006.

Rawls, John. A Theory of Justice. Cambridge, Massachusetts: Belknap Press of Harvard University Press, 1971.

Reardon, Betty. Sexism and the War System. New York: Teachers College Press, 1985.

Reves, Emery. Anatomy of Peace, Random House, Inc. 1945.

Richards, Howard. Letters from Quebec: a Philosophy for Peace and Justice. San Francisco and London: International Scholars Press, 1994.

Rieber, Robert W. (ed.), The Psychology of War and Peace; the Image of the Enemy. New York: Plenum Press, 1991.

Salamanca, Bonifacio S. The Filipino Reaction to American Rule: 1901 - 1913. np: The Shoe String Press, 1968.

Rodat, Ryan. "Saving Private Ryan." DreamWorks SKG & Paramount Pictures Corporation & Amblin Entertainment, Inc. 1998.

Screening Violence. Stephen Prince, ed. New Brunswick, New Jersey: Rutgers University Press. 2000.

Shakespeare, William. Henry V. 1599. Film interpretation written by Kenneth Branaugh. 1989.

Shlain, Leonard. The Alphabet Versus the Goddess: The Conflict Between word and Image. New York: Viking Penguin. 1998.

--------------. Sex, Time, and Power: How Women's Sexuality Shaped Evolution. New York: Viking Penguin. 2003.

Smith, Adam. An Inquiry into the Nature and Causes of the Wealth of Nations. London: Methuen and Co., Ltd., ed. Edwin Cannan, 1904. Fifth edition. (First published 1776).

Smoke, Richard, and Willis Harman. Paths to Peace: Exploring the Feasibility of Sustainable Peace. Boulder, Colorado: Westview Press. 1987.

Stone, Merlin. When God Was A Woman. New York: Barnes and Noble. 1976.

Suvorov, Vikor. Spetsnaz: The Inside Story of the Soviet Special Forces. David Floyd, tr. New York: W. W. Norton & Company. 1987.

Tacitus, P. Cornelius. Germania. In: Medieval Sourcebook: Tacitus's Germania in Latin. Paul Halsall, editor. ORB: The Online Reference Book for Medieval Studies. 1998. (accessed 8/99).

Takaki, Ronald. A Different Mirror: A History of Multicultural America. Boston:
Little, Brown and Company, 1993.

Taylor, Frederick W. The Scientific Principles of Management. New York: Harper and Row. 1911.

The Holy Bible New International Version. Grand Rapids Michigan: Zondervan Bible Publishers.1984.

Thucydides. History of the Peloponnesian War. Betty Radice, ed., New York: Penguin Books, 1972.

Townshend, Charles, ed. The Oxford Illustrated History of Modern War. New York: Oxford University Press. 1997.

Toynbee, Arnold J. War and Civilization. New York: Oxford University Press. 1950.

Trivers, Robert L. Social Evolution. Benjamin/Cummings, Menlo Park, CA. 1985.

Tsu, Lao. Tao Te Ching Translated by Jane English and Gia Fu-Feng. New York: Vintage Books, a Division of Random House. 1972.

Tuchman, Barbara W. A Distant Mirror: The Calamitous 14th Century. New York: Ballantine Books. 1978.

Turnbull, Stephen. The Lone Samurai and the Martial Arts. London, England: Arms and Armour Press.1990.

Turner, Frederick Jackson. The Significance of the Frontier in American History. Ann Arbor: University Microfilms, Incorporated, 1966.

Twain, Mark. A Pen Warmed-Up in Hell: Mark Twain in Protest, ed. Frederick Anderson. New York: Harper and Row, 1972.

-------------- Following the Equator and Anti-Imperialist Essays, ed. Shelley Fisher Fishkin. New York: Oxford Univ. Press, 1996.

-------------- Letters from the Earth, ed. Bernard DeVoto. New York: Harper and Row, 1962.

-------------- Mark Twain on the Damned Human Race, ed. Janet Smith. New York: Hill and Wang, 1962.

Tzu Sun. The Art of War. James Clavell, ed. New York: Delacorte Press. 1983.

Upshur, Jiu-Hwa, et al. World History. Belmont, California: Thomson Wadsworth. 2005.

War in the Age of Technology: The Myriad Faces of Modern Armed Conflict.   Geoffrey Jensen and Andrew Wiest, ed. Part of World Of War. Dennis Showalter, General Editor. New York: New York University Press. 2001.

War: Opposing Viewpoints. Tamara L. Roleff, ed. San Diego: Greenhaven Press. 1999.

Watts, David P. "Reciprocity and Interchange in the Social Relationships of Wild Male Chimpanzees." Behaviour, 2002.139, 343-370.

Welch, Richard E. Jr. Response to Imperialism: The United States and the Philippine-American War, 1899 - 1902. Chapel Hill, North Carolina: University of North Carolina Press, 1979.

Wertham, Frederic, MD. A Sign for Cain: An Exploration of Human Violence. New York: The Macmillan Company. 1966.

White, Matthew. Historical Atlas of the Twentieth Century, 2003.
http://users.erols.com/mwhite28/20centry.htm

Wilson, E.O. Sociobiology: The New Synthesis. Cambridge, Mass.: Harvard University Press. 1975.

Wolff, Leon. Little Brown Brothers: America's Forgotten Bid for Empire Which Cost 250,000 Lives. ; reprint, New York: Kraus Reprint Co., 1970.

Wolff, Robert Paul. In Defense of Anarchism. Berkeley: The University of California Press. 1970.

-------------- Understanding Rawls: A Reconstruction and Critique of A Theory of Justice. Princeton, N.J.: Princeton University Press, 1977.

Wolpoff, Milford H., et al. 2001. "Modern Human

Ancestry at the Peripheries: A Test of the Replacement Theory." Science 291:293-297.

Woodward, Bob. Veil: The Secret Wars of the CIA, 1981-1987. New York: Pocket Books, A Division of Simon & Schuster, Inc. 1987.

Wright, Quincy. A Study of War. Chicago: University of Chicago Press, 1942.

-------------- The Causes of War and the Conditions of Peace. London: Longmans, Green and Co., 1935.

Xenophon. Anabasis. Translated by Carleton L. Brownson, Revised by John Dillery. Cambridge, Massachusetts: Harvard University Press. 1998.

Yamamoto, Tsunetomo. Hagakure, The Book of the Samurai, Translated by William Scott Wilson, Kondansha International Ltd., 1979.

Zezima, Michael. Saving Private Power: The Hidden History of "The Good War." New York: Soft Skull Press. 2000.

Zinn, Howard. A People's History of the United States. New York: Harper Perennial. 2001.

------------- Terrorism and War. Canada: Seven Stories. 2002.

GOVERNMENT DOCUMENTS

The Constitution of the United States. Washington: Government Printing Office, 1787.

United States Bureau of Insular Affairs. War Department. Reports of the Philippine Commission the Civil Government and the Heads of the Executive Department of the Civil Government of the Philippine Islands. Washington: Government Printing Office, 1904.

United States Code, Title 50, Section 2441. War Crimes. Washington: Government Printing Office, 2002.

United States Code, Title 18, War and National Defense. Washington: Government Printing Office, 2002.

Project Related Websites

http://www.iep.utm.edu/w/war.htm#H1

http://www.antiwar.com/

http://en.wikipedia.org/wiki/Wikipedia:Text_of_the_GNU_Free_Documentation_License

http://en.wikipedia.org/wiki/Marius#ImportanceofGaius_Marius

http://www.howardri.org/ontheconcept.html

Japanese Americans. http://www.janm.org/nrc/militarych.php 2006.

Japanese Americans. http://www.goforbroke.org/learning/learning_teachers_lesson_military.asp 2006.

"Tony Poe."
http://www.atimes.com/atimes/Southeast_Asia/EG08
Ae02.html 2005.

Jihad. http://i-cias.com/e.o/jihad.htm 2006.

Haganah.
http://www.jewishvirtuallibrary.org/jsource/History/hag
        anah.html 2005.

"hilly flanks"
http://www.thamesandhudsonusa.com/web/humanpa
st/summaries/ch06.html 2005.

Selection, Sex and Fitness.
http://en.wikipedia.org/wiki/Evolutionary_psychology
2004.

Merriam-Webster Online. http://www.webster.com/
2006.

NOTES:

468